信息安全专业系列教材

信息安全专业科技英语

English for Information Security

李 剑 主编

北京邮电大学出版社
·北京·

内 容 简 介

本书采用英文方式介绍了信息安全领域最常用的知识。从技术方面来讲主要有黑客攻击技术、密码学、防火墙技术、入侵检测技术、网络安全协议、虚拟专用网技术、计算机病毒、公钥基础设施等。除此之外还介绍了当前信息安全管理方面的一些知识。

本书适合于信息安全专业的研究生或本科生。本书一方面可以作为"信息安全专业科技英语"课的教材,另一方面也可以作为信息安全专业"信息安全概论"课的英文版教材。

图书在版编目(CIP)数据

信息安全专业科技英语/李剑主编.—北京:北京邮电大学出版社,2007(2021.1重印)
ISBN 978-7-5635-1388-8

Ⅰ.信… Ⅱ.李… Ⅲ.信息系统—安全技术—英语—高等学校—教材 Ⅳ.H31

中国版本图书馆 CIP 数据核字(2007)第 001486 号

书　　名:	信息安全专业科技英语
作　　者:	李　剑
责任编辑:	李欣一
出版发行:	北京邮电大学出版社
社　　址:	北京市海淀区西土城路 10 号(邮编:100876)
发 行 部:	电话:010-62282185　传真:010-62283578
E-mail:	publish@bupt.edu.cn
经　　销:	各地新华书店
印　　刷:	北京九州迅驰传媒文化有限公司
开　　本:	787 mm×960 mm　1/16
印　　张:	18.75
字　　数:	408 千字
版　　次:	2007 年 2 月第 1 版　2021 年 1 月第 5 次印刷

ISBN 978-7-5635-1388-8　　　　　　　　　　　　　　　　　　　　定 价:28.00 元

・ 如有印装质量问题,请与北京邮电大学出版社营销中心联系 ・

前 言

目前信息安全专业已经在全国如火如荼地开展起来了,但是一直没有这门专业的专业英语教材。这对于培养全面发展的信息安全专业人员是不利的。主要有以下原因:

(1) 目前在信息安全领域,国内和国外的产品在很多方面还有很大差距,所以需要学习国外技术,这就需要有很高的信息安全专业英语水平;

(2) 学生在研究时,需要看国外信息安全方面的专业英文资料;

(3) 学生在学习中文专业词语的时候,不明白相应的英语应该怎么写,特别是在写科技论文的时候,如"漏洞"一词应该是"Vulnerability",许多同学就不会。

本教材就是为满足这些需求而编写的。

全书分为 9 章。第 1 章 "Hacker Attack Technology" 主要介绍黑客和攻击的概念以及目前常见的黑客攻击手法。第 2 章 "Cryptography",主要介绍当前各种密码学技术。第 3 章 "Firewall" 主要介绍防火墙技术及防火墙的结构。第 4 章 "Intrusion Detection System" 主要介绍入侵检测系统、入侵防御系统以及异常防御系统等。第 5 章 "Network Security Protocol" 主要介绍当前流行的一些网络安全协议,包括 Kerberos 协议、SSL 协议、SET 协议和 IPSec 协议。第 6 章 "Virtual Private Network" 主要介绍虚拟专用网技术。第 7 章 "Computer Virus" 主要介绍计算机病毒。第 8 章 "Public Key Infrastructure" 主要介绍公钥基础设施及 CA 证书。第 9 章 "Information Security Management" 简要介绍了当前信息安全管理方面的一些知识。

本教材包含了目前信息安全领域常用的攻击技术和防护技术,以及信息安全管理的知识。在讲解时,可以根据学生对象来选择要教的内容以及内容的深度。

本教材可以作为信息安全专业学生的"信息安全专业英语",也可以当做"信息安全概论"的英文版本。

感谢杨义先教授、罗群副教授,他们对本书的出版提出了宝贵的意见和建议。其他参与本书审阅编写等工作的还有景博、王智贤、许亮等,这里一并谢过!

由于本书作者水平有限,书中疏漏与错误之处在所难免,恳请广大同行和读者指正,我将在下一版中改正。我的电子邮箱是 securitydoctor@163.com。

李 剑

2006 年 11 月 30 日

北京邮电大学信息安全中心

目 录
Catalogue

Chapter 1 Hacker Attack Technology

1.1 Definition and Classification of Attack ·· 1
   1.1.1 Definition of Hacker ··· 1
   1.1.2 Definition of Attack ··· 2
   1.1.3 Classification of Attack ··· 2
1.2 The Process or Methodology Hackers Use to Attack ················· 3
   1.2.1 Performing Reconnaissance ··· 3
   1.2.2 Scanning and Enumeration ··· 4
   1.2.3 Gaining Access ··· 5
   1.2.4 Escalation of Privilege ··· 5
   1.2.5 Maintaining Access ··· 6
   1.2.6 Covering Tracks and Placing Backdoors ················· 6
1.3 The Methods and Ways of Attack ·· 7
   1.3.1 Network Scanning ··· 7
   1.3.2 Password Cracking Attack ··· 12
   1.3.3 IP Spoofing Attack ··· 18
   1.3.4 The Buffer Overflow Attack ··· 20
   1.3.5 DoS Attack ··· 24
   1.3.6 SQL Injection Attack ··· 30
   1.3.7 Trojan Horse Attack ··· 32
   1.3.8 Social Engineering ··· 34

Chapter 2 Cryptography

2.1 Cryptography Introduction ··· 41

	2.1.1	Terminology	41
	2.1.2	History of Cryptography and Cryptanalysis	43
	2.1.3	Modern Cryptography	47
	2.1.4	Legal Issues Involving Cryptography	54
2.2	Substitution Cryptography		56
	2.2.1	Simple Substitution	57
	2.2.2	Homophonic Substitution	59
	2.2.3	Polyalphabetic Substitution	60
	2.2.4	Polygraphic Substitution	61
	2.2.5	Mechanical Substitution Ciphers	63
	2.2.6	The One-time Pad	63
	2.2.7	Substitution in Modern Cryptography	64
2.3	Symmetric-key Cryptography		64
	2.3.1	Types of Symmetric-key Algorithms	65
	2.3.2	Speed	65
	2.3.3	Limitations	65
	2.3.4	Reversibility	66
	2.3.5	Attacks on Symmetric Ciphers	66
	2.3.6	Examples	67
2.4	Public-key Cryptography		67
	2.4.1	History	68
	2.4.2	Security	69
	2.4.3	Applications	70
	2.4.4	Practical Considerations	70
	2.4.5	Examples	76
2.5	Cryptographic Hash Function		79
	2.5.1	Overview	79
	2.5.2	Related Algorithms	80
	2.5.3	Cryptographic Properties	80
	2.5.4	Applications of Hash Functions	81
	2.5.5	Merkle-Damgård Hash Functions	82
	2.5.6	Hash Functions Based on Block Ciphers	83
	2.5.7	Hash Functions to Build other Cryptographic Primitives	83
	2.5.8	List of Cryptographic Hash Functions	83

Chapter 3 Firewall

- 3.1 Introduction ········ 88
- 3.2 Firewall Technologies ········ 94
  - 3.2.1 Packet Filtering Firewall ········ 94
  - 3.2.2 Circuit Level Gateway Firewall ········ 95
  - 3.2.3 Application Level Gateway Firewall ········ 95
  - 3.2.4 Stateful Multilayer Inspection Firewall ········ 96
- 3.3 Firewall Architectures ········ 97
  - 3.3.1 Single-Box Architectures ········ 97
  - 3.3.2 Screened Host Architectures ········ 101
  - 3.3.3 Screened Subnet Architectures ········ 103
- 3.4 Windows Firewall ········ 108
  - 3.4.1 Introduction ········ 108
  - 3.4.2 Using the Exceptions Tab ········ 110
- 3.5 Problems and Benefits of Firewall ········ 112
  - 3.5.1 Firewall Related Problems ········ 112
  - 3.5.2 Benefits of a Firewall ········ 113

Chapter 4 Intrusion Detection System

- 4.1 Introduction ········ 116
  - 4.1.1 Types of Intrusion Detection Systems ········ 116
  - 4.1.2 Passive System vs. Reactive System ········ 117
- 4.2 State of the Art ········ 118
  - 4.2.1 From Intrusion Detection to Anomaly Prevention ········ 118
  - 4.2.2 Focus on Anomaly Prevention Systems ········ 119
  - 4.2.3 Generic Functional Architecture ········ 120
- 4.3 Data Collection ········ 123
  - 4.3.1 Short Definition ········ 123
  - 4.3.2 NIDS ········ 124
  - 4.3.3 HIDS ········ 125
  - 4.3.4 NNIDS ········ 125
  - 4.3.5 Honeypot as a Sensor ········ 125
  - 4.3.6 IPS ········ 126

  4.3.7 DIDS ·· 126

  4.3.8 Multi-layered Integration ·· 127

  4.3.9 Correlation ·· 127

4.4 Data Processing for Detection ·· 128

  4.4.1 Short Definition ··· 128

  4.4.2 Misuse Detection (or Scenario Based Analysis) ················ 128

  4.4.3 Anomaly Detection (or Behavior Analysis) ····················· 129

  4.4.4 Emerging Algorithms ·· 131

4.5 Alarms, Logs and Actions ·· 133

  4.5.1 Passive Actions ··· 133

  4.5.2 Active Actions ·· 133

4.6 Example: Data Mining Approaches for IDS ····························· 134

  4.6.1 Introduction ··· 135

  4.6.2 The Architecture ··· 137

  4.6.3 Mining Audit Data ··· 141

  4.6.4 Feature Construction ·· 146

  4.6.5 Experiments ··· 149

4.7 Known Problems with IDS ··· 149

  4.7.1 Lack of Adaptivity ··· 149

  4.7.2 False Positive & False Negative ································· 151

  4.7.3 Field of Vision ·· 151

  4.7.4 Performance ··· 152

  4.7.5 Increasing Cost ··· 153

  4.7.6 Complex Management Issues ··································· 154

  4.7.7 Evasion Techniques ·· 155

Chapter 5 Network Security Protocol

5.1 Introduction ·· 159

5.2 Kerberos Protocol ··· 160

  5.2.1 History and Development ······································· 160

  5.2.2 Description ·· 161

  5.2.3 Use ·· 162

  5.2.4 The Protocol ·· 162

  5.2.5 Kerberos Operation ·· 163

5.2.6	Kerberos Drawbacks	165

5.3 SSL Protocol ………………………………………………………………… 165
    5.3.1 Description ……………………………………………………………… 165
    5.3.2 Ciphers Used with SSL ………………………………………………… 167
    5.3.3 The SSL Handshake …………………………………………………… 169
    5.3.4 Server Authentication ………………………………………………… 171
    5.3.5 Client Authentication ………………………………………………… 172
    5.3.6 Applications …………………………………………………………… 175

5.4 SET Protocol ………………………………………………………………… 176
    5.4.1 Introduction …………………………………………………………… 176
    5.4.2 Overview of SET Protocol …………………………………………… 177
    5.4.3 SET Cryptography …………………………………………………… 179
    5.4.4 SET Process …………………………………………………………… 180
    5.4.5 Certificates Insurance ………………………………………………… 181
    5.4.6 Security of SET ……………………………………………………… 181
    5.4.7 Future of SET ………………………………………………………… 182

5.5 IPSec Protocol ……………………………………………………………… 182
    5.5.1 Current Status as a Standard ………………………………………… 183
    5.5.2 Design Intent ………………………………………………………… 184
    5.5.3 Technical Details ……………………………………………………… 184
    5.5.4 IPSec Protocol Types ………………………………………………… 186
    5.5.5 Implementations ……………………………………………………… 191

Chapter 6 Virtual Private Network

6.1 Authentication Mechanism ………………………………………………… 195
6.2 Types of VPN ……………………………………………………………… 196
6.3 Characteristics in Application ……………………………………………… 197
6.4 Tunneling …………………………………………………………………… 198
    6.4.1 Two Types of VPN Tunneling ……………………………………… 199
    6.4.2 Point-to-Point Tunneling Protocol …………………………………… 199
    6.4.3 Layer 2 Tunneling Protocol ………………………………………… 201
    6.4.4 SSL VPN ……………………………………………………………… 207
    6.4.5 MPLS VPN …………………………………………………………… 208
6.5 Various Topology Scenarios ………………………………………………… 211

6.5.1	Topology 1	212
6.5.2	Topology 2	212
6.5.3	Topology 3	213
6.5.4	Topology 4	213
6.5.5	Topology 5	214
6.5.6	Topology 6	214
6.6	VPN Security Dialogs	215

Chapter 7 Computer Virus

7.1	Introduction	218
7.1.1	Comparison with Biological Viruses	218
7.1.2	Distinction between Malware and Computer Viruses	219
7.1.3	Effects of Computer Viruses	219
7.1.4	Use of the Word "Virus"	219
7.1.5	History	219
7.2	Virus Classification	221
7.2.1	Boot Sector Virus	221
7.2.2	Companion Virus	224
7.2.3	E-mail Virus	224
7.2.4	Logic Bomb	227
7.2.5	Macro Virus	228
7.2.6	Cross-site Scripting Virus	235
7.2.7	Trojan Horse	241
7.2.8	Computer Worm	241
7.3	Why People Create Computer Viruses	245
7.4	Replication Strategies	245
7.4.1	Nonresident Viruses	246
7.4.2	Resident Viruses	246
7.4.3	Host Types	247
7.5	Methods to Avoid Detection	247
7.5.1	Avoiding Bait Files and Other Undesirable Hosts	248
7.5.2	Stealth	249
7.5.3	Self-modification	249
7.5.4	Simple Self-modifications	249

7.5.5　Encryption with a Variable Key ……………………………………… 250
7.5.6　Polymorphic Code ……………………………………………………… 250
7.5.7　Metamorphic Code ……………………………………………………… 251
7.6　Vulnerability and Countermeasures …………………………………………… 251
7.6.1　The Vulnerability of Operating Systems to Viruses ………………… 251
7.6.2　The Role of Software Development ………………………………… 252
7.6.3　Anti-virus Software and Other Countermeasures ………………… 253

Chapter 8　Public-Key Infrastructure

8.1　PKI Introduction ………………………………………………………………… 256
8.1.1　Purpose ………………………………………………………………… 256
8.1.2　Functions ……………………………………………………………… 257
8.1.3　How Public and Private-key Cryptography Works ………………… 258
8.1.4　Who Provides the Infrastructure …………………………………… 259
8.1.5　PKI Typical Use ……………………………………………………… 260
8.1.6　Alternatives …………………………………………………………… 261
8.1.7　PKI History …………………………………………………………… 262
8.1.8　Usage Examples ……………………………………………………… 263
8.2　Certificate Authority …………………………………………………………… 263
8.2.1　Issuing a Certificate ………………………………………………… 264
8.2.2　Security ………………………………………………………………… 264
8.2.3　Public-Key Certificate ………………………………………………… 265
8.3　X.509 …………………………………………………………………………… 267
8.3.1　History and Usage …………………………………………………… 267
8.3.2　Certificates …………………………………………………………… 268
8.3.3　Sample X.509 Certificates …………………………………………… 269
8.3.4　Security ………………………………………………………………… 272
8.3.5　Public-Key Infrastructure Working Group ………………………… 272
8.3.6　Protocols and Standards Supporting X.509 Certificates ………… 273
8.4　Trusted Third Party …………………………………………………………… 273
8.4.1　An Example …………………………………………………………… 274
8.4.2　Actual Practice ……………………………………………………… 274
8.4.3　Parallels Outside Cryptography …………………………………… 274
8.5　Certificate Revocation List …………………………………………………… 275

8.5.1　CRL Introduction …… 275
8.5.2　Problems with All CRLs …… 276
8.6　An Example of a PKI in Action …… 277

Chapter 9　Information Security Management

9.1　ISO/IEC 17799 …… 282
9.2　ISO/IEC 27001 …… 284
9.3　ISM3 …… 284

参考文献 …… 287

Chapter 1

Hacker Attack Technology

With the rapid growth of interest in the Internet and the Windows operating system, network security has become a major concern to companies throughout the world. The fact that the information and tools needed to penetrate the security of corporate networks are widely available has only increased that concern.

1.1 Definition and Classification of Attack

1.1.1 Definition of Hacker

A hacker is someone who creates and modifies computer software and computer hardware, including computer programming, administration, and security-related items. The term usually bears strong connotations, but may be either favorable or denigrating depending on cultural context. Common definitions include:

In computer programming, a hacker is a software designer and programmer who builds elegant, beautiful programs and systems. A hacker can also be a programmer who hacks or reaches a goal by employing a series of modifications to exploit or extend existing codes or resources. For some, "hacker" has a negative connotation and refers to a person who "hacks" or uses kludges to accomplish programming tasks that are ugly, inelegant, and inefficient. This negative form of the noun "hack" is even used among users of the positive sense of "hacker".

In computer security, a hacker is a person who specializes in work with the security mechanisms for computer and network systems. While including those who endeavor to strengthen such mechanisms, it more often is used, especially in the mass media, to refer to those who seek access despite them.

In other technical fields, hacker is extended to mean a person who makes things work beyond perceived limits through their own technical skill, such as a hardware hacker, or reality hacker.

In hacker culture, a hacker is a person who has attained a certain social status and is recognized among members of the culture for commitment to the culture's values and a certain amount of technical knowledge.

1.1.2 Definition of Attack

Attack is an assault against a computer system or network as a result of deliberate, intelligent action; for example, denial of service attacks, penetration and sabotage. Such as brute force attack, dictionary attack, denial of service attack, replay attack, piggybacking, penetration and sabotage.

1.1.3 Classification of Attack

According to the different classification standard, there can be different attack classification. Based on the service of network is changed or not, attacks can be divided into two categories: passive attack and active attack.

Passive attacks are in the nature of eavesdropping on, or monitoring of, transmissions. The goal of the opponent is to obtain information that is transmitted.

Active attack involves modification of the data stream or the creation of the false stream. A typical active attack is one in which an intruder impersonates one end of the conversation, or acts as a man-in-the-middle. We can simply say that passive attack is trying to get the content of message and active attack try to do modification on the data and send the false message to the receiver. Passive attack can sub category to release of message contents and traffic analysis. Active attack has four categories: masquerade, replay, modification of messages and denial of service.

Another attack classification standard is based on the attacker is the system natural user or not. Attacks can be divided into two categories: exterior attack and interior attack.

Exterior attack is initiated by the user who is not the system's own user and enters the system through deviant way. Hacker attack belongs to the exterior attack.

Chapter 1 Hacker Attack Technology

Interior attack is initiated by the system natural user who has the system's account and authorization.

1.2 The Process or Methodology Hackers Use to Attack

Attackers follow a fixed methodology. To beat a hacker, you have to think like one, so it's important to understand the methodology. The steps a hacker follows can be broadly divided into six phases, which include pre-attack and attack phases:

(1) Performing reconnaissance

(2) Scanning and enumeration

(3) Gaining access

(4) Escalation of privilege

(5) Maintaining access

(6) Covering tracks and placing backdoors

NOTE: A denial of service (DoS) might be included in the preceding steps if the attacker has no success in gaining access to the targeted system or network.

Let's look at each of these phases in more detail so that you could understand the steps better.

1.2.1 Performing Reconnaissance

Reconnaissance is considered the first pre-attack phase and a systematic attempt to locate, gather, identify, and record information about the target. The hacker seeks to find out as much information as possible about the victim. This first step is considered a passive information gathering. As an example, many of you have probably seen a detective movie in which the policeman waits outside a suspect's house all night and then follows him from a distance when he leaves in the car. That's reconnaissance; it is passive in nature, and, if done correctly, the victim never even knows it is occurring.

Hackers can gather information in many different ways, and the information they obtained allows them to formulate a plan of attack. Some hackers might dumpster dive to find out more about the victim. Dumpster diving is the act of going through the victim's trash. If the organization does not have good media control policies, many types of sensitive information will probably go directly in the trash. Organizations should inform employees to shred sensitive information or dispose of it in an approved way.

Don't think that you are secure if you take adequate precautions with paper documents. Another favorite of the hacker is social engineering. A social engineer is a person who can smooth talk other individuals into revealing sensitive information. This might be accomplished by calling the help desk and asking someone to reset a password or by sending an E-mail to an insider telling him he needs to reset an account.

If the hacker is still struggling for information, he can turn to what many consider the hacker's most valuable reconnaissance tool, the Internet. That's right; the Internet offers the hacker a multitude of possibilities for gathering information. Let's start with the company website. The company website might have key employees listed, technologies used, job listings probably detailing software and hardware types used, and some sites even have databases with employee names and E-mail addresses.

TIP: Good security policies are the number one defense against reconnaissance attacks. They are discussed in more detail in later section "Social Engineering".

1.2.2 Scanning and Enumeration

Scanning and enumeration are considered the second pre-attack phase. Scanning is the active step of attempting to connect to systems to elicit a response. Enumeration is used to gather more in-depth information about the target, such as open shares and user account information. At this step in the methodology, the hacker is moving from passive information gathering to active information gathering. Hackers begin injecting packets into the network and might start using scanning tools such as Nmap. The goal is to map open ports and applications. The hacker might use techniques to lessen the chance that he will be detected by scanning at a very slow rate. As an example, instead of checking for all potential applications in just a few minutes, the scan might take days to verify what applications are running. Many organizations use Intrusion Detection Systems (IDS) to detect just this type of activity. Don't think that the hacker will be content with just mapping open ports. He will soon turn his attention to grabbing banners. He will want to get a good idea of what type of version of software applications you are running. And, he will keep a sharp eye out for down-level software and applications that have known vulnerabilities. An example of down-level software would be Windows 95.

One key defense against the hacker is the practice of deny all. The practice of deny all rule can help reduce the effectiveness of the hacker's activities at this step. Deny all means that all ports and applications are turned off, and only the minimum number of applications and services are turned on that are needed to accomplish the organization's goals.

NOTE: Practice of deny all rule can help reduce the effectiveness of the hacker's

Chapter 1 Hacker Attack Technology

activities at this step. Deny all means that all ports and applications are turned off and only the minimum number of applications and services are turned on that are needed to accomplish the organization's goals.

Unlike the elite blackhat hacker who attempts to remain stealth, script kiddies might even use vulnerability scanners such as Nessus to scan a victim's network. Although the activities of the blackhat hacker can be seen as a single shot in the night, the script kiddies scan will appear as a series of shotgun blasts, as their activity will be loud and detectable. Programs such as Nessus are designed to find vulnerabilities but are not designed to be hacking tools; as such, they generate a large amount of detectable network traffic.

TIP: The greatest disadvantage of vulnerability scanners is that they are very noisy.

1.2.3 Gaining Access

As far as potential damage, this could be considered one of the most important steps of an attack. This phase of the attack occurs when the hacker moves from simply probing the network to actually attacking it. After the hacker has gained access, he can begin to move from system to system, spreading his damage as he progresses.

Access can be achieved in many different ways. A hacker might find an open wireless access point that allows him a direct connection or the help desk might have given him the phone number for a modem used for out-of-band management. Access could be gained by finding vulnerability in the web server's software. If the hacker is really bold, he might even walk in and tell the receptionist that he is late for a meeting and will wait in the conference room with network access. Pity the poor receptionist who unknowingly provided network access to a malicious hacker. These things do happen to the company that has failed to establish good security practices and procedures.

The factors that determine the method a hacker uses to access the network ultimately comes down to his skill level, amount of access he achieves, network architecture, and configuration of the victim's network.

1.2.4 Escalation of Privilege

Although the hacker is probably happy that he has access, don't expect him to stop what he is doing with only a "Joe user" account. Just having the access of an average user probably won't give him much control or access to the network. Therefore, the attacker will attempt to escalate himself to administrator or root privilege. After all, these are the individuals who control the network, and that is the type of power the hacker seeks.

Privilege escalation can best be described as the act of leveraging a bug or vulnerability in an application or operating system to gain access to resources that normally would have been protected from an average user. The end result of privilege escalation is that the application performs actions that are running within a higher security context than intended by the designer, and the hacker is granted full access and control.

1.2.5 Maintaining Access

Would you believe that hackers are paranoid people? Well, many are, and they worry that their evil deeds might be uncovered. They are diligent at working on ways to maintain access to the systems they have attacked and compromised. They might attempt to pull down the etc/passwd file or steal other passwords so that they can access other user's accounts.

Rootkits are one option for hackers. A rootkit is a set of tools used to help the attacker maintain his access to the system and use it for malicious purposes. Rootkits have the capability to mask the hacker, hide his presence, and keep his activity secret.

Sometimes hackers might even fix the original problem that they used to gain access, where they can keep the system to themselves. After all, who wants other hackers around to spoil the fun? Sniffers are yet another option for the hacker and can be used to monitor the activity of legitimate users. At this point, hackers are free to upload, download, or manipulate data as they see fit.

1.2.6 Covering Tracks and Placing Backdoors

Nothing happens in a void, and that includes computer crime. Hackers are much like other criminals in that they would like to be sure to remove all evidence of their activities. This might include using rootkits or other tools to cover their tracks. Other hackers might hunt down log files and attempt to alter or erase them.

Hackers must also be worried about the files or programs they leave on the compromised system. File hiding techniques, such as hidden directories, hidden attributes, and Alternate Data Streams (ADS), can be used. As an ethical hacker, you will need to be aware of these tools and techniques to discover their activities and to deploy adequate countermeasures.

Backdoors are methods that the hacker can use to reenter the computer at will.

There are many tools and techniques used to perform such activities. At this point, what is important is to identify the steps.

1.3 The Methods and Ways of Attack

1.3.1 Network Scanning

Network Scanning is the use of a computer network for gathering information on computer systems, which may be used for system maintenance, security assessment and investigation, and for attack. This includes Ping Sweeps, network port scanning, operation system detection and vulnerability scanning.

1. Ping Sweeps

(1) ICMP Sweeps (ICMP ECHO requests)

We can use ICMP packets to determine whether a target IP address is alive or not, by simply sending an ICMP ECHO request (ICMP type 8) packets to the targeted system and waiting to see if an ICMP ECHO reply (ICMP type 0) is received. If an ICMP ECHO reply is received, it means that the target is alive; no response means the target is down.

Querying multiple hosts using this method is referred to as Ping Sweep (see Figure 1.1). Ping Sweeps is the most basic step in mapping out a network.

This is an older approach to mapping, and the scan is fairly slow. Some of the tools used for this kind of scan include:

Unix: fping & gping, nmap

Windows: Pinger, Ping Sweep, WS_Ping ProPack

Pinger is one of the fastest ICMP sweep scanners. Its advantage lies in its ability to send multiple ICMP ECHO packets concurrently and wait for the response. It also allows you to resolve host names and save the output to a file.

Blocking ICMP sweeps is rather easy, simply by not allowing ICMP ECHO requests into your network from the void.

If you are still not convinced that you should block ICMP ECHO requests, bear in mind that you can also perform Broadcast ICMP's.

(2) Broadcast ICMP

Sending ICMP ECHO request to the network or/and broadcast addresses will produce all the information you need for mapping a targeted network in even a simpler way.

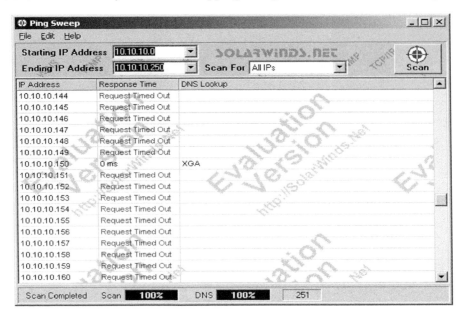

Figure 1.1 Ping Sweep

The request will be broadcast to all alive hosts on the target network, and they will send ICMP ECHO replies to the attacker source IP after only one or two packets have been sent by him.

Here we can first distinguish between Unix and Windows machines. While Unix machines often still answers to requests directed to the network address (the answer will be the fully qualified network address), Windows machines will ignore it.

(3) Non-ECHO ICMP

Blocking incoming ICMP ECHO requests is not enough. We can use non-ECHO ICMP protocols for gathering various information about a system.

Good examples are ICMP type 13 messages (TIMESTAMP), and ICMP type 17 messages (ADDRESS MASK REQUEST).

ICMP timestamp request and reply allow a system to query another for the current time.

The ICMP address mask request (and reply) is intended for diskless systems to obtain its subnet mask at bootstrap time. We can use it to request the netmask of a particular device.

We can use the icmpush & icmpquery tools to perform this kind of scanning.

Many firewalls are configured to block only ICMP ECHO traffic, and in this case it

Chapter 1 Hacker Attack Technology

makes the non-ECHO requests a valid form of host identification.

Even if ICMP traffic is blocked on the border router or firewall, there are additional techniques that can be used to determine which systems are actually alive, although these techniques are not as accurate as a normal ICMP Sweep.

(4) TCP Sweeps

The TCP connection establishment process is called "the three way handshake", and is combined of three segments.

- A client sends a SYN segment specifying the port number of a server that the client wants to connect to, and the client initial sequence number.
- If the server's service (or port) is active, the server will respond with its own SYN segment containing the server's initial sequence number. The server will also acknowledge the client's SYN by ACKing the client's SYN+1.

If the port is not active, the server will send a RESET segment, which will reset the connection.

- The client will acknowledge the server's SYN by ACKing the servers ISN+1.

When will a RESET be sent? —Whenever an arriving segment does not appear correct to the referenced connection. Referenced connection means the connection specified by the destination IP address and port number, and the source IP address and the port number.

With the TCP Sweep technique, instead of sending ICMP ECHO request packets we send TCP ACK or TCK SYN packets (depending if we have root access or not) to the target network. The port number can be selected to meet our needs. Usually a good pick would be one of the following ports—21 / 22 / 23 / 25 / 80 (especially if a firewall is protecting the targeted network). Receiving a response is a good indication that something is up there. The response depends on the target's operating system, the nature of the packet sent and some firewalls, routers or packet-filtering devices used.

Bear in mind that firewalls can spoof a RESET packet for an IP address, so TCP Sweeps may not be reliable.

Nmap and Hping are tools that support TCP Sweep, both for the Unix platform. Hping even adds an additional option to fragment packets, which allows the TCP packet to pass through certain access control devices.

(5) UDP Sweeps (Also known as UDP Scans)

This method relies on the ICMP PORT UNREACHABLE message, initiated by a closed UDP port. If no ICMP PORT UNREACHABLE message is received after sending a UDP datagram to a UDP port that we wish to examine on a targeted system, we may assume the port is opened.

UDP scanning is unreliable because of a number of reasons:
- Routers can drop UDP packets as they cross the Internet;
- Many UDP services do not respond when correctly probed;
- Firewalls are usually configured to drop UDP packets (except for DNS);
- UDP Sweep relies on the fact that a non-active UDP port will respond with an ICMP PORT UNREACHABLE message.

2. Network Port Scanning

Ping Sweeps help us identify which systems are alive. The next step is trying to determine what services (if any) are running or in a LISTENING state on the targeted system, by connecting to the TCP and UDP ports of that system. This is called—Port Scanning.

Network Port is a numeric identifier used to distinguish between different network services (i.e., HTTP, Telnet, FTP) on the same computing system. Although Port numbers range from 0 to 65 536, many well known services have reserved port numbers between 0 and 1 024 (i.e., HTTP uses port 80, Telnet uses port 23, and FTP uses ports 20 and 21). To establish a session with a host, a network request must be sent to the appropriate Port number on the host. That is, to establish an HTTP session with a web server, your workstation software will send a request to port 80 of the web server.

For the hacker it is critical to identify listening ports, because it helps him identify the operating system and application in use.

The services detected as listening may suffer from vulnerabilities which may result from two reasons:
- Misconfiguration of the service;
- The version of the software is known to have security flaws.

If identified, these vulnerabilities can lead to unprivileged access gained by the attacker.

Network Port Scanning is the process of sending data packets over the network to selected service port numbers (HTTP-80, Telnet-23, etc) of a computer system with the purpose of identifying available network services on that system. This process is helpful for troubleshooting system problems or tightening system security. Network Port Scanning is an information gathering process, and when performed by unknown individuals it is considered a prelude to attack.

3. Operating System Detection

Because many security holes are operating system dependent, identifying which

Chapter 1 Hacker Attack Technology

operating system runs on the target host / machine is of major importance.

An attacker can scan a range of IPs for opened TCP and UDP ports and the operating system type. Then he can put the list aside for a while.

When a security hole that is operating system dependent is discovered, all the attacker has to do is pull the list and look for matching information.

(1) Banner Grabbing

Some services can be used to identify an operating system. The TELNET service is the most notable example. If a system provides the TELNET service, just by telneting to the box and looking at the welcome banner we can, in most cases, identify the operating system:

```
[root@pooh]# telnet 192.168.1.188
Debian GNU/Linux 2.1 target.domain.com
target login:
```

Other services have banners that give the same information, for example the mail server:

```
220 target.domain.com ESMTP Sendmail 8.9.3/8.9.3/Debian/GNU; Thu, 28 Oct 1999 09:56:32 +0200
```

Today, an increasing number of systems keep their banners turned off or make their banners display forged information.

Some applications leak information. A good example is the SYST command on FTP servers and IIS server:

```
[root@pooh] # telnet 192.168.1.188
get
HTTP/1.1 400 Bad Request
Server: Microsoft-IIS/4.0
Date: Thu, 28 Oct 1999 08:29:46 GMT
Content-Type: text/html
Content-Length: 87
<html><head><title>Error</title></head><body>The parameter is incorrect.</body></html>
```

(2) DNS HINFO Record

The Host information record is a pair of strings identifying the host's hardware type and the operating system.

www IN HINFO "Sparc Ultra 5" "Solaris 2.6"

This is an old technique that is rarely effective today because administrators avoid using this record.

(3) TCP/IP Stack Fingerprinting

Stack fingerprinting is a technique that uses distinct variations in TCP stack implementation to determine the type of a remote operating system.

The idea is to send "specific" TCP packets to the target IP and observe the response. The response will be unique to a certain group or individual operating system(s). The response varies because one vendor's IP stack implementation is not the same as another. This comes from different interpretation of specific RFC guidelines when vendors wrote their TCP/IP stack.

The tools often used for stack fingerprinting are Queso written by Savage and Nmap. Nmap has a larger database of responses of operating systems than any other tools. In order to get maximum reliability, Nmap needs at least one port opened at the target.

4. Vulnerability Scanning

Vulnerability Scanning is the process of identifying known vulnerabilities of computing systems on the network. This process goes a step beyond identifying the available network services of a system as performed by a network port scan. The vulnerability scan will identify specific weaknesses in the operating system or application software, which can be used to compromise or crash the system. Vulnerability scanning is intrusive and should be performed with care, as some scans can cause systems to crash or to behave erratically. The vulnerability scan is also an information gathering process, and when performed by unknown individuals it is considered a prelude to attack.

1.3.2 Password Cracking Attack

Password cracking is the process of recovering secret passwords from data that has been stored in or transmitted by a computer system (see Figure 1.2). A common approach is to repeatedly try guesses for the password. The purpose of password cracking might be to help a user recover a forgotten password (though installing an entirely new password is less of a security risk, but involves system administration privileges), to gain unauthorized access to a system, or as a preventive measure by system administrators to check for easily crackable passwords.

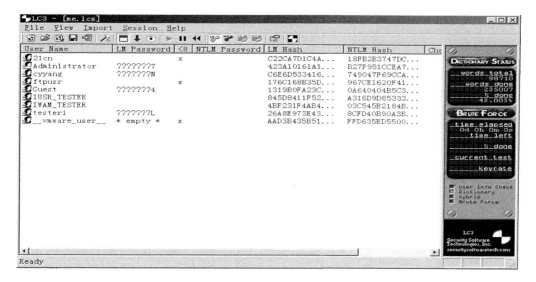

Figure 1.2 Password cracking

1. Background

Passwords to access computer systems are usually stored, typically not in clear text form, in a database so the system can perform passwords verification when users attempt to login. To preserve confidentiality of system passwords, the passwords verification data is typically generated by applying a one-way function to the password, possibly in combination with other data. For simplicity in this discussion, when the one-way function (which may be either an encryption function or cryptographic hash) does not incorporate a secret key, other than the password, we will refer to the one way function employed as a hash and its output as a hashed password.

Even though functions that create hashed passwords may be cryptographically secure, possession of a hashed password provides a quick way to test guesses for the password by applying the function to each guess, and comparing the result to the verification data. The most commonly used hash functions can be computed rapidly and the attacker can test guesses repeatedly with different guesses until one succeeds, meaning the plaintext password has been recovered.

The term password cracking is typically limited to recovery of one or more plaintext passwords from hashed passwords. Password cracking requires that an attacker can gain access to a hashed password, either by reading the password verification database (e.g., via a Trojan Horse, virus program, or social engineering) or intercepting a hashed password sent over an open network, or has some other way to rapidly and without limit test whether a guessed password is correct.

Without the hashed version of a password, the attacker can still attempt access to the computer system in question with guessed passwords. However, well designed systems limit the number of failed access attempts and can alert administrators to trace the source of the attack if that quota is exceeded. With the hashed passwords, the attacker can work undetected, and if the attacker has obtained several hashed passwords, the chances for cracking at least one is quite high.

There are also many other ways of obtaining passwords illicitly, such as social engineering, wiretapping, keystroke logging, login spoofing, dumpster diving, phishing, shoulder surfing, timing attack, acoustic cryptanalysis, identity management system attacks and compromising host security (see password for details). However, cracking usually designates a guessing attack.

Cracking may be combined with other techniques. For example, use of a hash-based challenge-response authentication method for password verification may provide a hashed password to an eavesdropper, who can then crack the password. A number of stronger cryptographic protocols exist that do not expose hashed-passwords during verification over a network, either by protecting them in transmission using a high-grade key, or by using a zero-knowledge password proof.

2. Principal Attack Methods

(1) Weak Encryption

If a system uses a cryptographically weak function to hash or encrypt passwords, exploiting that weakness can recover even "well-chosen" passwords. Decryption need not be a quick operation, and can be conducted while not connected to the target system. Any "cracking" technique of this kind is considered successful if it can decrypt the password in fewer operations than would be required by a brute force attack (see below). The fewer operations required, the "weaker" the encryption is considered to be (for equivalently well chosen passwords). One example is the LM hash that Microsoft Windows uses by default to store user passwords that are less than 15 characters in length. LM hash breaks the password into two 7-character fields which are then hashed separately, allowing each half to be attacked separately.

Progress in cryptography has made available functions which are believed to actually be "one way" hashes, such as MD5 or SHA-1. These are thought to be impossible to invert in practice. When quality implementations of good cryptographic hash functions are correctly used for authentication, password cracking through decryption can be

Chapter 1 Hacker Attack Technology

considered infeasible.

(2) Guessing

Not surprisingly, many users choose weak passwords, usually one related to themselves in some way. Repeated research over some 40 years has demonstrated that around 40% of user-chosen passwords are readily guessable by programs. Examples of insecure choices include:

- blank (none);
- the word "password", "passcode", "admin" and their derivates;
- the user's name or login name;
- the name of their significant other or another relative;
- their birthplace or date of birth;
- a pet's name;
- automobile licence plate number;
- a simple modification of one of the precedings, such as suffixing a digit or reversing the order of the letters;
- a row of letters from a standard keyboard layout (e. g. , the qwerty keyboard—qwerty itself, asdf, or qwertyuiop).

and so on.

Some users even neglect to change the default password that came with their account on the computer system. And some administrators neglect to change the default account passwords provided by the operating system vendor or hardware supplier. A famous example is the use of FieldService as a user name with Guest as the password. If not changed at system configuration time, anyone familiar with such systems will have "cracked" an important password; such service accounts often have higher access privileges than a normal user account.

The determined cracker can easily develop a computer program that accepts personal information about the user being attacked and generates common variations for passwords suggested by that information.

(3) Dictionary Attack

A dictionary attack also exploits the tendency of people to choose weak passwords, and is related to the previous attack. Password cracking programs usually come equipped with "dictionaries", or word lists, with thousands or even millions of entries of several kinds, including:

- words in various languages
- names of people

- places
- commonly used passwords

The cracking program encrypts each word in the dictionary, and simple modifications of each word, and checks whether any match an encrypted password. This is feasible because the attack can be automated and, on inexpensive modern computers, several thousand possibilities can be tried per second.

Guessing, combined with dictionary attacks, have been repeatedly and consistently demonstrated for several decades to be sufficient to crack perhaps as many as 50% of all account passwords on production systems.

(4) Brute Force Attack

A last resort is to try every possible password, known as a brute force attack. In theory, a brute force attack will always be successful since the rules for acceptable passwords must be publicly known, but as the length of the password increases, so does the number of possible passwords. This method is unlikely to be practical unless the password is relatively small. But, how small is too small? A common current length recommendation is 8 or more randomly chosen characters combining letters, numbers, and special (punctuation, etc) characters. Systems which limit passwords to numeric characters only, or upper case only, or, generally, which exclude possible password character choices make such attacks easier. Using longer passwords in such cases (if possible on a particular system) can compensate for a limited allowable character set. And, of course, even with an adequate range of character choice, users who ignore that range (using only upper case alphabetic characters, or digits alone, for instance) make brute force attacks much easier against those password choices.

Generic brute-force search techniques can be used to speed up the computation. But the real threat may be likely to be from smart brute-force techniques that exploit knowledge about how people tend to choose passwords. NIST SP 800-63 (2) provides further discussion of password quality, and suggests, for example, that an 8 character user-chosen password may provide somewhere between 18 and 30 bits of entropy, depending on how it is chosen.

NOTE: This number is very far less than what is generally considered to be safe for an encryption key.

How small is too small thus depends partly on an attacker's ingenuity and resources (e.g., available time, computing power, etc), the latter of which will increase as computers get faster. Most commonly used hashes can be implemented using specialized hardware, allowing faster attacks. Large numbers of computers can be harnessed in parallel, each trying a separate portion of the search space. Unused overnight and weekend time on office computers can also be used for this purpose.

The distinction between guessing, dictionary and brute force attacks is not strict. They are similar in that an attacker goes through a list of candidate passwords one by one; the list may be explicitly enumerated or implicitly defined, may or may not incorporate knowledge about the victim, and may or may not be linguistically derived. Each of the three approaches, particularly "dictionary attack", is frequently used as an umbrella term to denote all the three attacks and the spectrum of attacks encompassed by them.

(5) Precomputation

In its most basic form, precomputation involves hashing each word in the dictionary (or any search space of candidate passwords) and storing the 〈plaintext, ciphertext〉 pairs in a way that enables lookup on the ciphertext field. This way, when a new encrypted password is obtained, password recovery is instantaneous. Precomputation can be very useful for a dictionary attack if salt is not used properly (see below), and the dramatic decrease in the cost of mass storage has made it practical for fairly large dictionaries.

Advanced precomputation methods exist that are even more effective. By applying a time-memory tradeoff, a middle ground can be reached—a search space of size N can be turned into an encrypted database of size $O(2N/3)$ in which searching for an encrypted password takes time $O(2N/3)$. The theory has recently been refined into a practical technique, and the online implementation at http://passcracking.com/ achieves impressive results on 8 character alphanumeric MD5 hashes. Another example cracks alphanumeric Windows LAN Manager passwords in a few seconds. This is much faster than brute force attacks on the obsolete LAN Manager, which uses a particularly weak method of hashing the password. Current Windows systems still compute and store a LAN Manager hash by default for backwards compatibility.

A technique similar to precomputation, known generically as memoization, can be used to crack multiple passwords at the cost of cracking just one. Since encrypting a word takes much longer than comparing it with a stored word, a lot of efforts are saved by encrypting each word only once and comparing it with each of the encrypted passwords using an efficient list search algorithm. The two approaches may of course be combined: the time-space tradeoff attack can be modified to crack multiple passwords simultaneously in a shorter time than cracking them one after the other.

1.3.3　IP Spoofing Attack

In computer networking, the term Internet Protocol address spoofing is the creation of IP packets with a forged (spoofed) source IP address. Since "IP address" is sometimes just referred to as an IP, IP spoofing is another name for this term.

1. How Spoofing is Done

The header of every IP packet contains its source address. This is normally the address that the packet was sent from. By forging the header, so it contains a different address, an attacker can make it appear that the packet was sent by a different machine. This can be a method of attack used by network intruders to defeat network security measures, such as authentication based on IP addresses.

This method of attack on a remote system can be extremely difficult, as it involves modifying thousands of packets at a time and cannot usually be done using a Microsoft Windows computer. IP spoofing involves modifying the packet header, which lists, among other things, the source IP, destination IP, a checksum value, and most importantly, the order value in which it was sent. As when a box sends packets into the Internet, packets sent may, and probably will arrive out of order, and must be put back together using the order sent value. IP spoofing involves solving the algorithm that is used to select the order sent values, and to modify them correctly. This poses a major problem because if one evaluates the algorithm in the wrong fashion, the IP spoof will be unsuccessful.

This type of attack is most effective where trust relationships exist between machines. For example, it is common on some corporate networks to have internal systems trust each other, so that a user can log in without a username or password provided, they are connecting from another machine on the internal network (and so must already be logged in). By spoofing a connection from a trusted machine, an attacker may be able to access the target machine without authenticating.

2. Spoofing Attacks

There are a few variations on the types of attacks that successfully employ IP spoofing. Although some are relatively dated, others are very pertinent to current security concerns.

(1) Non-Blind Spoofing

This type of attack takes place when the attacker is on the same subnet as the victim. The sequence and acknowledgement numbers can be sniffed, eliminating the potential difficulty of calculating them accurately. The biggest threat of spoofing in this instance would be session hijacking. This is accomplished by corrupting the datastream of an established connection, then re-establishing it based on correct sequence and acknowledgement numbers with the attack machine. Using this technique, an attacker could effectively bypass any authentication measures taken place to build the connection.

(2) Blind Spoofing

It is a more sophisticated attack, because the sequence and acknowledgement numbers are unreachable. In order to circumvent this, several packets are sent to the target machine in order to sample sequence numbers. While not the case today, machines in the past used basic techniques for generating sequence numbers. It was relatively easy to discover the exact formula by studying packets and TCP sessions. Today, most OSs implement random sequence number generation, making it difficult to predict them accurately. If, however, the sequence number was compromised, data could be sent to the target. Several years ago, many machines used host-based authentication services (i. e., Rlogin). A properly crafted attack could add the requisite data to a system (i. e., a new user account), blindly, enabling full access for the attacker who was impersonating a trusted host.

(3) Man in the Middle Attack

Both types of spoofing are forms of a common security violation known as a man in the middle (MITM) attack, see Figure 1.3. In these attacks, a malicious party intercepts a legitimate communication between two friendly parties. The malicious host then controls the flow of communication and can eliminate or alter the information sent by one of the original participants without the knowledge of either the original sender or the recipient. In this way, an attacker can fool a victim into disclosing confidential information by "spoofing" the identity of the original sender, who is presumably trusted by the recipient.

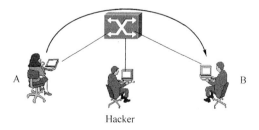

Figure 1.3 Man in the middle attack

(4) Denial of Service Attack

IP spoofing is almost always used in what is currently one of the most difficult attacks to defend against—denial of service attacks, or DoS. Since crackers are concerned only with consuming bandwidth and resources, they need not worry about properly completing handshakes and transactions. Rather, they wish to flood the victim with as many packets as possible in a short amount of time. In order to prolong the effectiveness of the attack, they spoof source IP addresses to make tracing and stopping the DoS as difficult as possible. When multiple compromised hosts are participating in the attack, all sending spoofed traffic, it is very challenging to quickly block traffic.

1.3.4 The Buffer Overflow Attack

A buffer overflow occurs when a program or process tries to store more data in a buffer (temporary data storage area) than it was intended to hold. Since buffers are created to contain a finite amount of data, the extra information—which has to go somewhere—can overflow into adjacent buffers, corrupting or overwriting the valid data held in them. Although it may occur accidentally through programming error, buffer overflow is an increasingly common type of security attack on data integrity. In buffer overflow attacks, the extra data may contain codes designed to trigger specific actions, in effect sending new instructions to the attacked computer that could, for example, damage the user's files, change data, or disclose confidential information. Buffer overflow attacks are said to have arisen because the C programming language supplied the framework, and poor programming practices supplied the vulnerability.

In July 2000, a vulnerability to buffer overflow attack was discovered in Microsoft Outlook and Outlook Express. A programming flaw made it possible for an attacker to compromise the integrity of the target computer by simply sending an E-mail message. Unlike the typical E-mail virus, users could not protect themselves by not opening attached files; in fact, the user did not even have to open the message to enable the attack. The programs' message header mechanisms had a defect that made it possible for senders to overflow the area with extraneous data, which allowed them to execute whatever type of code they desired on the recipient's computers. Because the process was activated as soon as the recipient downloaded the message from the server, this type of buffer overflow attack was very difficult to defend. Microsoft has since created a patch to elim-

Chapter 1 Hacker Attack Technology

inate the vulnerability.

Buffer overflow problems always have been associated with security vulnerabilities. In the past, lots of security breaches have occurred due to buffer overflow. This article attempts to explain what buffer overflow is, how it can be exploited and what countermeasures can be taken to avoid it.

Knowledge of C or any other high level language is essential to this discussion. Basic knowledge of process memory layout is useful, but not necessary. Also, all the discussions are based on Linux running on x86 platform. The basic concepts of buffer overflow, however, are the same no matter what platform and operating system is used.

1. Buffer Overflow: the Basics

A buffer is a contiguous allocated chunk of memory, such as an array or a pointer in C. In C and C++, there are no automatic bounds checking on the buffer, which means a user can write past a buffer. For example:

```
int main () {
    int buffer[10];
    buffer[20] = 10;
}
```

The above C program is a valid program, and every compiler can compile it without any errors. However, the program attempts to write beyond the allocated memory for the buffer, which might result in unexpected behavior. Over the years, some bright people have used only this concept to create havoc in the computer industry. Before we understand how they did it, let's first see what a process looks like in memory.

A process is a program in execution. An excutable program on a disk contains a set of binary instructions to be executed by the processor; some read-only datas, such as printf format strings; global and static data that lasts throughout the program execution; and a brk pointer that keeps track of the malloced memory. Function local variables are automatic variables created on the stack whenever functions execute, and they are cleaned up as the function terminates.

The Figure 1.4 shows the memory layout of a Linux process. A process image starts with the program's code and data. Code and data consists of the program's instructions and the initialized and uninitialized static and global data, respectively. After that is the run-time heap (created using malloc/calloc), and then at the top is the user stack. This stack is used whenever a function call is made.

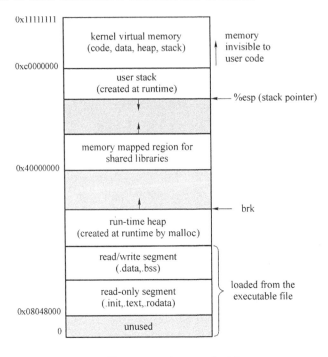

Figure 1.4　The memory layout of a Linux process

A stack is a contiguous block of memory containing data. A stack pointer (SP) points to the top of the stack. Whenever a function call is made, the function parameters are pushed onto the stack from right to left. Then the return address (address to be executed after the function returns), followed by a frame pointer (FP), is pushed on the stack. A frame pointer is used to reference the local variables and the function parameters, because they are at a constant distance from the FP. Local automatic variables are pushed after the FP. In most implementations, stacks grow from higher memory addresses to the lower ones.

Figure 1.5 depicts a typical stack region as it looks when a function call is being executed. Notice the FP between the local and the return addresses. For this C example:

```
void function (int a, int b, int c) {
    char buffer1[5];
    char buffer2[10];
}
```

```
int main() {
    function(1,2,3);
}
```

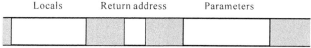

Figure 1.5 A typical stack region

The function stack looks like Figure 1.6.

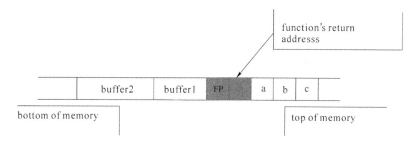

Figure 1.6 The function stack

As you can see, buffer1 takes 8 bytes and buffer2 takes 12 bytes, as memory can be addressed only in multiples of word size (4 bytes). In addition, an FP is needed to access a, b, c, buffer1 and buffer2 variables. All these variables are cleaned up from the stack as the function terminates. These variables take no space in the executable disk copy.

2. Buffer Overflow: the Details

Consider another C example:

```
void function (char * str) {
    char buffer[16];
    strcpy (buffer, str);
}
int main () {
    char * str = "I am greater than 16 bytes"; // length of str = 27 bytes
    function (str);
}
```

This program is guaranteed to cause unexpected behavior, because a string (str) of 27 bytes has been copied to a location (buffer) that has been allocated for only 16 bytes.

The extra bytes run past the buffer and overwrite the space allocated for the FP, return address and so on. This, in turn, corrupts the process stack. The function used to copy the string is strcpy, which completes no checking of bounds. Using strncpy would have prevented this corruption of the stack. However, this classic example shows that a buffer overflow can overwrite a function's return address, which in turn can alter the program's execution path. Recall that a function's return address is the address of the next instruction in memory, which is executed immediately after the function returns.

In addition to subroutine calls, an attacker must also understand enough assembly (the byte codes used by processors like the Intel Pentium) to code the exploit itself. In a buffer overflow exploit, code gets written on the stack, beyond the return address and function call arguments, and the return address gets modified so that it will point to the beginning (approximately) of the code. Then, when the function call returns, the attacker's code gets executed instead of normal program execution.

1.3.5 DoS Attack

In computer security, a denial-of-service attack (DoS attack) is an attempt to make a computer resource unavailable to its intended users. Typically the targets are high-profile web servers where the attack is aiming to cause the hosted web pages to be unavailable on the Internet. It is a computer crime that violates the Internet proper use policy as indicated by the Internet Architecture Board (IAB).

DoS attacks have two general forms:
- Force the victim computer(s) to reset or consume its resources such that it can no longer provide its intended service;
- Obstruct the communication media between the intended users and the victim in such that they can no longer communicate adequately.

Not all service outages, even those that result from malicious activity, are necessarily denial-of-service attacks. Other types of attack may include a denial of service as a component, but the denial of service may be part of a larger attack.

Illegitimate use of resources may also result in denial of service. For example, an intruder may use one's anonymous FTP area as a place to store illegal copies of commercial software, consuming disk space and generating network traffic. They are often used to bring down a server and stop a website from existing on the internet.

1. Methods of Attacks

A "denial of service" attack is characterized by an explicit attempt by attackers to

Chapter 1 Hacker Attack Technology

prevent legitimate users of a service from using that service. Examples include:
- Attempts to "flood" a network, thereby preventing legitimate network traffic;
- Attempts to disrupt a server by sending more requests than it can possibly handle, thereby preventing access to a service;
- Attempts to prevent a particular individual from accessing a service;
- Attempts to disrupt service to a specific system or person.

Attacks can be directed at any network device, including attacks on routing devices and Web, electronic mail, or Domain Name System servers.

A DoS attack can be perpetrated in a number of ways. There are three basic types of attack:
- Consumption of computational resources, such as bandwidth, disk space, or CPU time;
- Disruption of configuration information, such as routing information;
- Disruption of physical network components.

In addition, the US-CERT has provided tips on the manifestations of DoS attacks:
- Unusually slow network performance (opening files or accessing websites);
- Unavailability of a particular website;
- Inability to access any website;
- Dramatic increase in the number of spam E-mails received.

2. SYN Floods

SYN flood sends a flood of TCP/SYN packets, often with a forged sender address. Each of these packets are handled like a connection request, causing the server to spawn a half-open connection, by sending back a TCP/SYN-ACK packet, and waiting for a TCP/ACK packet in response from the sender address. However, because the sender address is forged, the response never comes. These half-open connections consume resources on the server and limit the number of connections the server is able to make, reducing the server's ability to respond to legitimate requests until after the attack ends.

When a computer wants to make a TCP/IP connection (the most common internet connection) to another computer, usually a server, an exchange of TCP/SYN and TCP/ACK packets of information occurs. The computer requests the connection, usually the client's or user's computer, sends a TCP/SYN packet which asks the server if it can connect. If the server will allow connections, it sends a TCP/SYN-ACK packet back to the client to say "Yes, you may connect" and reserves a space for the connection, waiting for the client to respond with a TCP/ACK packet detailing the specifics of its connection.

English for Information Security

In a SYN flood the address of the client is often forged so that when the server sends the go-ahead back to the client, the message is never received because the client either doesn't exist or wasn't expecting the packet and subsequently ignores it. This leaves the server with a dead connection, reserved for a client that will never respond. Usually this is done to one server many times in order to reserve all the connections for unresolved clients, which keeps legitimate clients from making connections.

The classic example is that of a party. Only 50 people can be invited to a party, and invitations are available on a first-come first-serve basis. Fifty letters are sent to request invitations, but the letters all have false return addresses. The invitations are mailed to the return addresses of the request letters. Unfortunately, all of the return addresses provided were fake, so nobody, or at least nobody of interest, receives the invitations. Now, when someone actually wants to come to the party (view the website), there are no invitations left because all the invitations (connections) have been reserved for 50 supposed people who will never actually show up.

3. LAND Attack

A LAND attack involves sending a spoofed TCP/SYN packet (connection initiation) with the target host's IP address with an open port as both source and destination. The attack causes the targeted machine to reply to itself continuously and eventually crash.

4. ICMP Floods

A smurf attack is one particular variant of a flooding DoS attack on the public Internet. It relies on misconfigured network devices that allow packets to be sent to all computer hosts on a particular network via the broadcast address of the network, rather than a specific machine. The network then serves as a smurf amplifier. In such an attack, the perpetrators will send large numbers of IP packets with the source address faked to appear to be the address of the victim. To combat DoS attacks on the Internet, services like the Smurf Amplifier Registry have given network service providers the ability to identify misconfigured networks and to take appropriate action such as filtering.

Ping flood is based on sending the victim an overwhelming number of ping packets, usually using the "pingf" command. It is very simple to launch, the primary requirement being access to greater bandwidth than the victim.

5. UDP Floods

UDP floods include "Fraggle attacks". In a fraggle attack an attacker sends a large amount of UDP echo traffic to IP broadcast addresses, all of them having a fake source address. It is a simple rewrite of the smurf attack code.

6. Teardrop Attack

The Teardrop attack involves sending IP fragments with overlapping oversized payloads to the target machine. A bug in the TCP/IP fragmentation re-assembly code caused the fragments to be improperly handled, crashing the operating system as a result. Windows 3.1x, Windows 95 and Windows NT operating systems, as well as versions of Linux prior to 2.0.32 and 2.1.63 are vulnerable to this attack.

7. Application Level Floods

On IRC, IRC floods are a common electronic warfare weapon.

Various DoS-causing exploits such as buffer overflow can cause server-running software to get confused and fill the disk space or consume all available memory or CPU time.

Other kinds of DoS rely primarily on brute force, flooding the target with an overwhelming flux of packets, oversaturating its connection bandwidth or depleting the target's system resources. Bandwidth-saturating floods rely on the attacker having higher bandwidth available than the victim; a common way of achieving this today is via Distributed Denial of Service(DDoS), employing a botnet. Other floods may use specific packet types or connection requests to saturate finite resources by, for example, occupying the maximum number of open connections or filling the victim's disk space with logs.

A "banana attack" is another particular type of DoS. It involves redirecting outgoing messages from the client back onto the client, preventing outside access, as well as flooding the client with the sent packets.

An attacker with access to a victim's computer may slow it until it is unusable or crash it by using a fork bomb.

A "Pulsing zombie" is a term referring to a special DoS attack. A network is subjected to hostile pinging by different attacker computers over an extended amount of time. This results in a degraded quality of service and increased workload for the network's resources. This type of attack is more difficult to detect than traditional DoS attacks due to their surreptitious nature.

8. Nukes

Nukes are malformed or specially crafted packets.

WinNuke is a type of nuke, exploiting the vulnerability in the NetBIOS handler in Windows 95. A string of out-of-band data is sent to TCP port 139 of the victim machine, causing it to lock up and display a Blue Screen of Death. This attack was very popular between IRC-dwelling script kiddies, due to easy availability of a user-friendly click-and-crash WinNuke program.

9. Distributed Attack

A DDoS as shown in Figure 1.7 occurs when multiple compromised systems flood the bandwidth or resources of a targeted system, usually a web server(s). These systems are compromised by attackers using a variety of methods.

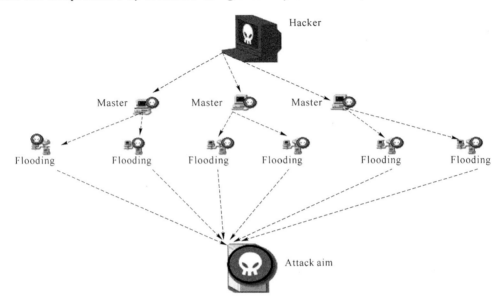

Figure 1.7　DDoS attack

Malware can carry DDoS attack mechanisms; one of the more well known examples of this was MyDoom. Its DoS mechanism was triggered on a specific date and time. This type of DDoS involved hardcoding the target IP address prior to release of the malware and no further interaction was necessary to launch the attack.

A system may also be compromised with a trojan, allowing the attacker to download a zombie agent (or the trojan may contain one). Attackers can also break into systems using automated tools that exploit flaws in programs that listen for connections from remote hosts. This scenario primarily concerns systems acting as servers on the web.

Stacheldraht is a classic example of a DDoS tool. It utilizes a layered structure where the attacker uses a client program to connect to handlers which are compromised systems that issue commands to the zombie agents which in turn facilitate the DDoS attack. Agents are compromised via the handlers by the attacker using automated routines to exploit vulnerabilities in programs that accept remote connections running on the targeted remote hosts. Each handler can control up to a thousand agents.

Chapter 1 Hacker Attack Technology

These collections of compromised systems are known as botnets, DDoS tools like stacheldraht still use classic DoS attack methods centered around IP spoofing and amplification like smurf and fraggle attacks (these are also known as bandwidth consumption attacks), SYN floods (also known as resource starvation attacks) may also be used. Newer tools can use DNS servers for DoS purposes.

Unlike MyDooms DDoS mechanism botnets can be turned against any IP address. Script kiddies use them to deny the availability of well known websites to legitimate users. More sophisticated attackers will use DDoS tools for the purposes of extortion and even against their business rivals.

It is important to note the differences between a DDoS and DoS attack. If an attacker mounts a smurf attack from a single host it would be classed as a DoS attack. In fact, any attack against availability (e. g. ,using High-energy radio-frequency weapons to render computer equipment inoperable) would be classed as a DoS attack albeit an exotic one. On the other hand, if an attacker uses a thousand zombie systems to simultaneously launch smurf attacks against a remote host this would be classed as a DDoS attack.

10. Reflected Attack

A distributed reflected DoS attack involves sending forged requests of some type to a very large number of computers that will reply to the requests. Using Internet protocol spoofing, the source address is set to that of the targeted victim, which means all the replies will go to (and flood) the target.

ICMP Echo Request attacks (described above) can be considered one form of reflected attack, as the flooding host(s) send Echo Requests to the broadcast addresses of misconfigured networks, thereby enticing a large number of hosts to send Echo Reply packets to the victim. Some early DDoS programs implemented a distributed form of this attack.

Many services can be exploited to act as reflectors, some harder to block than others. DNS amplification attacks involve a new mechanism that increased the amplification affect, using a much larger list of DNS servers than seen earlier.

11. Effects

DoS attacks can also lead to problems in the network "branches" around the actual computer being attacked. For example, the bandwidth of a router between the Internet and a LAN may be consumed by DoS, meaning not only will the intended computer be compromised, but the entire network will also be disrupted. This is another, more complex form of the DDoS, wherein the "zombies" can be located on the target system itself, thus increasing network traffic on either side of the target.

English for Information Security

If the DoS is conducted on a sufficiently large scale, entire geographical swathes of Internet connectivity can also be compromised by incorrectly configured or flimsy network infrastructure equipment without the attacker's knowledge or intent. For this reason, most, if not all, ISPs ban the practice.

1.3.6 SQL Injection Attack

A DoS is not an attack in itself, but rather a condition that can be created through a variety of means. One of the vectors of attack through which a DoS condition can be created is SQL Injection.

SQL Injection is a Layer 7 vulnerability that occurs when an application does not properly validate input. A user crafts malicious input containing SQL commands that the application, since there is no proper validation, unknowingly executes.

For example, assume we have a website running on a Windows server, using IIS and MS SQL server.

Note, below, that the database is being accessed with a user with administrative rights (like the default "sa" user).

Now, consider the following HTML page:

```
<html>
    <body>
        <form action="login.jsp">
            Username: <input name="htmlUsername" type="text"/><br/>
            Password: <input name="htmlPassword" type="text"/><br/>
            <input type="submit"/>
        </form>
    </body>
</html>
```

Now, suppose this is the jsp that processes the page:

```
<%@ taglib prefix="sql" uri="http://java.sun.com/jstl/sql" %>
<%@ taglib uri="http://java.sun.com/jstl/core" prefix="c" %>
<html>
<head>
    <title>JSP Page With SQL Injection Vulnerability</title>
```

```
    </head>
    <body>
        <sql:setDataSource
            var = "sampleDataSource"
            driver = "com.microsoft.sqlserver.jdbc.SQLServerDriver"
            url = "jdbc:sqlserver://127.0.0.1"
            user = "sa"
            password = "pass"
        />
        <sql:query var = "queryResults" dataSource = "sampleDataSource">
            SELECT * FROM user_table
            WHERE username = '${requestScope['htmlUsername']}' AND password = '${requestScope['htmlPassword']}';
        </sql:query>
        <c:if test = "${queryResults.rowCount > 0}">
            Logged in!
        </c:if>
        <c:if test = "${queryResults.rowCount == 0}">
            Could not log you in!
        </c:if>
    </body>
</html>
```

The jsp page gets the values submitted from the HTML, looks them up in the database, and displays a message according to the validity of the credentials submitted.

The problem with the jsp page is that the input, in the htmlUsername and htmlPassword parameters, is not validated before being sent to the database server. This vulnerability will allow a DoS condition to be created in the following manner.

Since we are accessing the database with a user with system administrator rights (the "sa" user), we are able to execute the infamous xp_cmdshell stored procedure which will execute arbitrary commands in the windows command line.

Now, suppose we type in the following username in the HTML form:

bogusUsername'; exec master..xp_cmdshell 'iisreset /STOP'--

By sending this carefully crafted username, the following SQL will be executed on the MS SQL server:

SELECT * FROM user_table

```
WHERE username = 'bogusUsername'; exec master..xp_cmdshell'iisreset /STOP'--
AND password = '';
```

Note that the single quote we inserted, followed by a semicolon, finished with a double dash (SQL comment), closes the SQL query and allows arbitrary execution of any code we wish. Using the xp_cmdshell stored procedure we send the iisreset /STOP command to windows. This command will cause the IIS server to be shut down, therefore creating a DoS condition.

1.3.7 Trojan Horse Attack

In the context of computer software, a Trojan horse is a malicious program that is disguised as or embedded within legitimate software. The term is derived from the classical myth of the Trojan Horse(see Figure 1.8). They may look useful or interesting (or at the very least harmless) to an unsuspecting user, but are actually harmful when executed(see Social engineering (security)).

Figure 1.8 Trojan Horse

Often the term is shortened to simply trojan, even though this turns the adjective into a noun, reversing the myth (Greeks, not Trojans, were gaining malicious access).

There are two common types of Trojan horses. One, is otherwise useful software that has been corrupted by a cracker inserting malicious code that executes while the program is used. Examples include various implementations of weather alerting programs, computer clock setting software, and peer to peer file sharing utilities. The other type is a standalone program that masquerades as something else, like a game or image file, in order to trick the user into some misdirected complicity that is needed to carry out the program's objectives.

Trojan horse programs cannot operate autonomously, in contrast to some other types of malware, like viruses or worms. Just as the Greeks needed the Trojans to bring the horse inside for their plan to work, Trojan horse programs depend on actions by the intended victims. As such, if trojans replicate and even distribute themselves, each new victim must run the program/trojan. Therefore their virulence is of a different nature, depending on successful implementation of social engineering concepts rather than flaws in a computer system's security design or configuration.

Chapter 1 Hacker Attack Technology

1. Types of Trojan Horses

Trojan horses are almost always designed to do various harmful things, but could be harmless. They are broken down in classification based on how they breach systems and the damage they cause. The main types of Trojan horses are:

- Remote Access Trojans
- Data Sending Trojans
- Destructive Trojans
- Proxy Trojans
- FTP Trojans
- Security software disabler Trojans
- DoS attack Trojans
- URL Trojans

Some examples are:

- Erasing or overwriting data on a computer.
- Encrypting files in a cryptoviral extortion attack.
- Corrupting files in a subtle way.
- Upload and download files.
- Allowing remote access to the victim's computer. This is called a RAT(remote administration tool).
- Spreading other malware, such as viruses. In this case the Trojan horse is called a "dropper" or "vector".
- Setting up networks of zombie computers in order to launch DDoS attacks or send spam.
- Spying on the user of a computer and covertly reporting data like browsing habits to other people (see the article on spyware).
- Make screenshots.
- Logging keystrokes to steal information such as passwords and credit card numbers (also known as a keylogger).
- Phish for bank or other account details, which can be used for criminal activities.
- Installing a backdoor on a computer system.
- Opening and closing CD-ROM tray.
- Harvest E-mail addresses and use them for spam.
- Restarts the computer whenever the infected program is started.

"Time bombs" and "logic bombs" are types of Trojan horses. "Time bombs" activate on particular dates and/or times. "Logic bombs" activate on certain conditions met by the computer.

Droppers perform two tasks at once. A dropper performs a legitimate task but also installs a computer virus or a computer worm on a system or disk at the same time.

2. Examples

A simple example of a Trojan horse would be a program named "waterfalls. scr. exe" claiming to be a free waterfall screensaver which, when run, instead begins erasing all the files on the victim's computer.

On the Microsoft Windows platform, an attacker might attach a Trojan horse with an innocent-looking filename to an E-mail message which entices the recipient into opening the file. The Trojan horse itself would typically be a Windows executable program file, and thus must have an executable filename extension such as . exe, . com, . scr, . bat, or . pif. Since Windows is configured by default to hide filename extensions from a user, the Trojan horse is an extension that might be "masked" by giving it a name such as "Readme. txt. exe". With file extensions hidden, the user would only see "Readme. txt" and could mistake it for a harmless text file. Icons can also be chosen to imitate the icon associated with a different and benign program, or file type.

When the recipient double-clicks on the attachment, the Trojan horse might superficially do what the user expects it to do (open a text file, for example), so as to keep the victim unaware of its real, concealed, objectives. Meanwhile, it might discreetly modify or delete files, change the configuration of the computer, or even use the computer as a base from which to attack local or other networks—possibly joining many other similarly infected computers as part of a DDoS attack.

A destructive program masquerades as a benign application. Unlike viruses, Trojan horses do not replicate themselves but they can be just as destructive. One of the most insidious types of Trojan horse is a program that claims to rid your computer of viruses but instead introduces viruses onto your computer. The term comes from a Greek story of the Trojan War, in which the Greeks give a giant wooden horse to their foes, the Trojans, ostensibly as a peace offering. But after the Trojans drag the horse inside their city walls, Greek soldiers sneak out of the horse's hollow belly and open the city gates, allowing their compatriots to pour in and capture Troy.

1.3.8 Social Engineering

Social engineering is a collection of techniques used to manipulate people into performing actions or divulging confidential information. While similar to a confidence trick or simple fraud, the term typically applies to trickery for information gathering or com-

Chapter 1 Hacker Attack Technology

puter system access and in most (but not all) cases the attacker never comes face-to-face with the victim.

The term has been popularized in recent years by well known (reformed) computer criminal and security consultant Kevin Mitnick who points out that it's much easier to trick someone into giving you his or her password for a system than to spend the effort to hack in. He claims it to be the single most effective method in his arsenal. David Mackey, director of security intelligence at IBM, stated "I think that in 2006 we're going to continue to see the computer user being the weak link", the underlying assumption being this is what makes social engineering possible.

As a "Social Engineering attack" example, the E-mail shown in Figure 1.9 is received from "CitiBank". It said that "In order to safeguard your account, we require that you confirm your banking details."

Figure 1.9 An E-mail from "CitiBank"

1. Social Engineering Techniques/Terms

All Social Engineering techniques are based on flaws in human logic known as cognitive biases. These bias flaws are used in various combinations to create attack techniques, some of which are listed here:

(1) Pretexting

Pretexting is the act of creating and using an invented scenario (the pretext) to persuade a target to release information or perform an action and is usually done over the telephone. It's more than a simple lie as it most often involves some prior research or set up and the use of pieces of known information (e.g., For impersonation: Birthday, Social Security Number, last bill amount) to establish legitimacy in the mind of the target.

This technique is often used to trick a business into disclosing customer information, and is used by private investigators to obtain telephone records, utility records, banking records and other information directly from junior company service representatives. The information can then be used to establish even greater legitimacy under tougher questioning with a manager (e.g., to make account changes, to get specific balances, etc).

As most U.S. companies still authenticate a client by asking only for a Social Security Number, Birthday, or Mother's maiden name—all of which are easily obtained from public records—the method is extremely effective and will likely continue to work well until a more stringent identification method is adopted.

Pretexting can also be used to impersonate co-workers, police, bank, IRS or insurance investigators—or any other individual who could have perceived authority or right-to-know in the mind of the target. The pretexter must simply prepare answers to questions that might be asked by the target. In some cases all that is needed is a voice of the right gender, an earnest tone and an ability to think on one's feet.

An example of pretexting can be seen on this the broken episode at time 8:55.

(2) Phishing

Phishing applies to E-mail appearing to come from a legitimate business— a bank, or credit card company —requesting "verification" of information and warning of some dire consequence if it is not done. The letter usually contains a link to a fradulent web page that looks legitimate—with company logos and content—and has a form requesting everything from a home address to an ATM card's PIN.

(3) Trojan Horse / Gimmes

Gimmes take advantage of curiosity or greed to deliver malware. Also known as a Trojan Horse, gimmes can arrive as an E-mail attachment promising anything from a cool or sexy screen saver, an important anti-virus or system upgrade, or even the latest

Chapter 1 Hacker Attack Technology

dirt on an employee. The recipient is expected to give in to the need to see the program and open the attachment. In addition, many users will blindly click on any attachments they receive that seem even mildly legitimate. See Trojan horse (computing) for more examples.

Another variation uses physical media and relies on the curiosity of the victim: The attacker leaves a malware infected floppy disc, CD-ROM or USB key in a location sure to be found (bathroom, elevator, sidewalk), gives it a legitimate looking and curiosity piquing label—and simply waits.

Example: Get corporate logo off target's website, make a disk label using logo and write "Executive Salary Summary 1Q 2006" on the front.

(4) Quid pro Quo

Something for something:

- An attacker calls random numbers at a company claiming to be calling back from technical support. Eventually they will hit someone with a legitimate problem, grateful that someone is calling back to help them. The attacker will "help" solve the problem and in the process have the user type commands that give the attacker access and/or launch malware.
- In a 2003 Infosecurity survey, 90% of office workers outside of their building gave away their password in answer to a survey question in exchange for a cheap pen.

2. Social Engineering in Popular Culture

In the film Hackers, the protagonist used a form of social engineering, where the main character accessed a TV network's control system by phoning the security guard for a modem number, posing as an important executive. Although the film is not highly accurate, the particular method demonstrates the power of social engineering.

A form of social engineering can frequently be found in the Online Internet Gaming community. Befriending a user with the intent of extorting account passwords and game serial numbers can give previously banned cheaters access to online play. Insecure personal password policies amongst gamers will often give the unscrupulous user access to gamer's other types of account, e.g., forum accounts or E-mail accounts. Gamers should secure their accounts with strong passwords and never share their serial numbers or they may face sharing the server/forum bans that the hackers earn.

Glossary

access	访问
arsenal	兵工厂
assault	攻击,袭击

English for Information Security

attack	攻击
authentication	认证
backdoor	后门
brute	强力
computer crime	计算机犯罪
confidence trick	骗局,欺诈
confidential information	机密消息
criminal	罪犯
denial	拒绝,否认
destructive	破坏性的
detective	侦探
deviant	不正常的
divulge	泄漏,暴露
eavesdropping	偷听
enumeration	列举
escalate	逐步升高,逐步增强
extortion	敲诈,勒索
fingerprinting	指纹识别
flaw	缺点,裂纹,瑕疵
fraud	欺骗,诡计
hacker	黑客
hostile	敌对的
illegitimate	违法的,不合理的
impersonate	模仿,扮演
intruder	入侵者
legitimacy	合法性,正确性
legitimate	合理的,合法的
malicious	恶意的
modification	更改,修改
monitor	监控器
password cracking	密码破解
penetrate	穿透,渗透
piggybacking	载答,借道法
privilege	特权
reconnaissance	搜查,搜索

rival	竞争者,对手
sabotage	阴谋破坏,怠工
safeguard	维护,保护,捍卫
security	安全
sniffer	嗅探器
spoofing	哄骗
subroutine	子程序
suspect	嫌疑犯
trickery	欺骗
victim	受害人,牺牲品
virulence	恶意
vulnerability	弱点

Translate the following sentences/passage into Chinese

(1) A hacker is someone who creates and modifies computer software and computer hardware, including computer programming, administration, and security-related items. In computer programming, a hacker is a software designer and programmer who builds elegant, beautiful programs and systems.

(2) Attack is an assault against a computer system or network as a result of deliberate, intelligent action; for example, denial of service attacks, penetration and sabotage. Such as brute force attack, dictionary attack, denial of service attack, replay attack, piggybacking, penetration and sabotage.

(3) Although the activities of the blackhat hacker can be seen as a single shot in the night, the script kiddies scan will appear as a series of shotgun blasts, as their activity will be loud and detectable.

(4) Privilege escalation can best be described as the act of leveraging a bug or vulnerability in an application or operating system to gain access to resources that normally would have been protected from an average user.

(5) Network Scanning is the use of a computer network for gathering information on computer systems, which may be used for system maintenance, security assessment and investigation, and for attack.

Translate the following sentences/passage into English

(1) 最初的黑客是指具有熟练的编写和调试计算机程序的技巧,并使用这些技巧来获得非法或未授权的网络或文件访问,入侵企业内部网的人。随着各种强大的黑客

English for Information Security

工具的广泛传播,对计算机技术了解很少的人也可以实施黑客攻击行为,因此网络系统受到黑客攻击的可能性大大增加了。

(2) 主动攻击会造成网络系统状态和服务的改变。主动攻击包括试图阻断或攻破保护机制、引入恶意代码、偷窃或篡改信息。主动进攻可能造成数据资料的泄露和散播,或导致拒绝服务以及数据的篡改,包括大多数的未授权用户企图以非正常手段和正常手段进入远程系统。

(3) 一般完整的攻击过程都是先隐藏自身,在隐藏好自己后再进行预攻击探测,检测目标机器的各种属性和具备的被攻击条件;然后采取相应的攻击方法进行破坏,达到自己的目的之后攻击者会删除自己的行为在目标系统中的日志。

(4) 缓冲区溢出攻击已成为目前较为主流的攻击方法,但缓冲区溢出的类型有多种,有针对操作系统的溢出,如 windows rpc dcom 溢出、windows lsass.dll 溢出等;也有针对应用服务的溢出,如 IIS SSL PCT 溢出、SERV-U mdtm 溢出、Exchange Server NNTP 溢出等。

(5) 拒绝服务(Denial of Servive,简称 DoS 攻击),就是通过非法独占受攻击的目标系统的服务,最终试图阻止合法用户使用受攻击目标提供的网络服务。拒绝服务攻击最常见的就是攻击者通过产生大量流向受害网络的数据包,消耗该网络所有的可用带宽。

Questions

(1) What is the process that hacker uses to attack?
(2) What is the spoofing attack?
(3) What is the buffer overflow attack?
(4) What is the DDoS attack?
(5) What is the SQL Injection Attack?

Chapter 2

Cryptography

2.1 Cryptography Introduction

Cryptography (or cryptology; derived from Greek κρυπτός kryptós "hidden" and the verb γράφω gráfo "write"). In modern times, it has become a branch of information theory, as the mathematical study of information and especially its transmission from place to place. The noted cryptographer Ron Rivest has observed that "cryptography is about communication in the presence of adversaries." It is a central contributor to several fields: information security and related issues, particularly, authentication, and access control. One of cryptography's primary purposes is hiding the meaning of messages, not usually the existence of such messages. In modern times, cryptography also contributes to computer science. Cryptography is central of the techniques used in computer and network security for such things as access control and information confidentiality. Cryptography is also used in many applications encountered in everyday life; the security of ATM cards, computer passwords, and electronic commerce all depend on cryptography.

As shown in Figure 2.1, the German Lorenz cipher machine used in World War II for encryption of very high-level general staff messages.

2.1.1 Terminology

The term is often used to refer to the field as a whole, as is cryptology ("the study of secrets"). The study of how to circumvent the confidentiality sought by using encryption is called cryptanalysis or, more loosely, "codebreaking". The field is a rich source of jargon, some of it humorous.

Figure 2.1 German Lorenz cipher machine

Until modern times, cryptography referred almost exclusively to encryption, the process of converting ordinary information (plaintext) into something unintelligible; this is a ciphertext. Decryption is the reverse, moving from unintelligible ciphertext to plaintext. A cipher (or cypher) is a pair of algorithms which perform this encryption and the reversing decryption. The detailed operation of a cipher is controlled both by the algorithm and, in each instance, by a key. This is a secret parameter (known only to the communicants) for the cipher algorithm. Historically, ciphers were often used directly for encryption or decryption without additional procedures.

In colloquial use, the term "code" is often used to mean any methods of encryption or concealment of meaning. However, within cryptography, code has a more specific meaning; it means the replacement of a unit of plaintext (i. e. , a meaningful word or phrase) with a code word (for example, apple pie replaces attack at dawn). Codes are no longer used in serious cryptography—except incidentally for such things as unit designations (e. g. , "Bronco Flight")—since properly chosen ciphers are both more practical and more secure than even the best codes, and better adapted to computers as well.

Chapter 2 Cryptography

Some use the English terms cryptography and cryptology interchangeably, while others use cryptography to refer to the use and practice of cryptographic techniques, and cryptology to refer to the subject as a field of study. In this respect, English usage is more tolerant of overlapping meanings than several European languages.

2.1.2　History of Cryptography and Cryptanalysis

As shown in Figure 2.2, the Ancient Greek scytale probably much like this modern reconstruction, may have been one of the earliest devices used to implement a cipher.

Before the modern era, cryptography was concerned solely with message confidentiality (i. e., encryption)—conversion of messages from a comprehensible form into an incomprehensible one, and back again at the other end, rendering it unreadable by interceptors or eavesdroppers without secret knowledge (namely, the key needed for decryption). In recent decades, the field has expanded beyond confidentiality concerns to include techniques for authentication of message integrity or sender/receiver identity, digital signatures, interactive proofs, and secure computation.

Figure 2.2　The Ancient Greek scytale

The earliest forms of secret writing required little more than pen and paper. The main classical cipher types are transposition ciphers, which rearrange the order of letters in a message (e. g. "help me" becomes "ehpl em" in a trivially simple rearrangement scheme); and substitution ciphers, which systematically replace letters or groups of letters with other letters or groups of letters (e. g., "fly at once" becomes "gmz bu podf" by replacing each letter with the one following it in the alphabet). Simple versions of either offered little confidentiality, and still don't. An early substitution cipher was the Caesar cipher, in which each letter in the plaintext was replaced by a letter some fixed number of positions further down the alphabet. It was named after Julius Caesar who is reported to have used it, with a shift of 3, to communicate with his generals during his military campaigns.

Encryption attempts to ensure secrecy in communications, such as those of spies, military leaders, and diplomats, but it has also had religious applications. For instance, early Christians used cryptography to obfuscate some aspects of their religious writings to avoid the near certain persecution they would have faced had they been less obscured; famously, 666, the Number of the Beast from the Christian New Testament Book of

Revelation, is sometimes thought to be a ciphertext referring to the Roman Emperor Nero, one of whose policies was persecution of Christians. There is record of several, even earlier, Hebrew ciphers as well. Cryptography is recommended in the Kama Sutra as a way for lovers to communicate without inconvenient discovery. Steganography (i.e., hiding even the existence of a message so as to keep it confidential) was also first developed in ancient times. An early example, from Herodotus, concealed a message—a tattoo on a slave's shaved head by regrown hair. More modern examples of steganography include the use of invisible ink, microdots, and digital watermarks to conceal information.

Ciphertexts produced by classical ciphers always reveal statistical information about the plaintext, which can often be used to break them. After the Arab discovery of frequency analysis (around the year 1000), nearly all such ciphers became more or less readily breakable by an informed attacker. Such classical ciphers still enjoy popularity today, though mostly as puzzles (see cryptogram). Essentially all ciphers remained vulnerable to cryptanalysis using this technique until the invention of the polyalphabetic cipher by Leon Battista Alberti around the year 1467. Alberti's innovation was to use different ciphers (i.e., substitution alphabets) for various parts of a message (often each successive plaintext letter). He also invented what was probably the first automatic cipher device, a wheel which implemented a partial realization of his invention. In the polyalphabetic Vigenère cipher encryption uses a key word, which controls letter substitution depending on which letter of the key word is used. Despite this improvement, polyalphabetic ciphers of this type remained partially vulnerable to frequency analysis techniques, though this was undiscovered until the mid 1800s by Babbage.

As shown in Figure 2.3, the Enigma machine used in several variants by the German military between the late 1920s and the end of World War II, implemented a complex electro-mechanical polyalphabetic cipher to protect sensitive communications. Breaking the Enigma cipher at the Biuro Szyfrów, and the subsequent large-scale decryption of Enigma traffic at Bletchley Park, was an important factor contributing to the Allied victory in World War II.

Although frequency analysis is a powerful and general technique, encryption was still often effective in practice; many a would-be cryptanalyst was unaware of the technique. Breaking a message without frequency analysis essentially required knowledge of the cipher used, thus encouraging espionage, bribery, burglary, defection, etc. to discover it. It was finally recognized in the 19th century that secrecy of a cipher's algorithm is not a sensible, nor practical, safeguard; in fact, any adequate cryptographic scheme (including ciphers) should remain secure even if the adversary knows the cipher algorithm itself. Secrecy of the key should alone be sufficient for confidentiality when under attack—for good ciphers. This fundamental principle was first explicitly stated in 1883 by Auguste Kerckhoffs and is called Kerckhoffs' principle; alternatively and more bluntly, it was restated by Claude Shannon as Shannon's Maxim—"the enemy knows the system".

Figure 2.3 The Enigma machine

Various physical devices and aids have been used to assist with ciphers. One of the earliest may have been the scytale of ancient Greece, a rod supposedly used by the Spartans as an aid for a transposition cipher. In medieval times, other aids were invented such as the cipher grille, also used for a kind of steganography. With the invention of polyalphabetic ciphers came more sophisticated aids such as Alberti's own cipher disk, Johannes Trithemius' tabula recta scheme, and Thomas Jefferson's multi-cylinder (invented independently by Bazeries around 1900). Early in the 20th century, several mechanical encryption/decryption devices were invented, and many patented, including rotor machines—most famously the Enigma machine used by Germany in World War II. The ciphers implemented by the better of these designs brought about a substantial increase in cryptanalytic difficulty.

The development of digital computers and electronics after World War II made possible much more complex ciphers. Furthermore, computers allowed for the encryption of any kinds of data that is represented by computers in binary unlike classical ciphers which only encrypted written text, dissolving the need for a linguistic approach to cryptanalysis. Many computer ciphers can be characterized by their operation on binary bits (sometimes in groups or blocks), unlike classical and mechanical schemes, which generally manipulate traditional characters (i. e., letters and digits). However, computers have also assisted cryptanalysis, which has compensated to some extent for increased cipher complexity. Nonetheless, good modern ciphers have stayed ahead of cryptanalysis: it is usually the case that use of a quality cipher is very efficient, while breaking it requires an effort many orders of magnitude larger, making cryptanalysis so inefficient and impractical as to be effectively impossible.

A credit card with smart card capabilities is shown in Figure 2.4. The 3 by 5 mm chip embedded in the card is shown enlarged in the inset. Smart cards attempt to combine portability with the power to compute modern cryptographic algorithms.

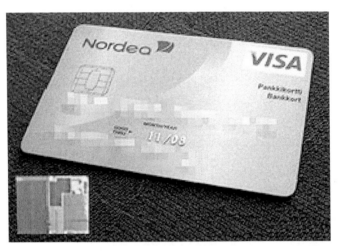

Figure 2.4 Credit card

Extensive open academic research into cryptography is relatively recent—it began only in the mid-1970s with the public specification of DES (the Data Encryption Standard) by the NBS, the Diffie-Hellman paper, and the public release of the RSA algorithm. Since then, cryptography has become a widely used tool in communications, computer networks, and computer security generally. The security of many modern cryptographic techniques is based on the difficulty of certain computational problems, such as the integer factorization problem or the discrete logarithm problem. In many

Chapter 2 Cryptography

cases, there are proofs that cryptographic techniques are secure if a certain computational problem cannot be solved efficiently. With one notable exception—the one-time pad—these contingent, and thus not definitive, proofs are the best available for cryptographic algorithms and protocols.

As well as being aware of cryptographic history, cryptographic algorithm and system designers must also sensibly consider probable future developments in their designs. For instance, the continued improvements in computer processing power have increased the scope of brute-force attacks when specifying key lengths. The potential effects of quantum computing are already being considered by some cryptographic system designers.

Essentially, prior to the early 20th century, cryptography was chiefly concerned with linguistic patterns. Since then the emphasis has shifted, and cryptography now makes extensive use of mathematics, including aspects of information theory, computational complexity, statistics, combinatorics, abstract algebra, and number theory. Cryptography is also a branch of engineering, but an unusual one as it deals with active, intelligent, and malevolent opposition (see cryptographic engineering and security engineering); all other kinds of engineering need deal only with neutral natural forces. There is also active research examining the relationship between cryptographic problems and quantum physics (see quantum cryptography and quantum computing).

2.1.3 Modern Cryptography

The modern field of cryptography can be divided into several areas of study. The primary ones are discussed here; see Topics in Cryptography for more.

1. Symmetric-key Cryptography Introduction

Symmetric-key cryptography refers to encryption methods in which both the sender and receiver share the same key (or, less commonly, in which their keys are different, but related in an easily computable way). This was the only kind of encryption publicly known until 1976.

As shown in Figure 2.5, one round (out of 8.5) of the patented IDEA cipher used in some versions of PGP for high-speed encryption of, for instance, E-mail.

The modern study of symmetric-key ciphers relates mainly to the study of block ciphers and stream ciphers and to their applications. A block cipher is, in a sense, a modern embodiment of Alberti's polyalphabetic cipher: block ciphers take as input a block of plaintext and a key, and output a block of ciphertext of the same size. Since messages are almost always longer than a single block, some method of knitting together successive blocks is required. Several have been developed, some with better security in one aspect of another than others. They are the mode of operations and must be carefully considered when using a block cipher in a cryptosystem.

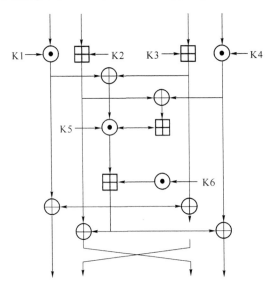

Figure 2.5 IDEA

DES and AES are block ciphers which have been designated cryptography standards by the US government (though DES's designation was finally withdrawn after the AES was adopted). Despite its deprecation as an official standard, DES (especially its still-approved and much more secure triple-DES variant) remains quite popular; it is used across a wide range of applications, from ATM encryption to E-mail privacy and secure remote access. Many other block ciphers have been designed and released, with considerable variation in quality; many have been thoroughly broken. See Category: Block ciphers.

Stream ciphers, in contrast to the "block" type, create an arbitrarily long stream of key material, which is combined with the plaintext bit-by-bit or character-by-character, somewhat like the one-time pad. In a stream cipher, the output stream is created based on an internal state which changes as the cipher operates. That state's change is controlled by the key, and, in some stream ciphers, by the plaintext stream as well. RC4 is an example of a well-known stream cipher.

Cryptographic hash functions (often called message digest functions) do not use keys, but are a related and important class of cryptographic algorithms. They take input data (often an entire message), and output a short, fixed length hash, and do so as a one-way function. For good ones, collisions (two plaintexts which produce the same hash) are extremely difficult to find.

Message authentication codes (MACs) are much like cryptographic hash functions, except that a secret key is used to authenticate the hash value on receipt.

2. Public-key Cryptography Introduction

Symmetric-key cryptosystems typically use the same key for encryption and decryption. A significant disadvantage of symmetric ciphers is the key management necessary to use them securely. Each distinct pair of communicating parties must, ideally, share a different key. The number of keys required increases as the square of the number of network members, which very quickly requires complex key management schemes to keep them all straight and secret. The difficulty of establishing a secret key between two communicating parties, when a secure channel doesn't already exist between them, also presents a chicken-and-egg problem which is a considerable practical obstacle for cryptography users in the real world.

In a groundbreaking 1976 paper, Whitfield Diffie and Martin Hellman (see Figure 2.6) proposed the notion of public-key (also, more generally, called asymmetric-key) cryptography in which two different but mathematically related keys are used—a public-key and a private-key. A public-key system is so constructed that calculation of the private-key is computationally infeasible from the public-key, even though they are necessarily related. Instead, both keys are generated secretly, as an interrelated pair. The historian David Kahn described public-key cryptography as "the most revolutionary new concept in the field since polyalphabetic substitution emerged in the Renaissance".

Figure 2.6　Whitfield Diffie and Martin Hellman

In public-key cryptosystems, the public-key may be freely distributed, while its paired private-key must remain secret. The public-key is typically used for encryption, while the private or secret key is used for decryption. Diffie and Hellman showed that public-key cryptography was possible by presenting the Diffie-Hellman key exchange protocol. In 1978, Ronald Rivest, Adi Shamir, and Len Adleman invented RSA, another public-key system. In 1997, it finally became publicly known that asymmetric key cryptography had been invented by James H. Ellis at GCHQ, a British intelligence organization, in the early 1970s, and that both the Diffie-Hellman and RSA algorithms had been previously developed (by Malcolm J. Williamson and Clifford Cocks, respectively).

Diffie-Hellman and RSA, in addition to being the first publicly known examples of high quality public-key cryptosystems, have been among the most widely used. Others include the Cramer-Shoup cryptosystem, ElGamal encryption, and various elliptic curve techniques. See Category: Asymmetric-key cryptosystems.

In addition to encryption, public-key cryptography can be used to implement digital signature schemes. A digital signature is reminiscent of an ordinary signature; they both have the characteristic that they are easy for a user to produce, but difficult for anyone else to forge. Digital signatures can also be permanently tied to the content of the message being signed; they cannot be "moved" from one document to another, for any attempt will be detectable. In digital signature schemes, there are two algorithms: one for signing, in which a secret key is used to process the message (or a hash of the message, or both), and one for verification, in which the matching public-key is used with the message to check the validity of the signature. RSA and DSA are two of the most popular digital signature schemes. Digital signatures are central to the operation of public-key infrastructures and to many network security schemes (SSL/TLS, many VPNs, etc).

Public-key algorithms are most often based on the computational complexity of "hard" problems, often from number theory. The hardness of RSA is related to the integer factorization problem, while Diffie-Hellman and DSA are related to the discrete logarithm problem. More recently, elliptic curve cryptography has developed in which security is based on number theoretic problems involving elliptic curves. Because of the complexity of the underlying problems, most public-key algorithms involve operations such as modular multiplication and exponentiation, which are much more computationally expensive than the techniques used in most block ciphers, especially with typical key sizes. As a result, public-key cryptosystems are commonly "hybrid" systems, in which a fast symmetric-key encryption algorithm is used for the message itself, while the relevant symmetric key is sent with the message, but encrypted using a public-key algorithm. Similarly, hybrid signature schemes are often used, in which a cryptographic hash function is computed, and only the resulting hash is digitally signed.

3. Cryptanalysis

The goal of cryptanalysis is to find some weakness or insecurity in a cryptographic scheme, thus permitting its subversion or evasion. Cryptanalysis might be undertaken by a malicious attacker, attempting to subvert a system, or by the system's designer (or others) attempting to evaluate whether a system has vulnerabilities, and so it is not inherently a hostile act. In modern practice, however, cryptographic algorithms and protocols must have been carefully examined and tested to offer any confidence in the system's quality (at least, under clear—and hopefully reasonable—assumptions). Without such an examination, no confidence in a crypto-system's quality is justified as there are few proofs of security in cryptography or cryptanalysis.

It is a commonly held misconception that every encryption method can be broken. In connection with his World War II work at Bell Labs, Claude Shannon proved that the one-time pad cipher is unbreakable, provided the key material is truly random, never reused, kept secret from all possible attackers, and of equal or greater length than the message. Most ciphers, apart from the one-time pad, can be broken with enough computational effort by brute force attack, but the amount of effort needed may be exponentially dependent on the key size, as compared to the effort needed to use the cipher. In such cases, effective security could be achieved if it is proven that any effort ("work factor" in Shannon's terms) is beyond the ability of any adversary. This means it must be proven that no efficient method (as opposed to the very inefficient brute force method) can be found to break the cipher. As of today, the one-time pad remains the only theoretically unbreakable cipher.

There are a wide variety of cryptanalytic attacks, and they can be classified in several ways. A common distinction turns on what an attacker knows and what capabilities are available. In a ciphertext-only attack, the cryptanalyst has access only to the ciphertext (good modern cryptosystems are usually effectively immune to ciphertext-only attacks). In a known-plaintext attack, the cryptanalyst has access to a ciphertext and its corresponding plaintext (or to many such pairs). In a chosen-plaintext attack, the cryptanalyst may choose a plaintext and learn its corresponding ciphertext (perhaps many times); an example is the gardening used by the British during World War II. Finally, in a chosen-ciphertext attack, the cryptanalyst may choose ciphertexts and learn their corresponding plaintexts. Also important, often overwhelmingly so, are mistakes (generally in the design or use of one of the protocols involved; see Cryptanalysis of the Enigma for some historical examples of this).

Cryptanalysis of symmetric-key ciphers typically involves looking for attacks against the block ciphers or stream ciphers that are more efficient than any attack that could be against a perfect cipher. For example, a simple brute force attack against DES requires one known plaintext and 255 decryptions, trying approximately half of the possible keys, to reach a point at which chances are better than even the key sought will be found. But this may not be enough assurance; a linear cryptanalysis attack against DES requires 243 known plaintexts and approximately 243 DES operations. This is a considerable improvement on brute force attacks.

Public-key algorithms are based on the computational difficulties of various problems. The most famous of these is integer factorization (the RSA cryptosystem is based on a problem related to factoring), but the discrete logarithm problem is also important. Much public-key cryptanalysis concerns numerical algorithms for solving these computational problems, or some of them, efficiently. For instance, the best known algorithms for solving the elliptic curve-based version of discrete logarithm are much more time-consuming than the best known algorithms for factoring, at least for problems of equivalent size. Thus, other things being equal, to achieve an equivalent strength of attack resistance, factoring-based encryption techniques must use larger keys than elliptic curve techniques. For this reason, public-key cryptosystems based on elliptic curves have become popular since their invention in the mid-1990s.

While pure cryptanalysis uses weaknesses in the algorithms themselves, other attacks on cryptosystems are based on actual use of the algorithms in real devices, known as side-channel attacks. If a cryptanalyst has access to, say, the amount of time the device took to encrypt a number of plaintexts or report an error in a password or PIN character, he may be able to use a timing attack to break a cipher that is otherwise resistant to analysis. An attacker might also study the pattern and length of messages to derive valuable information; this is known as traffic analysis, and can be quite useful to an alert adversary. And, of course, social engineering, and other attacks against the personnel who work with cryptosystems or the messages they handle (e.g., bribery, extortion, blackmail, espionage,…) may be most productive attacks of all.

4. Cryptographic Primitives

Much of the theoretical work in cryptography concerns cryptographic primitives—algorithms with basic cryptographic properties—and their relationship to other cryptographic problems. For example, a one-way function is a function intended to be easy to compute but hard to invert. In a very general sense, for any cryptographic application to be secure (if based on such computational feasibility assumptions), one-way functions must exist. However, if one-way functions exist, this implies that $P \neq NP$. Since the P versus NP problem is currently unsolved, we don't know if one-way functions exist. For instance, if one-way functions exist, then secure pseudorandom generators and secure pseudorandom functions exist.

Currently known cryptographic primitives provide only basic functionality. These are usually noted as confidentiality, message integrity, authentication, and non-repudiation. Any other functionality must be built into combinations of these algorithms and assorted protocols. Such combinations are called crypto systems and it is them which users will encounter. Examples include PGP and its variants, SSH, SSL/TLS, all PKIs, digital signatures, etc.

Other cryptographic primitives include cipher algorithms themselves, one-way permutations, trapdoor permutations, etc.

5. Cryptographic Protocols

In many cases, cryptographic techniques involve back and forth communication among two or more parties in space (e.g., between the home office and a branch office) or across time (e.g., cryptographically protected backup data). The term cryptographic protocol captures this general idea.

Cryptographic protocols have been developed for a wide range of problems, including relatively simple ones like interactive proofs, secret sharing, and zero-knowledge, and much more complex ones like electronic cash and secure multiparty computation.

When the security of a good cryptographic system fails, it is rare that the vulnerability leading to the breach will have been in a quality cryptographic primitive. Instead, weaknesses are often mistakes in the protocol design (often due to inadequate design procedures, or less than thoroughly informed designers), in the implementation (e.g., a software bug), in a failure of the assumptions on which the design was based (e.g., proper training of those who will use the system), or some other human error. Many cryptographic protocols have been designed and analyzed using ad hoc methods, but they rarely have any proof of security. Methods for formally analyzing the security of protocols, based on techniques from mathematical logic (see for example BAN logic), and more recently from concrete security principles, have been the subject of research for the past few decades. Unfortunately, to date these tools have been cumbersome and are not widely used for complex designs.

2.1.4 Legal Issues Involving Cryptography

1. Prohibitions

Because of its potential to assist the malicious in their schemes, cryptography has long been of interest to intelligence gathering agencies and law enforcement agencies. Because of its facilitation of privacy, and the diminution of privacy attendant on its prohibition, cryptography is also of considerable interest to civil rights supporters. Accordingly, there has been a history of controversial legal issues surrounding cryptography, especially since the advent of inexpensive computers has made possible widespread access to high quality cryptography.

In some countries, even the domestic use of cryptography is, or has been, restricted. Until 1999, France significantly restricted the use of cryptography domestically. In China, a license is still required to use cryptography. Many countries have tight restrictions on the use of cryptography. Among the more restrictive are laws in Belarus, China, Kazakhstan, Mongolia, Pakistan, Russia, Singapore, Tunisia, Venezuela, and Vietnam.

In the United States, cryptography is legal for domestic use, but there has been much conflicts over legal issues related to cryptography. One particularly important issue has been the export of cryptography and cryptographic software and hardware. Because of the importance of cryptanalysis in World War II and an expectation that cryptography would continue to be important for national security, many western governments have, at some point, strictly regulated export of cryptography. After World War II, it was illegal in the US to sell or distribute encryption technology overseas; in fact, encryption was classified as a munition, like tanks and nuclear weapons. Until the advent of the personal computer and the Internet, this was not especially problematic. Good cryptography is indistinguishable from bad cryptography for nearly all users, and in any case, most of the cryptographic techniques generally available were slow and error prone whether good or bad. However, as the Internet grew and computers became more widely available, high quality encryption techniques became well-known around the globe. As a result, export controls came to be seen to be an impediment to commerce and to research.

2. Export Controls

In the 1990s, there were several challenges to US export regulations of cryptography. One involved Philip Zimmermann's Pretty Good Privacy (PGP) encryption program; it was released in the US, together with its source code, and found its way onto the Internet in June of 1991. After a complaint by RSA Security (then called RSA Data

Chapter 2 Cryptography

Security, Inc., or RSADSI), Zimmermann was criminally investigated by the Customs Service and the FBI for several years. No charges were ever filed, however. Also, Daniel Bernstein, then a graduate student at UC Berkeley, brought a lawsuit against the US government challenging some aspects of the restrictions based on free speech grounds. The 1995 case Bernstein v. United States which ultimately resulted in a 1999 decision that printed source code for cryptographic algorithms and systems was protected as free speech by the United States Constitution.

In 1996, thirty-nine countries signed the Wassenaar Arrangement, an arms control treaty that deals with the export of arms and "dual-use" technologies such as cryptography. The treaty stipulated that the use of cryptography with short key-lengths (56-bit for symmetric encryption, 512-bit for RSA) would no longer be export-controlled. Cryptography exports from the US are now much less strictly regulated than in the past as a consequence of a major relaxation in 2000; there are no longer very many restrictions on key sizes in US-exported mass-market software. In practice today, since the relaxation in US export restrictions, and because almost each personal computer connected to the Internet, everywhere in the world, includes US-sourced web browsers such as Mozilla Firefox or Microsoft Internet Explorer, almost every Internet user worldwide has strong cryptography (i.e., using long keys) in their browser's Transport Layer Security or SSL stack. The Mozilla Thunderbird and Microsoft Outlook E-mail client programs similarly can connect to IMAP or POP servers via TLS, and can send and receive E-mail encrypted with S/MIME. Many Internet users don't realize that their basic application software contains such extensive cryptography systems. These browsers and E-mail programs are so ubiquitous that even governments whose intent is to regulate civilian use of cryptography generally don't find it practical to do much to control distribution or use of cryptography of this quality, so even when such laws are in force, actual enforcement is often effectively impossible.

3. NSA Involvement

Another contentious issue connected to cryptography in the United States is the influence of the National Security Agency in cipher development and policy. NSA was involved with the design of DES during its development at IBM and its consideration by the National Bureau of Standards as a possible Federal Standard for cryptography. DES was designed to be secure against differential cryptanalysis, a powerful and general cryptanalytic technique known to NSA and IBM, that became publicly known only when it was rediscovered in the late 1980s. According to Steven Levy, IBM rediscovered differential cryptanalysis, but kept the technique secret at NSA's request. The technique became publicly known only when Biham and Shamir rediscovered it some years later.

The entire affair illustrates the difficulty of determining what resources and knowledge an attacker might actually have.

Another instance of NSA's involvement was the 1993 Clipper chip affair, an encryption microchip intended to be part of the Capstone cryptography-control initiative. Clipper was widely criticized by cryptographers for two reasons: the cipher algorithm was classified (the cipher, called Skipjack, was declassified in 1998 long after the Clipper initiative lapsed), which caused concerns that NSA had deliberately made the cipher weak in order to assist its intelligence efforts. The whole initiative was also criticized based on its violation of Kerckhoffs' principle, as the scheme included a special escrow key held by the government for use by law enforcement, for example in wiretaps.

4. Digital Rights Management

Cryptography is central to Digital Rights Management (DRM), a group of techniques for technologically controlling use of copyrighted material, being widely implemented and deployed at the behest of some copyright holders. In 1998, Bill Clinton signed the Digital Millennium Copyright Act (DMCA), which criminalized the production, dissemination, and use of certain cryptanalytic techniques and technology; specifically, those that could be used to circumvent DRM technological schemes. This had a very serious potential impact on the cryptography research community since an argument can be made that any cryptanalytic research violated, or might violate, the DMCA. The FBI and the Justice Department have not enforced the DMCA as rigorously as had been feared by some, but the law, nonetheless, remains a controversial one. One well-respected cryptography researcher, Niels Ferguson, has publicly stated that he will not release some research into an Intel security design for fear of prosecution under the DMCA, and both Alan Cox (longtime number 2 in Linux kernel development) and Professor Edward Felten (and some of his students at Princeton) have encountered problems related to the Act. Dmitry Sklyarov was arrested during a visit to the US, and jailed for some months, for alleged violations of the DMCA which occurred in Russia, where the work for which he was arrested and charged was legal. Similar statutes have since been enacted in several countries. See for instance the EU Copyright Directive.

2.2 Substitution Cryptography

In cryptography, a substitution cipher is a method of encryption by which units of plaintext are substituted with ciphertext according to a regular system; the "units" may be a single letter (the most common), pairs of letters, triplets of letters, mixtures of the above, and so forth. The receiver deciphers the text by performing an inverse substitution.

Substitution ciphers can be compared with transposition ciphers. In a transposition cipher, units of the plaintext are rearranged in a different and usually quite complex order, but the units themselves are left unchanged. By contrast, in a substitution cipher, the units of the plaintext are retained in the same sequence in the ciphertext, but the units themselves are altered.

There are a number of different types of substitution cipher. If the cipher operates on a single letter, it is termed a simple substitution cipher; a cipher that operates on larger groups of letters is termed polygraphic. A monoalphabetic cipher uses fixed substitution over the entire message, whereas a polyalphabetic cipher uses a number of substitutions at different times in the message—such as with homophones, where a unit from the plaintext is mapped to one of several possibilities in the ciphertext.

2.2.1 Simple Substitution

Substitution over a single letter—simple substitution—can be demonstrated by writing out the alphabet in some order to represent the substitution. This is termed a substitution alphabet. The cipher alphabet may be shifted or reversed (creating the Caesar and Atbash ciphers, respectively) or scrambled in a more complex fashion, in which case it is called a mixed alphabet or deranged alphabet. Traditionally, mixed alphabets are created by first writing out a keyword, then all the remaining letters.

As shown in Figure 2.7, ROT13 is a Caesar cipher, a type of substitution cipher. In ROT13, the alphabet is rotated 13 steps.

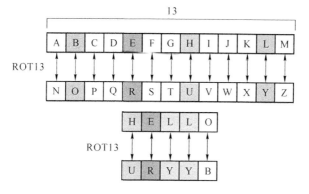

Figure 2.7　Simple substitution

1. Examples

Using this system, the keyword "zebras" gives us the following alphabets:

Plaintext alphabet:abcdefghijklmnopqrstuvwxyz

Ciphertext alphabet:ZEBRASCDFGHIJKLMNOPQTUVWXY

A message of

flee at once. we are discovered!

enciphers to

SIAA ZQ LKBA. VA ZOA RFPBLUAOAR!

Traditionally, the ciphertext is written out in blocks of fixed length, omitting punctuation and spaces; this is done to help avoid transmission errors and to disguise word boundaries from the plaintext. These blocks are called "groups", and sometimes a "group count" (i.e., the number of groups) is given as an additional check. Five letter groups are traditional, dating from when messages used to be transmitted by telegraph:

SIAAZ QLKBA VAZOA RFPBL UAOAR

If the length of the message happens not to be divisible by five, it may be padded at the end with "nulls". These can be any characters that decrypt to obvious nonsense, so the receiver can easily spot them and discard them.

The ciphertext alphabet is sometimes different from the plaintext alphabet; for example, in the pigpen cipher, the ciphertext consists of a set of symbols derived from a grid. For example:

X MARKS THE SPOT

Such features make little difference to the security of a scheme, however —at the very least, any set of strange symbols can be transcribed back into an A-Z alphabet and dealt with as normal.

2. Security for Simple Substitution Ciphers

A disadvantage of this method of derangement is that the last letters of the alphabet (which are mostly low frequency) tend to stay at the end. A stronger way of constructing a mixed alphabet is to perform a columnar transposition on the ordinary alphabet using the keyword, but this is not often done.

Although the number of possible keys is very large (26! ≈ 288.4, or about 88 bits), this cipher is not very strong, being easily broken. Provided the message is of

Chapter 2 Cryptography

reasonable length (see below), the cryptanalyst can deduce the probable meaning of the most common symbols by analyzing the frequency distribution of the ciphertext—frequency analysis. This allows formation of partial words, which can be tentatively filled in, progressively expanding the (partial) solution (see frequency analysis for a demonstration of this). In some cases, underlying words can also be determined from the pattern of their letters; for example, attract, osseous, and words with those two as the root are the only common English words with the pattern ABBCADB. Many people solve such ciphers for recreation, as with cryptogram puzzles in the newspaper.

According to the unicity distance of English, 27.6 letters of ciphertext are required to crack a mixed alphabet simple substitution. In practice, typically about 50 letters are needed, although some messages can be broken with fewer if unusual patterns are found. In other cases, the plaintext can be contrived to have a nearly flat frequency distribution, and much longer plaintexts will then be required.

2.2.2 Homophonic Substitution

An early attempt to increase the difficulty of frequency analysis attacks on substitution ciphers was to disguise plaintext letter frequencies by homophony. In these ciphers, plaintext letters map to more than one ciphertext symbol. Usually, the highest-frequency plaintext symbols are given more equivalents than lower frequency letters. In this way, the frequency distribution is flattened, making analysis more difficult.

Since more than 26 characters will be required in the ciphertext alphabet, various solutions are employed to invent larger alphabets. Perhaps the simplest is to use a numeric substitution "alphabet". Another method consists of simple variations on the existing alphabet; uppercase, lowercase, upside down, etc. More artistically, though not necessarily more securely, some homophonic ciphers employed wholly invented alphabets of fanciful symbols(see Poe's The Gold Bug for a literary example; cf. the Voynich manuscript).

An interesting variant is the nomenclator. Named after the public official who announced the titles of visiting dignitaries, this cipher combined a small codebook with large homophonic substitution tables. Originally the code was restricted to the names of important people, hence the name of the cipher; in later years it covered many common words and place names as well. The symbols for whole words (codewords in modern parlance) and letters (cipher in modern parlance) were not distinguished in the ciphertext. The Rossignols' Great Cypher used by Louis XIV of France was one; after it went out of use, messages in French archives were unbreakable for several hundred years.

Nomenclators were the standard fare of diplomatic correspondence, espionage, and advanced political conspiracy from the early fifteenth century to the late eighteenth century; most conspirators were and have remained less cryptographically sophisticated. Although government intelligence cryptanalysts were systematically breaking nomenclators by the mid-sixteenth century, and superior systems had been available since 1467, the usual response to cryptanalysis was simply to make the tables larger. By the late eighteenth century, when the system was beginning to die out, some nomenclators had 50 000 symbols.

Nevertheless, not all nomenclators were broken; today, cryptanalysis of archived ciphertexts remains a fruitful area of historical research.

The book cipher and straddling checkerboard are types of homophonic cipher.

2.2.3 Polyalphabetic Substitution

Polyalphabetic substitution ciphers were first described in 1467 by Leone Battista Alberti in the form of disks. Johannes Trithemius, in his book Steganographia (Ancient Greek for "hidden writing") introduced the now more standard form of a tableau (see below; ca. 1500 but not published until much later). A more sophisticated version using mixed alphabets was described in 1563 by Giovanni Battista della Porta in his book, De Furtivis Literarum Notis (Latin for "On concealed characters in writing").

In a polyalphabetic cipher, multiple cipher alphabets are used. To facilitate encryption, all the alphabets are usually written out in a large table, traditionally called a tableau. The tableau is usually 26×26, so that 26 full ciphertext alphabets are available. The method of filling the tableau, and of choosing which alphabet to use next, defines the particular polyalphabetic cipher. All such ciphers are easier to break than once believed, as substitution alphabets are repeated for sufficiently large plaintexts.

One of the most popular was that of Blaise de Vigenère. First published in 1585, it was considered unbreakable until 1863, and indeed was commonly called le chiffre indéchiffrable (French for "indecipherable cipher").

In the Vigenère cipher, the first row of the tableau is filled out with a copy of the plaintext alphabet, and successive rows are simply shifted one place to the left. (Such a simple tableau is called a tabula recta, and mathematically corresponds to adding the plaintext and key letters, modulo 26.) A keyword is then used to choose which ciphertext alphabet to use. Each letter of the keyword is used in turn, and then they are

Chapter 2 Cryptography

repeated again from the beginning. So if the keyword is "CAT", the first letter of plaintext is enciphered under alphabet "C", the second under "A", the third under "T", the fourth under "C" again, and so on. In practice, Vigenère keys were often phrases several words long.

In 1863, Friedrich Kasiski published a method (probably discovered secretly and independently before the Crimean War by Charles Babbage) which enabled the calculation of the length of the keyword in a Vigenère ciphered message. Once this was done, ciphertext letters that had been enciphered under the same alphabet could be picked out and attacked separately as a number of semi-independent simple substitutions—complicated by the fact that within one alphabet letters were separated and did not form complete words, but simplified by the fact that usually a tabula recta had been employed.

As such, even today a Vigenère type cipher should theoretically be difficult to break if mixed alphabets are used in the tableau, if the keyword is random, and if the total length of ciphertext is less than 27.6 times the length of the keyword. These requirements are rarely understood in practice, and so Vigenère enciphered message security is usually less than might have been.

Other notable polyalphabetics include:
- The Gronsfeld cipher. This is identical to the Vigenère except that only 10 alphabets are used, and so the "keyword" is numerical.
- The Beaufort cipher. This is practically the same as the Vigenère, except the tabula recta is replaced by a backwards one, mathematically equivalent to ciphertext = key−plaintext. This operation is self-inverse, so that exactly the same table is used in exactly the same way, for both encryption and decryption.
- The autokey cipher, which mixes plaintext in to the keying to avoid periodicity in the key.
- The running key cipher, where the key is made very long by using a passage from a book or similar text.

Modern stream ciphers can also be seen, from a sufficiently abstract perspective, to be a form of polyalphabetic cipher in which all the effort has gone into making the key stream as long and unpredictable as possible.

2.2.4 Polygraphic Substitution

In a polygraphic substitution cipher, plaintext letters are substituted for in larger groups (typically pairs, making a digraphic cipher), instead of substituting letters individually. The advantage of this is first that the frequency distribution of digraphs is much flatter than that of individual letters (though not actually flat in real languages; for example, "TH" is much more common than "XQ" in English). Second, the larger number of symbols requires correspondingly more ciphertext to productively analyze letter frequencies.

Because $26^2 = 676$, to substitute pairs with a substitution alphabet would take an alphabet 676 symbols long—which would be rather cumbersome. (Actually, not every combination would need to be created, or rare combinations could be split into individual letters, but this is negligible.) In the same De Furtivis Literarum Notis mentioned above, della Porta actually proposed such a system, with a 20×20 tableau (for the 20 letters of the Italian/Latin alphabet he was using) filled with 400 unique glyphs. However the system was impractical and probably never actually used. Algebraic or geometric methods are typically used to construct the substitution from simple operations.

The earliest practical digraphic substitution was the so-called Playfair cipher, actually invented by Sir Charles Wheatstone in 1854. It was in military use from the Boer War through World War II. In this cipher, a 5×5 grid is filled with the letters of a mixed alphabet (two letters, usually I and J, are combined). A digraphic substitution is then simulated by taking pairs of letters as two corners of a rectangle, and using the other two corners as the ciphertext (see the Playfair cipher main article for a diagram). Special rules handle double letters and pairs falling in the same row or column.

Several other practical polygraphics were introduced in 1901 by Felix Delastelle, including the bifid and four-square ciphers (both digraphic) and the trifid cipher (probably the first practical trigraphic).

The Hill cipher is a polygraphic substitution which can combine much larger groups of letters simultaneously, using linear algebra. It was invented in 1929 by Lester S. Hill. Each letter is treated as a digit in base 26: $A = 0$, $B = 1$, and so on. (In a variation, 3 extra symbols are added to make the basis prime.) A block of n letters is then considered as a vector of n dimensions, and multiplied by a $n \times n$ matrix, modulo 26. The components of the matrix are the key. Astonishingly, a Hill cipher of dimension 6 was once implemented mechanically!

Unfortunately, the Hill cipher is vulnerable to a known-plaintext attack because it is completely linear, so it must be combined with some non-linear step to defeat this attack. The combination of wider and wider weak, linear diffusive steps like a Hill cipher, with non-linear substitution steps, ultimately leads to a substitution-permutation network (e.g., a Feistel cipher), so it is possible—from this extreme perspective—

Chapter 2 Cryptography

to consider modern block ciphers as a type of polygraphic substitution.

2.2.5 Mechanical Substitution Ciphers

Between circa World War I and the widespread availability of computers (for some governments this was approximately the 1950s or 1960s; for other organizations it was a decade or more later; for individuals it was no earlier than 1975), mechanical implementations of polyalphabetic substitution ciphers were widely used. Several inventors had similar ideas about the same time, and rotor cipher machines were patented four times in 1919. The most important of the resulting machines was the Enigma, especially in the versions used by the German military from approximately 1930. The Allies also developed and used rotor machines (e.g., SIGABA and Typex).

All of these were similar in the substituted letter was chosen electrically from amongst the huge number of possible combinations resulting from the rotation of several letter disks. Since one or more of the disk rotated mechanically with each plaintext letter enciphered, the number of alphabets used was substantially more than astronomical. Early versions of these machines were, nevertheless, breakable. William F. Friedman of the US Army's SIS early found vulnerabilities in Hebern's rotor machine, and GC&CS's Dillwyn Knox solved versions of the Enigma machine (those without the "plugboard") well before World War II began. Traffic protected by essentially all of the German military Enigmas was broken by Allied cryptanalysts, most notably those at Bletchley Park, beginning with the German Army variant used in the early 1930s. This version was broken by inspired mathematical insight by Marian Rejewski in Poland.

No messages protected by the SIGABA and Typex machines were ever, so far as is publicly known, broken.

2.2.6 The One-time Pad

One type of substitution cipher, the one-time pad, is quite special. It was invented near the end of World War I by Gilbert Vernam and Joseph Mauborgne in the US. It was mathematically proved unbreakable by Claude Shannon, probably during World War II; his work was first published in the late 1940s. In its most common implementation, the one-time pad can be called a substitution cipher only from an unusual perspective; typically, the plaintext letter is combined (not substituted) in some manner (e.g., XOR) with the key material character at that position.

The one-time pad is, in most cases, impractical as it requires that the key material be as long as the plaintext, actually random, used once and only once, and kept entirely secret from all except the sender and intended receiver. When these conditions are violated, even marginally, the one-time pad is no longer unbreakable. Soviet one-time pad messages sent from the US for a brief time during World War II used non-random key material. US cryptanalysts, beginning in the late 1940s, were able to, entirely or partially, break a few thousand messages out of several hundred thousand(see VENONA).

In a mechanical implementation, rather like the ROCKEX equipment, the one-time pad was used for messages sent on the Moscow-Washington hot line established after the Cuban missile crisis.

2.2.7 Substitution in Modern Cryptography

Substitution ciphers as discussed above, especially the older pencil-and-paper hand ciphers, are no longer in serious use. However, the cryptographic concept of substitution carries on even today. From a sufficiently abstract perspective, modern bit-oriented block ciphers (e.g., DES, or AES) can be viewed as substitution ciphers on an enormously large binary alphabet. In addition, block ciphers often include smaller substitution tables called S-boxes. See also substitution-permutation network.

2.3 Symmetric-key Cryptography

Symmetric-key algorithms are a class of algorithms for cryptography that use trivially related cryptographic keys for both decryption and encryption.

The encryption key is trivially related to the decryption key, in that they may be identical or there is a simple transform to go between the two keys. The keys, in practice, represent a shared secret between two or more parties that can be used to maintain a private information link.

Other terms for symmetric-key encryption are single-key, one-key and public-key encryption. Use of the latter term can sometimes conflict with the term private-key in public-key cryptography.

2.3.1 Types of Symmetric-key Algorithms

Symmetric-key algorithms can be divided into stream ciphers and block ciphers. Stream ciphers encrypt the bits of the message one at a time, and block ciphers take a number of bits and encrypt them as a single unit. Blocks of 64 bits have been commonly used; the Advanced Encryption Standard algorithm approved by NIST in December 2001 uses 128-bit blocks.

Symmetric-key algorithms are not always used alone. In modern cryptosystem designs, both asymmetric (public-key) and symmetric algorithms are used to take advantages of the virtues of both. Such systems include SSL, PGP and GPG, etc. Asymmetric key algorithms make key distribution for faster symmetric key algorithms.

2.3.2 Speed

Symmetric-key algorithms are generally much less computationally intensive than asymmetric-key algorithms. In practice, this means that a quality asymmetric-key algorithm is hundreds or thousands of times slower than a quality symmetric-key algorithm.

2.3.3 Limitations

The disadvantage of symmetric-key algorithms is the requirement of a shared secret key, with one copy at each end. Since keys are subject to potential discovery by a cryptographic adversary, they need to be changed often and kept secure during distribution and in service. The consequent requirement to choose, distribute and store keys without error and without loss, known as key management, is difficult to reliably achieve.

In order to ensure secure communications between everyone in a population of n people a total of $n(n-1)/2$ keys are needed. Very often these days, the much slower asymmetric algorithms are used to distribute symmetric-keys at the start of a session, then the higher speed symmetric-key algorithms take over (see Transport Layer Security). The same problems of reliable key distribution still exist at the asymmetric level, but they are somewhat more tractable. However, the symmetric key is nearly always generated in real-time.

The symmetric-key algorithms can't be used for authentication or non-repudiation purposes.

2.3.4 Reversibility

Encryption functions must, by definition, be reversible since you need to be able to both encrypt and (provided you have the right key) decrypt messages.

Various methods have been used historically to manage this. There have been book ciphers, in which the shared key is related to some contents in a book, auto-key ciphers in which the key is partially derived from the plaintext, grill ciphers (supposedly first invented by the Italian mathematician Gerolamo Cardano), etc. In modern times, after computers became available, most symmetric ciphers have been based on repeated "rounds". Usually a rather simple scheme for each round is used repeatedly as in the following generic example. This general method is usually ascribed to Horst Feistel. For a more indepth description of this method (with diagrams) see Feistel cipher.

The bits to be encoded are split into two parts p_1 and p_2. p_1 is unchanged, p_2 is added (or exclusive-or'd) to a one-way hashed function f (varied by a key or "salt") of p_1. The two results are then swapped over. This is called "a round".

i.e., where p_1, p_2, key are bit vectors; "," is a concatenation operator and f is a function $p_1, p_2 \mapsto p'_2, p_1$ such that:

$$p'_2 = p_2 + f(p_1, \text{key})$$

Since the output of the round still has access to the value p_1, and the addition is a reversible operation, then this operation may be undone, for any one-way function f.

Whilst a single round is insecure, p_1 having been unchanged, repeating the operation more than once, often with different functions and "round keys", greatly improves the strength.

To decrypt multiple rounds, each round is undone in reverse order hence, for decryption, the keys are applied in reverse order.

After several rounds (typically between 8 and 64) of processing, the output becomes so scrambled that, in the case of well designed ciphers, nothing faster than brute force key search is feasible. With a long enough key, a brute force attack can be made infeasible.

2.3.5 Attacks on Symmetric Ciphers

Symmetric ciphers have historically been susceptible to known-plaintext attacks, chosen plaintext attacks, differential cryptanalysis and linear cryptanalysis. Careful construction of the functions for each round can greatly reduce the chances of a successful attack.

When used with asymmetric ciphers for key transfer, pseudorandom key generators are nearly always used to generate the symmetric cipher session keys. However, lack of randomness in those generators or in their initialization vectors is disastrous and has led to cryptanalytic breaks in the past. Very careful implementation and deployment, with initialization based on high quality sources of entropy, is essential lest security be lost.

2.3.6 Examples

Some examples of popular and well-respected symmetric algorithms include Twofish, Serpent, AES (aka Rijndael), Blowfish, CAST5, RC4, TDES, and IDEA.

2.4 Public-key Cryptography

Public-key cryptography is a form of cryptography which generally allows users to communicate securely without having prior access to a shared secret key. This is done by using a pair of cryptographic keys, designated as public-key and private-key, which are related mathematically.

In public-key cryptography, the private-key is kept secret, while the public-key may be widely distributed. In a sense, one key "locks" a lock; while the other is required to unlock it. It should not be feasible to deduce the private-key of a pair given the private-key, and in high quality algorithms no such technique is known.

One analogy is that of a locked store front door with a mail slot. The mail slot is exposed and accessible to the public; its location (the street address) is in essence the public-key. Anyone knowing the street address can go to the door and drop a written message through the slot. However, only the person who possesses the matching private-key, the store owner in this case, can open the door and read the message.

The term asymmetric key cryptography is a synonym for public-key cryptography though a somewhat misleading one. There are asymmetric key encryption algorithms that do not have the public key-private key property noted above. For these algorithms, both keys must be kept secret, that is both are private-keys.

There are many forms of public-key cryptography, including:
- Public-key encryption—keeping a message secret from anyone who does not pos-

sess a specific private-key.
- Public-key digital signature—allowing anyone to verify that a message was created with a specific private-key.
- Key agreement—generally, allowing two parties that may not initially share a secret key to agree on one.

Typically, public-key techniques are much more computationally intensive than purely symmetric algorithms, but the judicious use of these techniques enables a wide variety of applications.

2.4.1 History

For most of the histories of cryptography, a key had to be kept absolutely secret and would be agreed upon beforehand using a secure, but non-cryptographic, method; for example, a face-to-face meeting or a trusted courier. There are a number of significant practical difficulties in this approach to distributing keys. Public-key cryptography was invented to address these drawbacks—with public-key cryptography, users can communicate securely over an insecure channel without having to agree upon a shared key beforehand.

In 1874, a book by William Stanley Jevons described the relationship of one-way functions to cryptography and went on to discuss specifically the factorization problem used to create the trapdoor function in the RSA system. In July 1996, one observer commented on the Jevons book in this way.

In his book The Principles of Science: A Treatise on Logic and Scientific Method, written and published in the 1890s, William S. Jevons observed that there are many situations where the "direct" operation is relatively easy, but the "inverse" operation is significantly more difficult. One example mentioned briefly is that enciphering (encryption) is easy while deciphering (decryption) is not. Much more attention is devoted to the principle that multiplication of integers is easy, but finding the (prime) factors of the product is much harder. Thus, Jevons anticipated a key feature of the RSA Algorithm for public-key cryptography, though he certainly did not invent the concept of public-key cryptography.

The first invention of asymmetric key algorithms was by James H. Ellis, Clifford Cocks, and Malcolm Williamson at GCHQ in the UK in the early 1970s; these inventions were what later become known as Diffie-Hellman key exchange, and a special case of RSA. This fact was kept secret until 1997.

An asymmetric key cryptosystem was published in 1976 by Whitfield Diffie and Martin Hellman, who, influenced by Ralph Merkle's work on public-key distribution, disclosed a method of public-key agreement. This method of exponential key exchange, which came to be known as Diffie-Hellman key exchange, was the first published practical method for establishing a shared secret key over an unprotected communications channel without using a prior shared secret. Merkle's public-key agreement technique became known as Merkle's Puzzles, and was published in 1978.

A generalization of the Cocks method was reinvented in 1977 by Rivest, Shamir and Adleman, all then at MIT. The latter authors published their works in 1978, and the algorithm appropriately came to be known as RSA. RSA uses exponentiation modulo a product of two large primes to encrypt and decrypt, performing both public-key encryption and public-key digital signature, and its security is connected to the presumed difficulty of factoring large integers, a problem for which there is no known efficient (i.e., practicably fast) general technique.

Since the 1970s, a large number and varieties of encryption, digital signature, key agreement, and other techniques have been developed in the field of public-key cryptography. The ElGamal cryptosystem (invented by Taher ElGamal then of Netscape) relies on the (similar, and related) difficulty of the discrete logarithm problem, as does the closely related DSA developed by the NSA and NIST. The introduction of elliptic curve cryptography by Neal Koblitz in the mid 1980s has yielded a new family of analogous public-key algorithms. Although mathematically more complex, elliptic curves appear to provide a more efficient way to leverage the discrete logarithm problem, particular with respect to key size.

2.4.2 Security

Regarding security, there is nothing especially more secure about asymmetric key algorithms than symmetric key algorithms. There are popular ones and unpopular ones. There are broken ones and ones that are, for now, not broken. Unfortunately, popularity is not a reliable indicator of security. Some algorithms have security proofs with various properties, and of varying quality. Many proofs claim that breaking an algorithm, with respect to some well-defined security goals, is equivalent to solving one of the more popular mathematical problems that are presumed to be intractable, like factoring large integers or finding discrete logarithms. Some proofs have also been shown to be broken. In general, none of these algorithms have been proved secure in as absolute a sense as the one-time pad has. As with all cryptographic algorithms, these algorithms must be chosen and used with care.

2.4.3 Applications

The most obvious application of a public-key encryption system is confidentiality; a message which a sender encrypts using the recipient's public-key can only be decrypted by the recipient's paired public-key.

Public-key digital signature algorithms can be used for sender authentication and non-repudiation. For instance, a user can encrypt a message with his own private-key and send it. If another user can successfully decrypt it using the corresponding public-key, this provides assurance that the first user (and no other) sent it. In practice, a cryptographic hash value of the message is calculated, encrypted with the private-key and sent along with the message (resulting in a cryptographic signature of the message). The receiver can then verify message integrity and origin by calculating the hash value of the received message and comparing it against the decoded signature (the original hash). If the hash from the sender and the hash on the receiver side do not match, then the received message is not identical to the message which the sender "signed", or the sender's identity is wrong.

To achieve authentication, non-repudiation, and confidentiality, the sender would first encrypt the message using his private-key, and then a second encryption is performed using the recipient's public-key.

These characteristics are useful for many other, sometimes surprising, applications, like digital cash, password-authenticated key agreement, multi-party key agreement, etc.

2.4.4 Practical Considerations

1. A Postal Analogy

An analogy which can be used to understand the advantages of an asymmetric system is to imagine two people, Alice and Bob, sending a secret message through the public mail. In this example, Alice has the secret message and wants to send it to Bob, after which Bob sends a secret reply.

With a symmetric key system, Alice first puts the secret message in a box, and then locks the box using a padlock to which she has a key. She then sends the box to

Chapter 2 Cryptography

Bob through regular mail. When Bob receives the box, he uses an identical copy of Alice's key (which he has somehow obtained previously, maybe by a face-to-face meeting) to open the box, and reads the message. Bob can then use the same padlock to send his secret reply.

In an asymmetric key system, Bob and Alice have separate padlocks. First, Alice asks Bob to send his open padlock to her through regular mail, keeping his key to himself. When Alice receives it, she uses it to lock a box containing her message, and sends the locked box to Bob. Bob can then unlock the box with his key and read the message from Alice. To reply, Bob must similarly get Alice's open padlock to lock the box before sending it back to her.

The critical advantage in an asymmetric key system is that Bob and Alice never need to send a copy of their keys to each other. This substantially reduces the chance that a third party (perhaps, in the example, a corrupt postal worker) will copy a key while it is in transit, allowing said the third party to spy on all future messages sent between Alice and Bob. In addition, if Bob were to be careless and allow someone else to copy his key, Alice's messages to Bob would be compromised, but Alice's messages to other people would remain secret, since the other people would be providing different padlocks for Alice to use.

2. Actual Algorithms—Two Linked Keys

Not all asymmetric key algorithms operate in precisely this fashion. The most common have the property that Alice and Bob each own two keys, one for encryption and one for decryption. In a secure asymmetric key encryption scheme, the decryption key should not be deducible from the encryption key. This is known as public-key encryption, since the encryption key can be published without compromising the security of encrypted messages. In the analogy above, Bob might publish instructions on how to make a lock ("public-key"), but the lock is such that it is impossible (so far as is known) to deduce from these instructions how to make a key which will open that lock ("private-key"). Those wishing to send messages to Bob use the private-key to encrypt the message; Bob uses his private-key to decrypt it.

3. Weaknesses

Of course, there is the possibility that someone could "pick" Bob's or Alice's lock. Unlike the case of the one-time pad or its equivalents, there is no currently known asymmetric key algorithm which has been proven to be secure against a mathematical attack. That is, it is not known to be impossible that some relation between the keys in a key pair, or a weakness in an algorithm's operation, might be found which would allow decryption without either key, or using only the encryption key. The security of asymmetric key algorithms is based on estimates of how difficult the underlying mathematical problem is to solve. Such estimates have changed both with the decreasing cost of computer power, and with new mathematical discoveries.

These possible insecurities may not be as weak as imagined though. If an estimate of how long (by brute force attack) it takes to crack a code is say 1 000 years (and there is no better attack found) then if it were used to encrypt your credit card details, they would be perfectly safe—because the time to decrypt the details is longer than the useful life of those details (your credit card expires after a few years).

Weaknesses have been found for promising asymmetric key algorithms in the past. The "knapsack packing" algorithm was found to be insecure when an unsuspected attack came to light. Recently, some attacks based on careful measurements of the exact amount of time which takes known hardware to encrypt plain text have been used to simplify the search for likely decryption keys. Thus, use of asymmetric key algorithms does not ensure security; it is an area of active research to discover and protect against new and unexpected attacks.

Another potential weakness in the process of using asymmetric keys is the possibility of a man in the middle attack (MITM attack), whereby the communication of public-keys is intercepted by a third party and modified to provide the third party's own public-keys instead. The encrypted response also must be intercepted, decrypted and re-encrypted using the correct public-key in all instances however to avoid suspicion, making this attack difficult to implement in practice. The attack is not impossible, and an evil staff member at Alice or Bob's ISP might find it outright easy. This form of attack is being addressed by the development of key distribution methods that can ensure sender authenticity and message integrity, even over insecure channels. This attack is especially interesting when the attacker is the government as they potentially have the power to persuade a certificate authority to sign a bogus public-key. Then the government can plug off the cable at Bob's ISP and insert their bogus web server. The function of this server is to present itself as Alice (validated by the certificate obtained by coercion), log all messages and forward them to the "real" Alice web server.

4. Computational Cost

Note that most public-key algorithms are relatively computationally costly, in comparison with many symmetric key algorithms of apparently equivalent security. This fact has important implications for their practical use. Most are used in hybrid cryptosystems for reasons of efficiency; in such a cryptosystem, a shared secret key ("session key") is generated by one party, this much briefer session key is then encrypted by each recipient's public-key. Each recipient uses the corresponding private-key to decrypt the session key. Once all parties have obtained the session key, they can use a much faster symmetric algorithm to encrypt and decrypt messages.

5. Associating Public-Keys with Identities

Furthermore, the binding between a public-key and its "owner" must be correct, lest the algorithm function perfectly and yet be entirely insecure in practice. As with most cryptography, the protocols used to establish and verify this binding are critically important. Associating a public-key with its owner is typically done by protocols implementing a public-key infrastructure; these allow the validity of the association to be formally verified by reference to a trusted third party, either in the form of a hierarchical certificate authority (e. g., X. 509), a local trust model (e. g., SPKI), or a web of trust scheme (e. g., that originally built into PGP and GPG and still to some extent usable with them). Whatever the cryptographic assurance of the protocols themselves, the association between a public-key and its owner is ultimately a matter of subjective judgement on the part of the trusted third party, since the key is a mathematical entity whilst the owner, and the connection between owner and key, are not. For this reason, the formalism of a public-key infrastructure must provide for explicit statements of the policy followed when making this judgement. For example, the complex and never fully implemented X. 509 standard allows a certificate authority to identify its policy by means of an object identifier which functions as an index into a catalogue of registered policies. Policies may exist for many different purposes, ranging from anonymity to military classification.

6. Relation to Real World Events

A public key will be known to a large, in practice, unknown set of users. All events requiring revocation or replacement of a public-key can take a long time to take full effect with all who must be informed (i. e., all those users who possess that key). For this reason, systems which must react to events in real time (e. g., safety-critical systems or national security systems) should not use public-key encryption without taking great care. There are four issues of interest.

(1) Privilege of Key Revocation

A malicious (or erroneous) revocation of some, or all, of the keys in the system is likely, in the second case, certain, to cause a complete failure of the system. If public-keys can be revoked individually, this is a possibility. However, there are design approaches which can reduce the practical chance of this occurring. For example, by means of certificates we can create what is called a "compound principal"; one such principal could be "Alice and Bob have Revoked Authority". Now only Alice and Bob (in concert) can revoke a key, and neither Alice nor Bob can revoke keys alone. However, revoking a key now requires both Alice and Bob to be available, and this creates a problem of reliability. In concrete terms, from a security point of view, there is now a single point of failure in the public-key revocation system. A successful DoS attack against either Alice or Bob (or both) will block a required revocation. In fact, any partition of authority between Alice and Bob will have this effect, regardless of how it comes about.

Because the principal having revocation authority for keys is very powerful, the mechanisms used to control it should involve both as many participants as possible (to guard against malicious attacks of this type), while at the same time as few as possible (to ensure that a key can be revoked without dangerous delay). Public-key certificates which include an expiry date are unsatisfactory in that the expiry date may not correspond with a real world revocation need, but at least such certificates need not all be tracked down system wide, nor must all users be in constant contact with the system at all times.

(2) Distribution of a New Key

After a key has been revoked, or when a new user is added to a system, a new key must be distributed in some pre-determined manner.

Assume that Carol's key has been revoked (e.g., automatically by exceeding its use-before date, or less so, because of a compromise of Carol's matching private-key). Until a new key has been distributed, Carol is effectively out of contact. No one will be able to send his messages without violating system protocols (i.e., without a valid public-key, no one can encrypt messages to him), and messages from him cannot be signed for the same reason. Or, in other words, the "part of the system" controlled by Carol is essentially unavailable. Security requirements have been ranked higher than system availability in such designs.

One could leave the authority to create new keys (and certify them) and the authority to revoke them in the hands of each user, and the original PGP design did so, but this raises problems of user understanding and operation. For security reasons, this approach has considerable difficulties; if nothing else, some users will be forgetful or inattentive or confused. On one hand, a public-key certificate revoking message should be spread as fast as possible while, on the other hand, (parts of) the system might be ren-

Chapter 2 Cryptography

dered inoperable before a new key can be installed. The time window can obviously be reduced to zero by always issuing the new key together with the certificate that revokes the old one, but this requires co-location of both authorities to revoke and to generate new keys.

It is most likely a system-wide failure if the (possibly combined) principal that issues new keys fails by issuing keys improperly. It is an instance of a common mutual exclusion; a design can make the reliability of a system high, but only at the cost of system availability, and vice versa.

(3) Spreading the Revocation

Notification of a key certificate revocation must be spread to all those who might potentially hold it, and as rapidly as possible.

There are two means of spreading information (e.g., a key revocation here) in a distributed system: either the information is pushed to users from a central point(s), or it is pulled from a central point(s) to end users.

Pushing the information is the simplest solution in that a message is sent to all participants. However, there is no way of knowing that all participants will actually receive the message, and if the number of participants is large and some of their physical or network distance great, the probability of complete success (which is, ideally, required for system security) will be rather low. In a partially updated state, the system is particularly vulnerable to DoS attacks as security has been breached, and a vulnerability window will continue to exist as long as some users have not "gotten the word". In other words, pushing certificate revocation messages is not very securable nor very reliable.

The alternative to pushing is pulling. In the extreme, all certificates contain all the keys needed to verify that the public-key of interest (i.e., the one belonging to the user to whom one wishes to send a message, or whose signature is to be checked) is still valid. In this case, at least some use of the system will be blocked if a user cannot reach the verification service (i.e., one of those systems which can establish the current validity of another user's key). Again, such a system design can be made as reliable as one wishes, at the cost of lowering security (the more servers to check for the possibility of a key revocation, the longer the window of vulnerability).

Another tradeoff is to use a somewhat less reliable, but more secure, verification service but to include an expiry data for each of the verification sources. How long this timeout should be is a decision which embodies a tradeoff between availability and security that will have to be decided in advance, at system design time.

(4) Recovery from a Leaked Key

Assume that the principal authorized to revoke a key has decided that a certain key must be revoked. In most cases this happens after the fact; for instance, it becomes known that at some time in the past an event occurred that endangered a private-key. Let us denote the time at which it is decided that the compromise occurred with T.

Such a compromise has two implications. Messages encrypted with the matching public-key (now or in the past) can no longer be assumed to be secret. Second, signatures made with the no_longer_trusted_to_be_actually_private-key after time T, can no longer be assumed to be authentic without additional information about who, where, when, etc. of the events leading up to digital signature. These will not always be available, and so all such digital signatures will be less than credible.

Loss of secrecy and/or authenticity even for a single user, has system wide security implications, and a strategy for recovery must thus be established. Such a strategy will determine who has authority and under what conditions to revoke a public-key certificate, how to spread the revocation, but also, ideally, how to deal with all messages signed with the key since time T (which will rarely be known precisely). Messages sent to that user which require the proper, now compromised, private-key to decrypt must be considered compromised as well, no matter when they were sent.

Such a recovery procedure can be quite complex, and while it is in progress the system will likely be very vulnerable against DoS attacks, among other things.

2.4.5 Examples

Examples of well-regarded asymmetric key techniques for varied purposes include:
- Diffie-Hellman
- DSS (Digital Signature Standard), which incorporates the Digital Signature Algorithm
- ElGamal
- Various Elliptic Curve techniques
- Various Password-authenticated key agreement techniques
- Paillier cryptosystem
- RSA encryption algorithm (PKCS)

Examples of poorly regarded asymmetric key algorithms include:
- Merkle-Hellman the "knapsack" algorithms

Examples of protocols using asymmetric key algorithms include:
- GPG, an implementation of OpenPGP
- IKE
- PGP
- Secure Socket Layer, now implemented as an IETF standard TLS
- SILC
- SSH

As shown in Figure 2.8, a big random number is used to make a public-key pair.

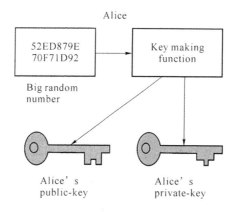

Figure 2.8　A public-key pair

As shown in Figure 2.9, anyone can encrypt using the public-key, but only the private-key can decrypt. Secrecy depends on the security of the private-key.

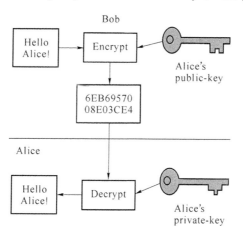

Figure 2.9　Encrypt

As shown in Figure 2.10, Using a private-key to encrypt (thus signing) a message; anyone can check the signature using the public-key. Validity depends on private-key security.

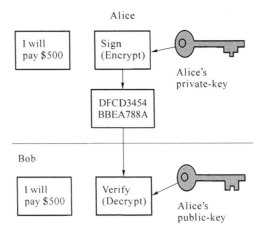

Figure 2.10 Signature

As shown in Figure 2.11, by combining your own private-key with the other user's public-key you can calculate a shared secret that only the two of you know. The shared secret can be used as the key for a symmetric cipher.

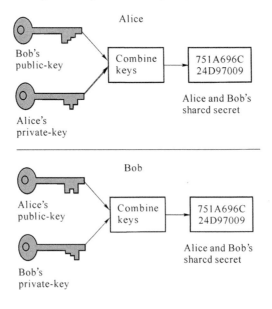

Figure 2.11 Combing private-key and public-key

2.5　Cryptographic Hash Function

In cryptography, a cryptographic hash function is a hash function with certain additional security properties to make it suitable for use as a primitive in various information security applications, such as authentication and message integrity. A hash function takes a long string (or message) of any length as input and produces a fixed length string as output, sometimes termed a message digest or a digital fingerprint (see Figure 2.12).

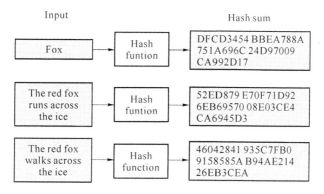

Figure 2.12　A hash function at work

In various standards and applications, the two most-commonly used hash functions are MD5 and SHA-1. In 2005, security flaws were identified in both algorithms.

2.5.1　Overview

Broadly speaking, a cryptographic hash function should behave as much as possible like a random function while still being deterministic and efficiently computable.

A cryptographic hash function is considered insecure if either of the following is computationally feasible:
- Finding a (previously unseen) message that matches a given digest;
- Finding "collisions", wherein two different messages have the same message digest.

An attacker who can do either of these things might, for example, use them to substitute an unauthorized message for an authorized one.

Ideally, it should not even be feasible to find two messages whose digests are substantially similar; nor would one want an attacker to be able to learn anything useful about a message given only its digest besides the digest itself.

2.5.2 Related Algorithms

Checksums and cyclic redundancy checks (CRCs) are quite distinct from cryptographic hash functions, and are used for different applications. If used for security, they are vulnerable to attack, for example, a CRC was used for message integrity in the WEP encryption standard, but an attack was readily discovered which exploited the linearity of the checksum specified.

A message authentication code or MAC takes a message and a secret key and generates a "MAC tag", such that it is difficult for an attacker to generate a valid pair (message, tag) that doesn't match one they've already seen; they are used to prevent attackers forging messages, among other uses. Though it is sometimes referred to as a "keyed hash function", a MAC serves a very different purpose and has very different security properties than a cryptographic hash function; for example, it is not considered a flaw if it is easy for someone who knows the MAC key to generate two messages that have the same MAC. Hash functions can be used to create MAC functions; see for example HMAC.

2.5.3 Cryptographic Properties

There is no formal definition which captures all of the properties considered desirable for a cryptographic hash function. These properties below are generally considered prerequisites:

- Preimage resistant (see one way for a related but slightly different property): given h it should be hard to find any m such that $h = \text{hash}(m)$.
- Second preimage resistant: given an input m_1, it should be hard to find another input, m_2 (not equal to m_1) such that $\text{hash}(m_1) = \text{hash}(m_2)$.
- Collision-resistant: it should be hard to find two different messages m_1 and m_2 such that $\text{hash}(m_1) = \text{hash}(m_2)$. Due to a possible birthday attack, this means the hash function output must be at least twice as large as what is required for preimage-resistance.

A hash function meeting these criteria may still have undesirable properties. For instance, most popular hash functions are vulnerable to length-extension attacks: given

Chapter 2 Cryptography

$h(m)$ and $\text{len}(m)$ but not m, by choosing a suitable m' an attacker can calculate $h(m \| m')$, where $\|$ denotes concatenation. This property can be used to break naive authentication schemes based on hash functions. The HMAC construction works around these problems.

An ideal hash function would be maximally "boring": it would have no interesting properties such as length extension, and the only interesting way it would differ from a random function would be in that it was deterministic and efficiently computable. This criterion is of course deeply resistant to formal expression; the closest thing to formal expression is the random oracle model, which is an idealization no real hash function can satisfy.

2.5.4 Applications of Hash Functions

A typical use of a cryptographic hash would be as follows: Alice poses to Bob a tough math problem and claims she has solved it. Bob would like to try it himself, but would yet like to be sure that Alice is not bluffing. Therefore, Alice writes down her solution, appends a random nonce, computes its hash and tells Bob the hash value (whilst keeping the solution and nonce secret). This way, when Bob comes up with the solution himself a few days later, Alice can prove that she had the solution earlier by revealing the nonce to Bob.

In actual practice, Alice and Bob will often be computer programs, and the secret would be something less easily spoofed than a claimed puzzle solution. The above application is called a commitment scheme. Another important application of secure hashes is verification of message integrity. Determination of whether or not any changes have been made to a message (or a file), for example, can be accomplished by comparing message digests calculated before, and after, transmission (or any other event) (for example, see Tripwire, a system using this property as a defense against malware and malfeasance). A message digest can also serve as a means of reliably identifying a file. A related application is password verification. Passwords are usually not stored in clear text, for obvious reasons, but instead in digest form. To authenticate a user, the password presented by the user is hashed and compared with the stored hash.

For both security and performance reasons, most digital signature algorithms specify that only the digest of the message be "signed", not the entire message. Hash functions can also be used in the generation of pseudorandom bits.

SHA-1, MD5, and RIPEMD-160 are among the most commonly-used messages digest algorithms as of 2005. In August 2004, researchers found weaknesses in a number of hash functions, including MD5, SHA-0 and RIPEMD. This has called into question the long-term security of later algorithms which are derived from these hash functions—in particular, SHA-1 (a strengthened version of SHA-0), RIPEMD-128, and RIPEMD-160 (both strengthened versions of RIPEMD). Neither SHA-0 nor RIPEMD are widely used since they were replaced by their strengthened versions. In February 2005, an attack on SHA-1 was reported, finding collisions in about 2^{69} hashing operations, rather than the 2^{80} expected for a 160-bit hash function. In August 2005, another attack on SHA-1 was reported, finding collisions in 2^{63} operations.

Hashes are used to identify files on peer-to-peer filesharing networks. For example, in an ed2k link, a MD4-variant hash is combined with the file size, providing sufficient information for locating file sources, downloading the file and verifying its contents. Magnet links are another example. Such file hashes are often the top hash of a hash list or a hash tree which allows for additional benefits.

2.5.5 Merkle-Damgård Hash Functions

A hash function must be able to process an arbitrary-length message into a fixed-length output. This can be achieved by breaking the input up into a series of equal-sized blocks, and operating on them in sequence using a compression function, see Figure 2.13. The compression function can either be specially designed for hashing or be built from a block cipher. A hash function build with the Merkle-Damgård is as resistant to collisions as is its compression function; any collision for the full hash function can be traced back to a collision in the compression function.

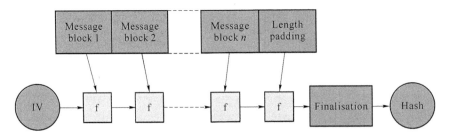

Figure 2.13 Hash function process

The last block processed should also be unambiguously length padded; this is crucial to the security of this construction. This construction is called the Merkle-Damgård construction. Most widely used hash functions, including SHA-1 and MD5, take this form.

Chapter 2 Cryptography

2.5.6 Hash Functions Based on Block Ciphers

There are several methods to use a block cipher to build a cryptographic hash function. The methods resemble the block cipher modes of operation usually used for encryption.

Using a block cipher as a hash function is usually much slower than using a specially designed hash function. But, in some cases it is easier because a single implementation of a block cipher can be used for both block cipher and a hash function. It can also save code space in very tiny embedded systems like for instance smart cards or nodes in cars or other machines.

2.5.7 Hash Functions to Build other Cryptographic Primitives

Hash functions can be used to build other cryptographic primitives. For these other primitives to be cryptographically secure care has to be taken to build them the right way.

Message authentication codes (MACs) are often built from hash functions. HMAC is such a MAC.

Just as block ciphers can be used to build hash functions, hash functions can be used to build block ciphers. Examples of such block ciphers are SHACAL, BEAR and LION.

Pseudorandom number generators (PRNGs) can be built using hash functions. This is done by combining a (secret) random seed with a counter and hashing it. If the counter is a bignum (allowed to count to any size) then the PRNG can have an infinite period.

Stream ciphers can be built using hash functions. Often this is done by first building a cryptographically secure pseudorandom number generator and then using its stream of random bytes as key tream and XOR that onto the cleartext to get the ciphertext. SEAL is such a stream cipher which is based on SHA-1.

2.5.8 List of Cryptographic Hash Functions

Some of the algorithms as shown in table 2.1 are known to be insecure; consult the

English for Information Security

article for each specific algorithm for more information on the status of each algorithm.

Table 2.1 Hash algorithm

Algorithun	Output size	Internal state size	Block size	Length size	Word size	Collision
HAVAL	256/224/192/160/128	256	1 024	64	32	Yes
MD2	128	384	128	No	8	Almost
MD4	128	128	512	64	32	Yes
MD5	128	128	512	64	32	Yes
PANAMA	256	8 736	256	No	32	With flaws
RIPEMD	128	128	512	64	32	Yes
RIPEMID-128/256	128/256	128/256	512	64	32	No
RIPEMD-160/320	160/320	160/320	512	64	32	No
SHA-0	160	160	512	64	32	Yes
SHA-1	160	160	512	64	32	With flaws
SHA-256/224	256/224	256	512	64	32	No
SHA-512/384	512/384	512	1 024	128	64	No
Tiger(2)-192/160/128	192/160/128	192	512	64	64	No
VEST-4/8(hash mode)	160/256	176/304	8	80	1	No
VEST-16/32(hash mode)	320/512	424/680	8	88	1	No
WHIRLPOOL	512	512	512	256	8	No

The SHA hash functions are a series of functions developed by the NSA: SHA, also known as SHA-0, SHA-1 and four flavors of a function known as SHA-2.

NOTE: The internal state here means the "internal hash sum" after each compression of a data block. Most hash algorithms also internally use some additional variables such as length of the data compressed so far since that is needed for the length padding in the end. See the Merkle-Damgård construction for details.

Glossary

adversary	敌手,对手
block cipher	分组密码
brute-force attack	暴力破解攻击
ciphertext	密文
confidentiality	机密性
cryptanalysis	密码分析学

Chapter 2 Cryptography

cryptanalyst	密码破译者
cryptographer	译解密码者
cryptography	密码系统
cryptology	密码研究
cryptosystem	密码系统
decryption	解密
derangement	扰乱
digital rights management (DRM)	数据版权管理
digital signatures	数据版权管理
discrete logarithm	离散对数
disguise	假装,伪装,掩饰
drawback	缺点,障碍
elliptic curve cryptography(ECC)	椭圆曲线加密算法
encryption	加密
entropy	熵
espionage	间谍,侦探
factorization problem	因子分解问题
hash function	哈希函数
immune	免疫者
integer factorization	整数分解
malevolent	有恶意的
message authentication codes (MACs)	消息认证码
message digest	消息摘要
message integrity	消息完整性
monoalphabetic cipher	单码代换密码
plaintext	明文
polyalphabetic cipher	多码代替密码
privacy	隐私权,保密性
pseudorandom	伪随机的
public-key cryptography	公钥加密算法
smart card	智能卡
stream cipher	流密码
substitution cipher	替代密码
symmetric-key cryptography	对称密钥密码学
transposition cipher	移位密码

English for Information Security

unicity	单一性
verification	确认验证
wiretap	窃听偷录

Translate the following sentences/passage into Chinese

(1) Until modern times, cryptography referred almost exclusively to encryption, the process of converting ordinary information (plaintext) into something unintelligible; this is a ciphertext. Decryption is the reverse, moving from unintelligible ciphertext to plaintext.

(2) In cryptography, a cryptographic hash function is a hash function with certain additional security properties to make it suitable for use as a primitive in various information security applications, such as authentication and message integrity.

(3) Before the modern era, cryptography was concerned solely with message confidentiality (i.e., encryption)—conversion of messages from a comprehensible form into an incomprehensible one, and back again at the other end, rendering it unreadable by interceptors or eavesdroppers without secret knowledge (namely, the key needed for decryption).

(4) Symmetric-key cryptography refers to encryption methods in which both the sender and receiver share the same key (or, less commonly, in which their keys are different, but related in an easily computable way).

(5) In addition to encryption, public-key cryptography can be used to implement digital signature schemes. A digital signature is reminiscent of an ordinary signature; they both have the characteristic that they are easy for a user to produce, but difficult for anyone else to forge.

Translate the following sentences/passage into English

(1) 现代密码学的一个基本原则是:一切秘密都存在于密钥之中。其含义是,在设计加密系统时,总是假设密码算法是公开的,真正需要保密的是密钥。这是因为密码算法相对密钥来说更容易泄漏。

(2) 对称密码体制的密码需要实现经过安全的密码通道由发方传给收方。这种密码体制的优点是:安全性高,加密速度快。缺点是:随着网络规模的扩大,密钥的管理成为一个难点;无法解决消息确认问题;缺乏自动检测密钥泄露的能力。

(3) 密码协议具有以下特点:协议自始至终是有序的过程,每一个步骤必须执行,在前一步没有执行完之前,后面的步骤不可能执行;协议至少需要两个参与者;通过协议必须能够完成某项任务;协议必须满足一定的安全需求。

(4) 由于密码学为通信提供强大的安全性,攻击者把目光转向了系统漏洞。系统漏洞是软件系统、网络协议等在设计编写时出现的安全缺陷,攻击者可以利用这些漏洞对系统进行攻击。对于这类攻击,目前有多种不同的应对技术,而密码学也在一定程度上可以发挥作用。

(5) 公开密钥密码也称为非对称密钥密码。使用公开密钥密码的每一个用户都分别拥有两个密钥:加密密钥和解密密钥,它们两者并不相同,并且由加密密钥得到解密密钥在计算机上是不可行的。每一个用户的加密密钥都是公开的(因此,加密密钥也称为公开密钥)。

Questions

(1) What are the advantages and disadvantages of public-key cryptography?
(2) What are the advantages and disadvantages of symmetric-key cryptography?
(3) Why symmetric-key cryptography can not be used in authentication?
(4) How public-key cryptography is used for signature?
(5) How hash function is used for message integrity?

Chapter 3

Firewall

3.1 Introduction

If you have been using the Internet for a length of time, especially if you work at a larger company and browse the Web while you are at work, you have probably heard the term firewall used. For example, you often hear people in companies say things like, "I can't use that site because they won't let it through the firewall."

If you have a fast Internet connection into your home (either a DSL connection or a cable modem), you may have found yourself hearing about firewalls for your home network as well(see Figure 3.1). It turns out that a small home network has many of the same security issues that a large corporate network does. You can use a firewall to protect your home network and family from offensive Web sites and potential hackers.

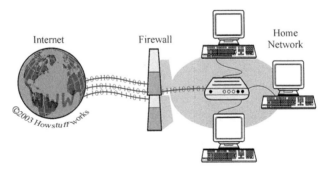

Figure 3.1 Firewall

Chapter 3 Firewall

Basically, a firewall is a barrier to keep destructive forces away from your property. In fact, that's why it's called a firewall. Its job is similar to a physical firewall that keeps a fire from spreading from one area to the next. As you read through this article, you will learn more about firewalls, how they work and what kinds of threats they can protect you from.

A firewall protects networked computers from intentional hostile intrusion that could compromise confidentiality or result in data corruption or denial of service. It may be a hardware device (see Figure 3.2) or a software program (see Figure 3.3) running on a secure host computer. In either case, it must have at least two network interfaces, one for the network it is intended to protect, and one for the network it is exposed to.

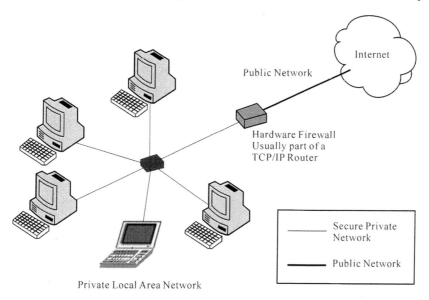

Figure 3.2 Hardware firewall

(Hardware firewall providing protection to a local network)

A firewall sits at the junction point or gateway between the two networks, usually a private network and a public network such as the Internet. The earliest firewalls were simply routers. The term firewall comes from the fact that by segmenting a network into different physical subnetworks, they limited the damage that could spread from one subnet to another just like firedoors or firewalls.

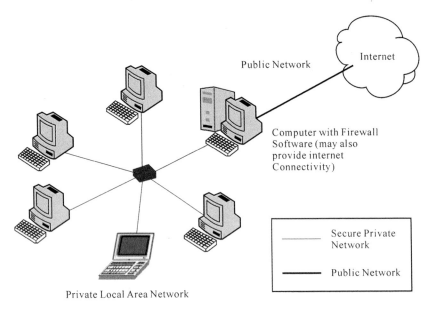

Figure 3.3 Computer with firewall software

(Computer running firewall software to provide protection)

1. What does a firewall do?

A firewall examines all traffic routed between the two networks to see if it meets certain criteria. If it does, it is routed between the networks, otherwise it is stopped. A firewall filters both inbound and outbound traffic. It can also manage public access to private networked resources such as host applications. It can be used to log all attempts to enter the private network and trigger alarms when hostile or unauthorized entry is attempted. Firewalls can filter packets based on their source and destination addresses and port numbers. This is known as address filtering. Firewalls can also filter specific types of network traffic. This is also known as protocol filtering because the decision to forward or reject traffic is dependant upon the protocol used, for example HTTP, FTP or Telnet. Firewalls can also filter traffic by packet attribute or state.

2. What can't a firewall do?

A firewall cannot prevent individual users with modems from dialing into or out of the network, by passing the firewall altogether. Employee misconduct or carelessness cannot be controlled by firewalls. Policies involving the use and misuse of passwords and user accounts must be strictly enforced. These are management issues that should be raised during the planning of any security policy but that cannot be solved with firewalls alone.

The arrest of the Phonemasters cracker ring brought these security issues to light.

Although they were accused of breaking into information systems run by AT&T Corp., British Telecommunications Inc., GTE Corp., MCI WorldCom, Southwestern Bell, and Sprint Corp., the group did not use any high tech methods such as IP spoofing (see question 10). They used a combination of social engineering and dumpster diving. Social engineering involves skills not unlike those of a confidence trickster. People are tricked into revealing sensitive information. Dumpster diving or garbology, as the name suggests, is just plain old looking through company trash. Firewalls cannot be effective against either of these techniques.

3. Who needs a firewall?

Anyone who is responsible for a private network that is connected to a public network needs firewall protection. Furthermore, anyone who connects so much as a single computer to the Internet via modem should have personal firewall software. Many dial-up Internet users believe that anonymity will protect them. They feel that no malicious intruder would be motivated to break into their computer. Dial-up users who have been victims of malicious attacks and who have lost entire days of work, perhaps having to reinstall their operating system, know that this is not true. Irresponsible pranksters can use automated robots to scan random IP addresses and attack whenever the opportunity presents itself.

4. How does a firewall work?

There are two access denial methodologies used by firewalls (see Figure 3.4). A firewall may allow all traffic through unless it meets certain criteria, or it may deny all traffic unless it meets certain criteria. The type of criteria used to determine whether traffic should be allowed through varies from one type of firewall to another. Firewalls may be concerned with the type of traffic, or with source or destination addresses and ports. They may also use complex rule bases that analyze the application data to determine if the traffic should be allowed through. How a firewall determines what traffic to let through depends on which network layer it operates at. A discussion on network layers and architecture follows.

5. What are the OSI and TCP/IP Network models?

To understand how firewalls work helps to understand how the different layers of a network interact. Network architecture is designed around a seven layer model, see Figure 3.5. Each layer has its own set of responsibilities, and handles them in a well-defined manner. This enables networks to mix and match network protocols and physical supports. In a given network, a single protocol can travel over more than one physical support (layer one) because the physical layer has been dissociated from the protocol layers (layers three to seven). Similarly, a single physical cable can carry more than one protocol. The TCP/IP model is older than the OSI industry standard model which is why it does not comply in every respect. The first four layers are so closely analogous to OSI layers however that interoperability is a day to day reality.

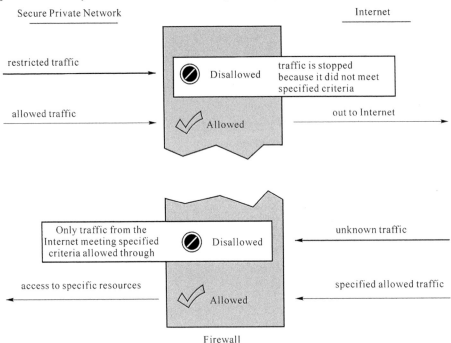

Figure 3.4 Basic firewall operation

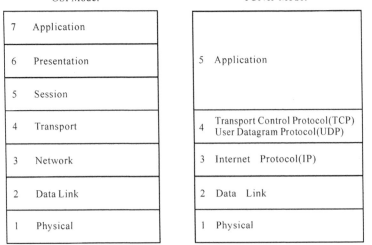

Figure 3.5 The OSI and TCP/IP models

Firewalls operate at different layers to use different criteria to restrict traffic. The lowest layer at which a firewall can work is layer three. In the OSI model this is the network layer. In TCP/IP it is the Internet Protocol layer. This layer is concerned with routing packets to their destination. At this layer a firewall can determine whether a packet is from a trusted source, but cannot be concerned with what it contains or what other packets it is associated with. Firewalls that operate at the transport layer know a little more about a packet, and are able to grant or deny access depending on more sophisticated criteria. At the application level, firewalls know a great deal about what is going on and can be very selective in granting access.

It would appear then, that firewalls functioning at a higher level in the stack must be superior in every respect. This is not necessarily the case. The lower in the stack the packet is intercepted, the more secure the firewall. If the intruder cannot get past level three, it is impossible to gain control of the operating system.

Professional firewall(see Figure 3.6) products catch each network packet before the operating system does, thus, there is no direct path from the Internet to the operating system's TCP/IP stack. It is therefore very difficult for an intruder to gain control of the firewall host computer then "open the doors" from the inside.

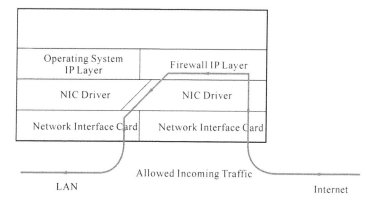

Figure 3.6 Professional firewalls have their own IP layer

According To Byte Magazine, traditional firewall technology is susceptible to misconfiguration on non-hardened OSes. More recently, however, "…firewalls have moved down the protocol stack so far that the OS doesn't have to do much more than act as a bootstrap loader, file system and GUI". The author goes on to state that newer firewall code bypasses the operating system's IP layer altogether, never permitting "potentially hostile traffic to make its way up the protocol stack to applications running on the system".

3.2 Firewall Technologies

Firewalls fall into four broad categories: packet filters, circuit level gateways, application level gateways and stateful multilayer inspection firewalls.

3.2.1 Packet Filtering Firewall

Packet filtering firewalls work at the network level of the OSI model (see Figure 3.7), or the IP layer of TCP/IP. They are usually part of a router. A router is a device that receives packets from one network and forwards them to another network. In a packet filtering firewall each packet is compared to a set of criteria before it is forwarded. Depending on the packet and the criteria, the firewall can drop the packet, forward it or send a message to the originator. Rules can include source and destination IP address, source and destination port number and protocol used. The advantages of packet filtering firewalls are their low cost and low impact on network performance. Most routers support packet filtering. Even if other firewalls are used, implementing packet filtering at the router level affords an initial degree of security at a low network layer. This type of firewall only works at the network layer however and does not support sophisticated rule based models. Network Address Translation (NAT) routers offer the advantages of packet filtering firewalls but can also hide the IP addresses of computers behind the firewall, and offer a level of circuit-based filtering.

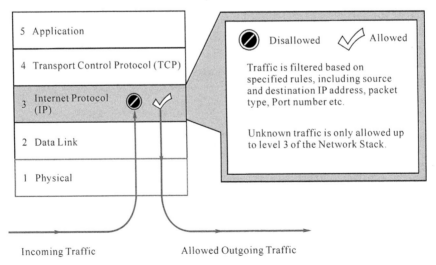

Figure 3.7　Packet filtering firewall

3.2.2 Circuit Level Gateway Firewall

Circuit level gateways work at the session layer of the OSI model(see Figure 3.8), or the TCP layer of TCP/IP. They monitor TCP handshaking between packets to determine whether a requested session is legitimate. Information passed to remote computer through a circuit level gateway appears to have originated from the gateway. This is useful for hiding information about protected networks. Circuit level gateways are relatively inexpensive and have the advantage of hiding information about the private network they protect. On the other hand, they do not filter individual packets.

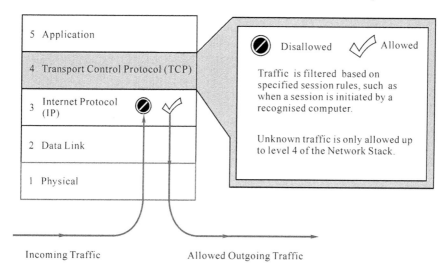

Figure 3.8 Circuit level gateway

3.2.3 Application Level Gateway Firewall

Application level gateways, also called proxies, are similar to circuit level gateways except that they are application specific(see Figure 3.9). They can filter packets at the application layer of the OSI model. Incoming or outgoing packets cannot access services for which there is no proxy. In plain terms, an application level gateway that is configured to be a web proxy will not allow any FTP, Gopher, Telnet or other traffic through. Because they examine packets at application layer, they can filter application specific commands such as http: post and get, etc. This cannot be accomplished with either packet filtering firewalls or circuit level neither of which knows anything about the application level information. Application level gateways can also be used to log user activity and logins. They offer a high level of security, but have a significant impact on network performance. This is because of context switches that slow down network access dramatically. They are not transparent to end users and require manual configuration of each client computer.

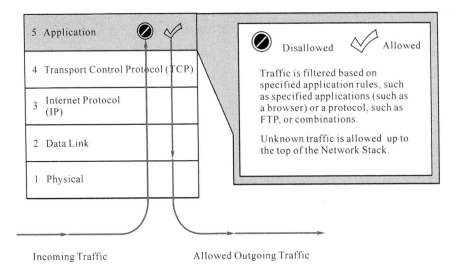

Figure 3.9　Application level gateway

3.2.4　Stateful Multilayer Inspection Firewall

Stateful multilayer inspection firewalls combine the aspects of the other three types of firewalls (see Figure 3.10). They filter packets at the network layer, determine whether session packets are legitimate and evaluate contents of packets at the application layer. They allow direct connection between client and host, alleviating the problem caused by the lack of transparency of application level gateways. They rely on algorithms to recognize and process application layer data instead of running application specific proxies. Stateful multilayer inspection firewalls offer a high level of security, good performance and transparency to end users. They are expensive however, and due to their complexity are potentially less secure than simpler types of firewalls if not administered by highly competent personnel.

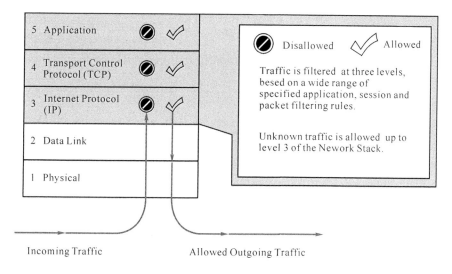

Figure 3.10　Stateful multilayer inspection firewall

3.3　Firewall Architectures

This secession describes a variety of ways to put firewall components together, and discusses their advantages and disadvantages. We'll tell you what some appropriate uses are for each architecture.

3.3.1　Single-Box Architectures

The simplest firewall architectures have a single object that acts as the firewall. In general, the security advantage of single-box architectures is that they provide a single place that you can concentrate on and be sure that you have correctly configured, while the disadvantage is that your security is entirely dependent on a single place. There is no defense in depth, but on the other hand, you know exactly what your weakest link is and how weak it is, which is much harder with multiple layers.

In practice, the advantages of single-box architectures are not in their security but in other practical concerns. Compared to a multiple-layer system that's integrated with your network, single-box architecture is cheaper, easier to understand and explain to management, and easier to get from an external vendor. This makes it the solution of choice for small sites. It also makes it a tempting solution for people who are looking for magic security solutions that can be put in once and forgotten about. While there are very good single-box firewalls, there are no magic firewalls, and single-box solutions require the same difficult decisions, careful configuration, and ongoing maintenance that all other firewalls do.

1. Screening Router

It is possible to use a packet filtering system by itself as a firewall, as shown in Figure 3.11, using just a *screening router* to protect an entire network. This is a low-cost system, since you almost always need a router to connect to the Internet anyway, and you can simply configure packet filtering in that router. On the other hand, it's not very flexible; you can permit or deny protocols by port number, but it's hard to allow some operations while denying others in the same protocol, or to be sure that what's coming in on a given port is actually the protocol you wanted to allow. In addition, it gives you no depth of defense. If the router is compromised, you have no further security.

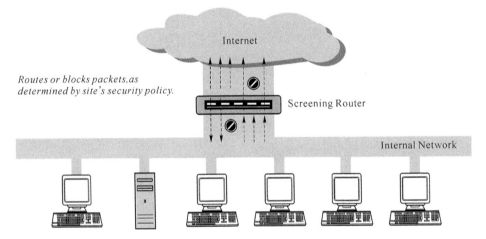

Figure 3.11 Using a screening router to do packet filtering

Appropriate Uses: A screening router is an appropriate firewall for a situation where:

- The network being protected already has a high level of host security;
- The number of protocols being used is limited, and the protocols themselves are straightforward;
- You require maximum performance and redundancy.

Screening routers are most useful for internal firewalls and for networks that are dedicated to providing services to the Internet. It's not uncommon for Internet service providers to use nothing but a screening router between their service hosts and the Internet, for instance.

2. Dual-Homed Host

Dual-homed host architecture is built around the dual-homed host computer, a computer that has at least two network interfaces. Such a host could act as a router between the networks these interfaces are attached to; it is capable of routing IP packets from one network to another. However, to use a dual-homed host as a firewall, you disable this routing function. Thus, IP packets from one network (e. g. , the Internet) are not directly routed to the other network (e. g. , the internal, protected network). Systems inside the firewall can communicate with the dual-homed host, and systems outside the firewall (on the Internet) can communicate with the dual-homed host, but these systems can't communicate directly with each other. IP traffic between them is completely blocked.

Some variations on the dual-homed host architecture use IP to the Internet and some other network protocol (for instance, NetBEUI) on the internal network. This helps to enforce the separation between the two networks, making it less likely that host misconfigurations will let traffic slip from one interface to another, and also reducing the chance that if this does happen there will be vulnerable clients. However, it does not make a significant difference to the overall security of the firewall.

The network architecture for a dual-homed host firewall is pretty simple: the dual-homed host sits between, and is connected to, the Internet and the internal network. Figure 3.12 shows this architecture.

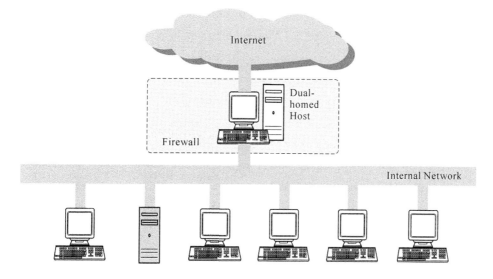

Figure 3.12 Dual-homed host architecture

Dual-homed hosts can provide a very high level of control. If you aren't allowing packets to go between external and internal networks at all, you can be sure that any packet on the internal network that has an external source is evidence of some kind of security problem.

On the other hand, dual-homed hosts aren't high-performance devices. A dual-homed host has more work to do for each connection than a packet filter does, and correspondingly needs more resources. A dual-homed host won't support as much traffic as an equivalent packet filtering system.

Since a dual-homed host is a single point of failure, it's important to make certain that its host security is absolutely impeccable. An attacker who can compromise the dual-homed host has full access to your site (no matter what protocols you are running). An attacker who crashes the dual-homed host has cut you off from the Internet. This makes dual-homed hosts inappropriate if being able to reach the Internet is critical to your business.

You are particularly vulnerable to problems with the host's IP implementation, which can crash the machine or pass traffic through it. These problems exist with packet filtering routers as well, but they are less frequent and usually easier to fix. Architectures that involve multiple devices are usually more resilient because multiple different IP implementations are involved.

A dual-homed host can provide services only by proxying them, or by having users log into the dual-homed host directly. You want to avoid having users log into the dual-homed host directly. As we discuss in later section, "Bastion Hosts", user accounts present significant security problems by themselves. They present special problems on dual-homed hosts, where users may unexpectedly enable services you consider insecure. Furthermore, most users find it inconvenient to use a dual-homed host by logging into it.

Proxying is much less problematic but may not be available for all services you're interested in "Proxy Systems", discusses some workarounds for this situation, but they do not apply in every case. Using a dual-homed host as your only network connection actually slightly eases some problems with proxying; if the host pretends to be a router, it can intercept packets bound for the outside world and transparently proxy them without anybody else's cooperation.

Proxying is much better at supporting outbound services (internal users using resources on the Internet) than inbound services (users on the Internet using resources on the internal network). In a dual-homed host configuration, you will normally have to provide services to the Internet by running them on the dual-homed host. This is not usually advisable because providing services to the Internet is risky, and the dual-homed host is a security-critical machine that you don't want to put risky services on. It might be acceptable to put a minimally functional web server on the dual-homed host (for instance, one that was only capable of providing HTML files and had no active content features, additional protocols, or forms processing), but it would clearly be extremely dangerous to provide a normal web server there.

The screened subnet architecture we describe in a later section offers some extra options for providing new, untrusted, or inbound services (e. g. , you can add a worthless machine to the screened subnet that provides only an untrusted service).

Appropriate Uses: A dual-homed host is an appropriate firewall for a situation where:
- Traffic to the Internet is small;
- Traffic to the Internet is not business-critical;
- No services are being provided to Internet-based users;
- The network being protected does not contain extremely valuable data.

3.3.2 Screened Host Architectures

Whereas a dual-homed host architecture provides services from a host that's attached to multiple networks (but has routing turned off), a screened host architecture provides services from a host that's attached to only the internal network, using a separate router. In this architecture, the primary security is provided by packet filtering. (For example, packet filtering is what prevents people from going around proxy servers to make direct connections.)

Figure 3.13 shows a simple version of a screened host architecture. The bastion host sits on the internal network. The packet filtering on the screening router is set up in such a way that the bastion host is the only system on the internal network that hosts on the Internet can open connections to (for example, to deliver incoming E-mail). Even then, only certain types of connections are allowed. Any external system trying to access internal systems or services will have to connect to this host. The bastion host thus needs to maintain a high level of host security.

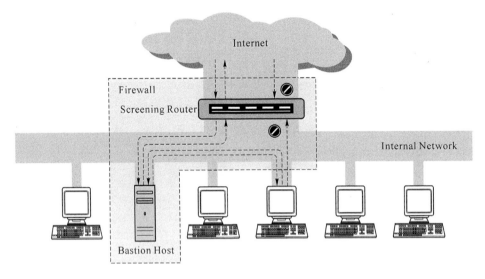

Figure 3.13　Screened host architecture

Packet filtering also permits the bastion host to open allowable connections (what is "allowable" will be determined by your site's particular security policy) to the outside world.

The packet filtering configuration in the screening router may do one of the following:
- Allow other internal hosts to open connections to hosts on the Internet for certain services (allowing those services via packet filtering, as "Packet Filtering");
- Disallow all connections from internal hosts (forcing those hosts to use proxy services via the bastion host, as "Proxy Systems").

You can mix and match these approaches for different services; Some may be allowed directly via packet filtering, while others may be allowed only indirectly via proxy. It all depends on the particular policy your site is trying to enforce.

Because this architecture allows packets to move from the Internet to the internal networks, it may seem more risky than a dual-homed host architecture, which is designed so that no external packet can reach the internal network. In practice, however, the dual-homed host architecture is also prone to failures that let packets actually cross from the external network to the internal network. (Because this type of failure is completely unexpected, there are unlikely to be protections against attacks of this kind.) Furthermore, it's easier to defend a router than it is to defend a host. For most purposes, the screened host architecture provides both better security and better usability than the dual-homed host architecture.

Compared to other architectures, however, such as the screened subnet architecture, there are some disadvantages to the screened host architecture. The major one is that if an attacker manages to break in to the bastion host, nothing is left in the way of network security between the bastion host and the rest of the internal hosts. The router also presents a single point of failure; if the router is compromised, the entire network is available to an attacker. For this reason, the screened subnet architecture, discussed next, has become increasingly popular.

Because the bastion host is a single point of failure, it is inappropriate to run high-risk services like web servers on it. You need to provide the same level of protection to it that you would provide to a dual-homed host that was the sole firewall for your site.

Appropriate Uses: A screened host architecture is appropriate when:
- Few connections are coming from the Internet (in particular, it is not an appropriate architecture if the screened host is a public web server);
- The network being protected has a relatively high level of host security.

3.3.3 Screened Subnet Architectures

The screened subnet architecture adds an extra layer of security to the screened host architecture by adding a perimeter network that further isolates the internal network from the Internet.

Why do this? By their nature, bastion hosts are the most vulnerable machines on your network. Despite your best efforts to protect them, they are the machines most likely to be attacked because they're the machines that can be attacked. If, as in the screened host architecture, your internal network is wide open to attack from your bastion host, then your bastion host is a very tempting target. No other defenses are between it and your other internal machines (besides whatever host security they may have, which is usually very little). If someone successfully breaks into the bastion host in the screened host architecture, that intruder has hit the jackpot. By isolating the bastion host on a perimeter network, you can reduce the impact of a break-in on the bastion host. It is no longer an instantaneous jackpot; it gives an intruder some access but not all.

With the simplest type of screened subnet architecture, there are two screening routers, each connected to the perimeter net. One site between the perimeter net and the internal network, and the other sits between the perimeter net and the external network (usually the Internet). To break into the internal network with this type of architecture, an attacker would have to get past both routers. Even if the attacker somehow broke in to the bastion host, he'd still have to get past the interior router. There is no single vulnerable point that will compromise the internal network.

Figure 3.14 shows a possible firewall configuration that uses the screened subnet architecture. The next few sections describe the components in this type of architecture.

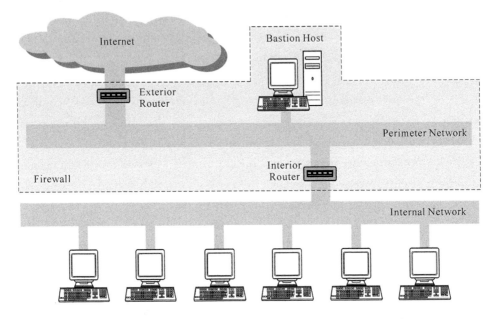

Figure 3.14 Screened subnet architecture (using two routers)

1. Perimeter Network

The perimeter network is another layer of security, an additional network between the external network and your protected internal network. If an attacker successfully breaks into the outer reaches of your firewall, the perimeter net offers an additional layer of protection between that attacker and your internal systems.

Here's an example of why a perimeter network can be helpful. In many network setups, it's possible for any machines on a given network to see the traffic for every machine on that network. This is true for most Ethernet-based networks (and Ethernet is by far the most common local area networking technology in use today); it is also true for several other popular technologies, such as token ring and FDDI. Snoopers may succeed in picking up passwords by watching for those used during Telnet, FTP, and rlogin sessions. Even if passwords aren't compromised, snoopers can still peek at the contents of sensitive files people may be accessing, interesting E-mail they may be reading, and so on; the snooper can essentially "watch over the shoulder" of anyone using the network. A large number of tools are available that attackers used to do this sort of snooping and to conceal that it's being done.

Chapter 3 Firewall

With a perimeter network, if someone breaks into a bastion host on the perimeter net, they'll be able to snoop only on traffic on that net. All the traffic on the perimeter net should be either to or from the bastion host, or to or from the Internet. Because no strictly internal traffic (that is, traffic between two internal hosts, which is presumably sensitive or proprietary) passes over the perimeter net, internal traffic will be safe from prying eyes if the bastion host is compromised.

Obviously, traffic to and from the bastion host, or the external world, will still be visible. Part of the work in designing a firewall is ensuring that this traffic is not itself confidential enough that reading it will compromise your site as a whole.

2. Bastion Host

With the screened subnet architecture, you attach a bastion host (or hosts) to the perimeter net; this host is the main point of contact for incoming connections from the outside world; for example:

- For incoming E-mail (SMTP) sessions to deliver electronic mail to the site;
- For incoming FTP connections to the site's anonymous FTP server;
- For incoming Domain Name System (DNS) queries about the site;

and so on.

Outbound services (from internal clients to servers on the Internet) are handled in either of these ways:

- Set up packet filtering on both the exterior and interior routers to allow internal clients to access external servers directly.
- Set up proxy servers to run on the bastion host (if your firewall uses proxy software) to allow internal clients to access external servers indirectly. You would also set up packet filtering to allow the internal clients to talk to the proxy servers on the bastion host and vice versa, but to prohibit direct communications between internal clients and the outside world.

In either case, packet filtering allows the bastion host to connect to, and accept connections from hosts on the Internet; which hosts, and for what services, are dictated by the site's security policy.

Such of what the bastion host does is act as proxy server for various services, either by running specialized proxy server software for particular protocols (such as HTTP or FTP), or by running standard servers for self-proxying protocols (such as SMTP).

3. Interior Router

The interior router (sometimes called the choke router in firewalls literature) protects the internal network both from the Internet and from the perimeter net.

The interior router does most of the packet filtering for your firewall. It allows

English for Information Security

selected services outbound from the internal net to the Internet. These services are the services your site can safely support and safely provide using packet filtering rather than proxies. (Your site needs to establish its own definition of what "safe" means. You'll have to consider your own needs, capabilities, and constraints; there is no one answers for all sites.) The services you allow might include outgoing HTTP, Telnet, FTP, and others, as appropriate for your own needs and concerns. (For detailed information on how you can use packet filtering to control these services, see section, "Packet Filtering".)

The services the interior router allows between your bastion host (on the perimeter net itself) and your internal net are not necessarily the same services the interior router allows between the Internet and your internal net. The reason for limiting the services between the bastion host and the internal network is to reduce the number of machines (and the number of services on those machines) that can be attacked from the bastion host, should it be compromised.

You should limit the services allowed between the bastion host and the internal net to just those that are actually needed, such as SMTP (so the bastion host can forward incoming E-mail), DNS (so the bastion host can answer questions from internal machines, or ask them, depending on your configuration), and so on. You should further limit services, to the extent possible, by allowing them only to or from particular internal hosts; for example, SMTP might be limited only to connections between the bastion host and your internal mail server or servers. Pay careful attention to the security of those remaining internal hosts and services that can be contacted by the bastion host, because those hosts and services will be what an attacker goes after—indeed, will be all the attacker can go after—if the attacker manages to break in to your bastion host.

4. Exterior Router

In theory, the exterior router (sometimes called the access router in firewalls literature) protects both the perimeter net and the internal net from the Internet. In practice, exterior routers tend to allow almost anything outbound from the perimeter net, and they generally do very little packet filtering. The packet filtering rules to protect internal machines would need to be essentially the same on both the interior router and the exterior router; if there's an error in the rules that allows access to an attacker, the error will probably be present on both routers.

Frequently, the exterior router is provided by an external group (for example, your Internet provider), and your access to it may be limited. An external group that's maintaining a router will probably be willing to put in a few general packet filtering rules but won't want to maintain a complicated or frequently changing rule set. You also may not trust them as much as you trust your own routers. If the router breaks and they install

Chapter 3 Firewall

a new one, are they going to remember to reinstall the filters? Are they even going to bother to mention that they replaced the router so that you know to check?

The only packet filtering rules that are really special on the exterior router are those that protect the machines on the perimeter net (that is, the bastion hosts and the internal router). Generally, however, not much protection is necessary, because the hosts on the perimeter net are protected primarily through host security (although redundancy never hurts).

The rest of the rules that you could put on the exterior router are duplicates of the rules on the interior router. These are the rules that prevent insecure traffic from going between internal hosts and the Internet. To support proxy services, where the interior router will let the internal hosts send some protocols as long as they are talking to the bastion host, the exterior router could let those protocols through as long as they are coming from the bastion host. These rules are desirable for an extra level of security, but they're theoretically blocking only packets that can't exist because they've already been blocked by the interior router. If they do exist, either the interior router has failed, or somebody has connected an unexpected host to the perimeter network.

So, what does the exterior router actually need to do? One of the security tasks that the exterior router can usefully perform—a task that usually can't easily be done anywhere else—is the blocking of any incoming packets from the Internet that have forged source addresses. Such packets claim to have come from within the internal network but actually are coming in from the Internet.

The interior router could do this, but it can't tell if packets that claim to be from the perimeter net are forged. While the perimeter net shouldn't have anything fully trusted on it, it's still going to be more trusted than the external universe; being able to forge packets from it will give an attacker most of the benefits of compromising the bastion host. The exterior router is at a clearer boundary. The interior router also can't protect the systems on the perimeter net against forged packets.

Another task that the exterior router can perform is to prevent IP packets containing inappropriate source addresses from leaving your network. All traffic leaving your network should come from one of your source addresses. If not, then either you have a serious configuration problem, or somebody is forging source addresses.

Although filtering inappropriate source addresses outbound doesn't provide any network protection to you, it prevents an intruder from using your systems to launch certain types of attacks on other sites. If the exterior router is configured to alert you when forged source addresses are seen, this may be just the early warning alarm you need in order to detect a serious network problem. The practice of being a good network citizen may also be enough to keep the name of your site out of a possibly embarrassing news headline.

Appropriate Uses: A screened subnet architecture is appropriate for most uses.

3.4 Windows Firewall

3.4.1 Introduction

Windows Firewall, previously known as Internet Connection Firewall or ICF, is a protective boundary that monitors and restricts information that travels between your computer and a network or the Internet. This provides a line of defense against someone who might try to access your computer from outside the Windows Firewall without your permission.

If you're running Windows XP Service Pack 2 (SP2), Windows Firewall is turned on by default. However, some computer manufacturers and network administrators might turn it off.

To open Windows Firewall

(1) Click **Start** and then click **Control Panel**;

(2) In the control panel, click **Windows Security Center** (see Figure 3.15);

(3) Click **Windows Firewall**.

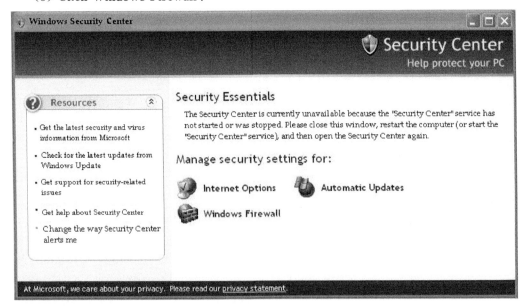

Figure 3.15   Windows firewall

Chapter 3 Firewall

Note you do not have to use Windows Firewall—you can install and run any firewall that you choose. Evaluate the features of other firewalls and then decide which firewall best meets your needs. If you choose to install and run another firewall, turn off Windows Firewall.

How Windows Firewall Works: When someone on the Internet or on a network tries to connect to your computer, we call that attempt an "unsolicited request". When your computer gets an unsolicited request, Windows Firewall blocks the connection. If you run a program such as an instant messaging program or a multiplayer network game that needs to receive information from the Internet or a network, the firewall asks if you want to block or unblock (allow) the connection. You should see a window like the one below(Figure 3.16).

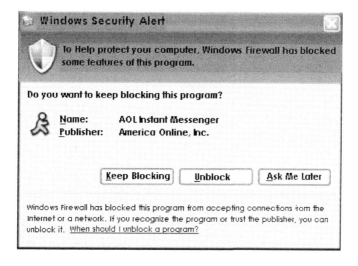

Figure 3.16 Firewall security alert

If you choose to unblock the connection, Windows Firewall creates an exception so that the firewall won't bother you when that program needs to receive information in the future. To learn more about exceptions, see the Using the Exceptions Tab section of this article.

TIP: Although you can turn off Windows Firewall for specific Internet and network connections, doing this increases the risk to your computer's security.

Table 3.1 shows what Windows Firewall does and does not do.

Table 3.1 What Windows Firewall Does and Does Not Do

It does	It does not
Help block computer viruses and worms from reaching your computer.	Detect or disable computer viruses and worms if they are already on your computer. For that reason, you should also install antivirus software and keep it updated to help prevent viruses, worms, and other security threats from damaging your computer or using your computer to spread viruses to others. For more information, see Frequently Asked Questions About Antivirus Software.
Ask for your permission to block or unblock certain connection requests.	Stop you from opening E-mail with dangerous attachments. Don't open E-mail attachments from senders that you don't know. Even if you know and trust the source of the E-mail you should still be cautious. If someone you know sends you an E-mail attachment, look at the subject line carefully before opening it. If the subject line is gibberish or does not make any sense to you, check with the sender before opening it.
Create a record (a security log), if you want one, that records successful and unsuccessful attempts to connect to your computer. This can be useful as a troubleshooting tool.	Block spam or unsolicited E-mail from appearing in your inbox. However, some E-mail programs can help you do this. Check the documentation for your E-mail program or see Fighting Unwanted Spam to learn more.

3.4.2 Using the Exceptions Tab

If you're running Windows XP Service Pack 2 (SP2) the Windows Firewall is turned on by default. This means that most programs will not be allowed to accept unsolicited communications from the Internet unless you choose to list those programs as exceptions. There are two programs that, by default, are already added to the exceptions list and can accept unsolicited communications from the Internet: Files and Settings Transfer Wizard and File and Printer Sharing.

Because firewalls restrict communication between your computer and the Internet, you might need to adjust settings for some other programs that prefer an open connection. You can make an exception for these programs, so that they can communicate through the Windows Firewall.

Allowing Exceptions—the Risks: Each time you allow an exception for a program to communicate through Windows Firewall, your computer is made more vulnerable. To allow an exception is like poking a hole through the firewall. If there are too many holes, there's not much wall left in your firewall. Hackers often use software that scans the Internet looking for computers with unprotected connections. If you have lots of exceptions and open ports, your computer can become more vulnerable.

To help decrease your security risk:
- Only allow an exception when you really need it;
- Never allow an exception for a program that you don't recognize;
- Remove an exception when you no longer need it.

Allowing Exceptions Despite the Risks: Sometimes you might want someone to be able to connect to your computer, despite the risk—such as when you expect to receive a file sent through an instant messaging program, or play a multiplayer game over the Internet.

For example, if you're exchanging instant messages with someone who wants to send you a file (a photo, for example), Windows Firewall will ask you if you want to unblock the connection and allow the photo to reach your computer. Or, if you want to play a multiplayer network game with friends over the Internet, you can add the game as an exception so that the firewall will allow the game information to reach your computer.

To add a program to the exceptions list:

(1) Click **Start** and then click **Control Panel**;

(2) In the control panel, click **Security Center**, and then click **Windows Firewall**;

(3) On the **Exceptions** tab, under **Programs and Services**, select the check box for the program or service that you want to allow, and then click **OK** (see Figure 3.17).

Figure 3.17 Windows firewall exceptions tab

If the program (or service) that you want to allow is not listed:

(1) Click **Add Program**;

(2) In the **Add a Program** dialog box, click the program that you want to add, and then click OK. The program will appear, selected, on the **Exceptions** tab, under **Programs and Services**;

(3) Click OK.

Tip: If the program (or service) that you want to allow is not listed in the Add a Program dialog box click Browse, locate the program that you want to add, and then double-click it. (Programs are usually stored in the Program Files folder on your computer.) The program will appear under Programs, in the Add a Program dialog box.

As a Last Resort, Open a Port: If you still do not find the program, you can open a port instead. A port is like a small door in the firewall that allows communications to pass through. To specify which port to open, on the Exceptions tab, click Add Port. (When you open a port, remember to close it again when you are done using it.)

Adding an exception is preferable to opening a port because:
- It is easier to do;
- You do not need to know which port number to use;
- It is more secure than opening a port, because the firewall is only open while the program is waiting to receive the connection.

Advanced Options: Advanced users can open ports for, and configure the scope of, individual connections to minimize opportunities for intruders to connect to a computer or network. To do this, open Windows Firewall, click the Advanced tab, and use the settings under Network Connection Settings.

3.5 Problems and Benefits of Firewall

3.5.1 Firewall Related Problems

Firewalls introduce problems of their own. Information security involves constraints, and users don't like this. It reminds them that Bad Things can and do happen. Firewalls restrict access to certain services. The vendors of information technology are constantly telling us "anything, anywhere, any time", and we believe them naively. Of course they forget to tell us we need to log in and out, to memorize our 27 different passwords, not to write them down on a sticky note on our computer screen and so on.

Firewalls can also constitute a traffic bottleneck. They concentrate security in one spot, aggravating the single point of failure phenomenon. The alternatives however are either no Internet access, or no security, neither of which are acceptable in most organizations.

3.5.2 Benefits of a Firewall

Firewalls protect private local area networks from hostile intrusion from the Internet. Consequently, many LANs are now connected to the Internet where Internet connectivity would otherwise have been too great a risk.

Firewalls allow network administrators to offer access to specific types of Internet services to selected LAN users. This selectivity is an essential part of any information management program, and involves not only protecting private information assets, but also knowing who has access to what. Privileges can be granted according to job description and need rather than on an all-or-nothing basis.

Glossary

application level gateway	应用级网关
attachment	附件
bastion host	堡垒主机
bootstrap	引导装入程序
bottleneck	瓶颈
circuit level gateway	电路级网关
control panel	控制面板
defense	防卫
dual-homed host	双重宿主主机
exterior router	外部路由器
firewall	防火墙
impeccable	没有缺点的
instant messages	及时消息
interior router	内部路由器
modem	调制解调器
Network Address Translation (NAT)	网络地址转换
packet filter	包过滤

English for Information Security

perimeter net	周边网络
prohibit	禁止
redundancy	冗余
screened host	屏蔽主机
screened subnet	屏蔽子网
screening router	筛选路由器
snooper	刺探者,窥探者
spam	垃圾邮件
threat	恐吓,威胁
token ring	令牌网
trickster	骗子,魔术师

Translate the following sentences/passage into Chinese

(1) A firewall sits at the junction point or gateway between the two networks, usually a private network and a public network such as the Internet. The earliest firewalls were simply routers.

(2) Professional firewall products catch each network packet before the operating system does, thus, there is no direct path from the Internet to the operating system's TCP/IP stack.

(3) Circuit level gateways work at the session layer of the OSI model, or the TCP layer of TCP/IP. They monitor TCP handshaking between packets to determine whether a requested session is legitimate. Information passed to remote computer through a circuit level gateway appears to have originated from the gateway.

(4) Stateful multilayer inspection firewalls combine the aspects of the other three types of firewalls. They filter packets at the network layer, determine whether session packets are legitimate and evaluate contents of packets at the application layer.

(5) Whereas a dual-homed host architecture provides services from a host that's attached to multiple networks (but has routing turned off), a screened host architecture provides services from a host that's attached to only the internal network, using a separate router.

Translate the following sentences/passage into English

(1) 如果对Internet的往返访问都通过防火墙,那么,防火墙可以记录各次访问,并提供有关网络使用率的有价值的统计数字。如果一个防火墙能在可疑活动发生时发出音响报警,则还提供防火墙和网络是否受到试探或攻击的细节。

(2) 目前防火墙只提供对外部网络用户攻击的防护,对来自内部网络用户的攻击只能依靠内部网络主机系统的安全性。防火墙无法禁止变节者或公司内部存在的间谍将敏感数据复制到软盘或 PCMCIA 卡上,并将其带出公司。

(3) 防火墙不能防止数据驱动式攻击。如果用户抓来一个程序在本地运行,那个程序很可能就包含一段恶意的代码。随着 Java、JavaScript 和 Active X 控件的大量使用,这一问题变得更加突出和尖锐。

(4) 数据包过滤技术,顾名思义是在网络中适当的位置对数据包实施有选择的通过,选择依据,即为系统内设置的过滤规则(通常称为访问控制表——Access Control List),只有满足过滤规则的数据包才被转发至相应的网络接口,其余数据包则被从数据流中删除。

(5) 不同类型的防火墙均提供标识和认证功能,内网中的用户通常认为是可信的,外网用户在访问内网资源时通常要经过认证。口令认证从目前技术来看,不是一种很强的认证方式,基于口令的攻击是一种常用的攻击方式,在防火墙中,其他过滤访问的认证方式有:一次时间口令、基于时间的口令和挑战-响应方案等。

Questions

(1) How does a Packet Filtering firewall work?

(2) How does a Circuit Level Gateway firewall work?

(3) How does a Application Level Gateway firewall work?

(4) How does a Screened Subnet Architecture firewall work?

(5) What is bastion host? How does it work?

Chapter 4

Intrusion Detection System

An Intrusion Detection System (IDS) generally detects unwanted manipulations to computer systems, mainly through the internet. There are many different types of IDS. Some of them are described here. The manipulations may take the form of attacks by skilled malicious hackers, or script kiddies using automated tools.

An Intrusion Detection System is used to detect all types of malicious network traffic and computer usage that can't be detected by a conventional firewall. This includes network attacks against vulnerable services, data driven attacks on applications, host based attacks such as privilege escalation, unauthorized logins and access to sensitive files, and malware (viruses, trojan horses, and worms).

An IDS is composed of several components: Sensors which generate security events, a Console to monitor events and alerts and control the sensors, and a central Engine that records events logged by the sensors in a database and uses a system of rules to generate alerts from security events received. There are several ways to categorize an IDS depending on the type and location of the sensors and the methodology used by the engine to generate alerts. In many simple IDS implementations all three components are combined in a single device or appliance.

4.1 Introduction

4.1.1 Types of Intrusion Detection Systems

In a Network-based Intrusion Detection System (NIDS), the sensors are located at

Chapter 4 Intrusion Detection System

choke points in the network to be monitored, often in the Demilitarized Zone(DMZ) or at network borders. The sensor captures all network traffic flows and analyzes the content of individual packets for malicious traffic. In systems, Protocol-based Intrusion Detection System(PIDS) and APIDS are used to monitor the transport and protocols illegal or inappropriate traffic or constricts of language (say SQL). In a host-based system, the sensor usually consists of a software agent which monitors all activity of the host on which it is installed. Hybrids of these two types of system also exist.

1. A Network Intrusion Detection System is an independent platform which identifies intrusions by examining network traffic and monitors multiple hosts. Network Intrusion Detection Systems gain access to network traffic by connecting to a hub, network switch configured for port mirroring, or network tap. An example of a NIDS is Snort.

2. A Protocol-based Intrusion Detection System consists of a system or agent that would typically sit at the front end of a server, monitoring and analyzing the communication protocol between a connected device (a user/PC or system). For a web server this would typically monitor the HTTPS protocol stream and understand the HTTP protocol relative to the web server/system it is trying to protect. Where HTTPS is in use then this system would need to reside in the "shim" or interface between where HTTPS is un-encrypted and immediately prior to it entering the Web presentation layer.

3. An Application Protocol-based Intrusion Detection System consists of a system or agent that would typically sit within a group of servers, monitoring and analyzing the communication on application specific protocols. For example, in a web server with database this would monitor the SQL protocol specific to the middleware/business-login as it transacts with the database.

4. A Host-based Intrusion Detection System consists of an agent on a host which identifies intrusions by analyzing system calls, application logs, file-system modifications (binaries, password files, capability/acl databases) and other host activities and state.

5. A Hybrid Intrusion Detection System combines one or more approaches. Host agent data is combined with network information to form a comprehensive view of the network. An example of a Hybrid IDS is Prelude.

4.1.2 Passive System vs. Reactive System

In a passive system, the IDS sensor detects a potential security breach, logs the information and signals an alert on the console. In a reactive system, also known as an Intrusion Prevention System (IPS), the IDS responds to the suspicious activity by resetting the connection or by reprogramming the firewall to block network traffic from the suspected malicious source. This can happen automatically or at the command of an operator.

Though they both relate to network security, an IDS differs from a firewall in that a firewall looks outwardly for intrusions in order to stop them from happening. Firewalls limit access between networks to prevent intrusion and do not signal an attack from inside the network. An IDS evaluates a suspected intrusion once it has taken place and signals an alarm. An IDS also watches for attacks that originate from within a system.

This is traditionally achieved by examining network communications, identifying heuristics and patterns (often known as signatures) of common computer attacks, and taking action to alert operators. A system which terminates connections is called an intrusion-prevention system, and is another form of an application layer firewall.

4.2　State of the Art

4.2.1　From Intrusion Detection to Anomaly Prevention

A complex sets of information security technologies are traditionally deployed to keep the bad guys out of the enterprise. However, everyone knows that information security breaches are inevitable. Intrusion Detection Systems (IDSs) have emerged to help detect perimeter breaches and intrusion.

When using an IDS, organizations quickly find that in order to be effective, they need a process to immediately respond to the alarms raised. And so Intrusion Prevention Systems (IPSs) were created, with the idea that knowing about an intrusion was a good thing but being able to react accordingly and dynamically was better. These new solutions interact tightly with other security components, and thus enable IT administrators to define specific actions to be taken by the IPS. It can, for example, add a new rule to a firewall when the attack severity reaches a pre-determined threshold.

Finally, different IT administrator came to the same conclusion: a huge part of information needed for monitoring and intrusion detection is the same. Using several different solutions (and agent for monitoring the network, one for intrusion detection, the other to collect performance data, etc.) raises several management issues. It produces duplicated data and increases the complexity of correlation (need for a common log format, time synchronization, etc.). So, why not consider every kind of anomaly, since it can have an indirect link with an intrusion. In addition, the more data I have the more efficient my detection can be. That's the main idea of Anomaly Prevention Systems (APSs).

4.2.2 Focus on Anomaly Prevention Systems

1. Defining an Anomaly

Strictly speaking, an anomaly is a deviation from a typical or normal condition. Anomaly detection is based on the premise that anything outside the realm of "normal" behavior is, by definition, "abnormal" (i. e. , it is an anomaly), and therefore constitutes an attack. This means knowing what "normal" behavior is.

However, what we mean by anomaly in an APS stands for a more generic purpose. It represents all kinds of "problems" faced by the information system, be it an intrusion, and unexpected behavior, a CPU overload, etc. In fact, a complete APS system will use several monitoring techniques and several algorithms to detect anomalies such as misuse detection, anomaly detection, strict anomaly detection, etc.

To have a complete overview of the Information System the ideal APS has to cope with various different kinds of anomaly that can be classified within categories:

- Physical anomalies
- Network anomalies
- Application-specific anomalies
- Performances anomalies
- Configuration anomalies
- Fault tolerance anomalies
- Usage anomalies
- Policy security anomalies

This leads to a huge amount of information coming from very different kinds of sensors (detecting a physical anomaly is a slightly different process compared to an application anomaly). It implies the need for powerful correlation techniques, data normalization and a standard for defining an anomaly and exchanging alerts from sensors to the correlation engine. These are complex challenges that next generation APS systems have to face.

2. Putting it All Together

The Philosophy of an APS is to collect information about all these anomalies only one time, and use powerful techniques of correlation and various algorithms of detection (protocol analysis, behavior analysis…) to process the data. Then using a role management system (based on LDAP technologies for example) it can produce the appropriate data, alarm or action for each specific role (security team, performance team, web admin, etc.).

4.2.3 Generic Functional Architecture

Be it an IDS, IPS or APS, all these solutions are built more or less using the same functional architecture. Here's an overview of the most well-known one.

1. CIDF Architecture

The Common Intrusion Detection Framework (CIDF) is an effort to develop protocols and application programming interfaces so that intrusion detection research projects can share information and resources and so that intrusion detection components can be reused in other systems. CIDF adopts a view of Intrusion Detection Systems in which they consist of discrete components that communicate via message passing. Several kinds of components, known as boxes, are envisaged:

- Event (E-) Box
- Analysis (A-) Box
- Countermeasure (C-) Box
- Storage/Data (D-) Box

The even box is responsible for the seamless collection of audit data, such as raw network packets and user-level and/or kernel-level log data. The data is then converted into a unified format and sent to the analysis box. Depending on the configuration, the data is also sent to the data box for a more detailed analysis later on, if needed. This is illustrated in Figure 4.1.

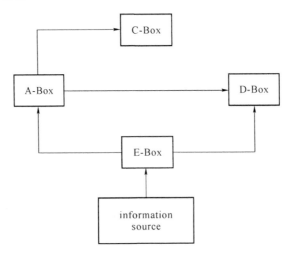

Figure 4.1 CIDF architecture

The bulk of IDS work occurs in the analysis box. This is where the data from the event box is examined for attack patterns, anomalies and non-compliance with security provisions. If there is a user-defined action in response to the overall analysis result, the countermeasure box, also known as the intrusion response unit, executes this action. Moreover the analysis result is sent to the data box.

Note that some of the CIDF ideas have been further developed by the IETF's Intrusion Detection Working Group(IDWG).

2. IDWG Architecture

The purpose of the IETF's Intrusion Detection Working Group (IDWG) is "to define data formats and exchange procedures for sharing information of interest to intrusion detection and response systems, and to management systems which may need to interact with them"—i. e. , IDS interoperability Specifications. Internet drafts have been issued by this working group, as follows:

- Intrusion Detection Message Exchange Requirements;
- Intrusion Detection Message Exchange Format Data Model and XML DTD;
- The Intrusion Detection Exchange Protocol (IDXP).

These drafts describe quite the same architectures (see Figure 4.2) using different names:

- **The Data Source** is the raw information that an intrusion detection system user to detect unauthorized or undesired activity. Common data sources include (but are not limited to) raw network packets, operating system audit logs, application audit logs, and system-generated checksum data.
- **The Sensor** is the component that collects data from the data source.
- **The Analyzer** is the component that analyzers the data collected by the sensor for signs of unauthorized or undesired activity or for events that might be of interest to the security administrator.
- **The manager** is the component from which the operator manages the various components of the IDS. Management functions typically include (but are not limited to) sensor configuration, analyzer configuration, event notification management, data consolidation and reporting.

They also define specific roles:

- **The Operator** is the human that is the primary user of the IDS manager. The operator often monitors the output of the IDS and initiates or recommends further action.
- **The administrator** is the human with overall responsibility for setting the security policy of the organization, and, thus for decisions about deploying and configuring the IDS. This may or may not be the same person as the operator of the

IDS. In some organizations, the administrator is associated with the network or systems administration groups. In other organizations, it's an independent position.

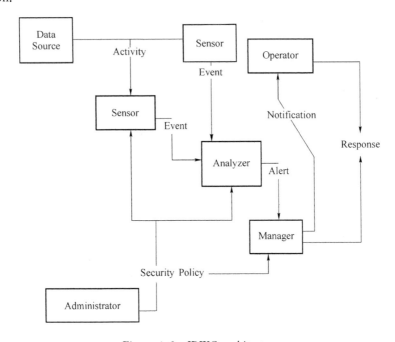

Figure 4.2 IDWG architecture

3. Verwoerd & Hunt Model

Another alternative is described by Verwoerd & Hunt as including the following common functional blocks:

- Sensor or Probe: these provide the most primitive data-gathering components. They track network traffic, log files, etc., translating log files into events useable by IDS monitors.
- Monitor: these receive events from sensors and process them. Events are correlated against IDS behavior models, resulting in model updates or alerts. An alert is a special case of an event. Alerts may be forwarded to higher-level monitors or to resolvers.
- Resolver: These receive alerts from monitors and determine the appropriate response—logging, adding firewall rules, operator notification, etc.
- Controller: These permit configuration and control of the other components. They also provide centralized administration of components, interrogation capabilities, etc.

4. Simplified Model

Going through all these architectures we can see that the main difference is mainly a matter of naming the components but we always find the same main functional blocks. First we collect data, then we process it using different algorithms and technique, then we take actions like logging in a database, sending an E-mail, interacting with a firewall, etc.

We organize the study according to the following simplified model: Data Collection, Data processing for detection, Alarms, Logs, Actions (see Figure 4.3).

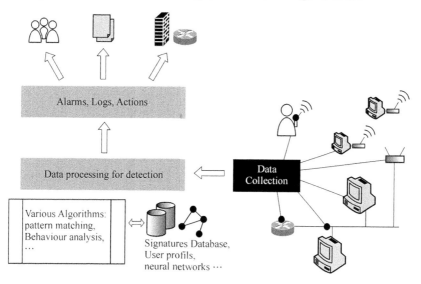

Figure 4.3 Simplified IDS model

4.3 Data Collection

4.3.1 Short Definition

Data collection is the cornerstone of an APS. Its goal is to get in an efficient manner all the data needed for processing intrusion detection. Historically, the collection procedure defines the IDS name:
- NIDS: network intrusion detection system.
- HIDS: host intrusion detection system.
- NNIDS: network node intrusion detection system.

- DIDS: distributed intrusion detection system.

These types of IDSs are illustrated in Figure 4.4, and will be described in more detail in the following sections.

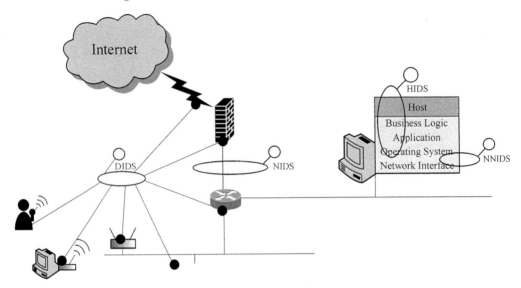

Figure 4.4 Types of IDS

4.3.2 NIDS

Network Intrusion Detection Systems (NIDS) monitor traffic on the wire or in case of a wireless network on the radio link. They examine packets in order to detect patterns of misuse or attack. NIDS see all the packets before they reach their destinations and can therefore initiate potential protection measures. They do this by matching one or a couple of packets against a repository of know attack signatures or performing anomaly detection.

When suspicious activity is detected, a network based IDS is raising an alert and/or taking actions to terminate the offending connection. Most of the network based IDSs work in what is known as "promiscuous mode". This means that they examine every packet on the local segment, whether or not those packets are destined for the IDS machine. If a NIDS is running on a network segment with a lot of traffic, usually a dedicated lost is required which just does the IDS task due to the heavy use of system resources.

Most attacks are not based on the contents of a single packet but are made up of several which can be sent over a lengthy period of time. This means that the IDS has to store a number of packets in an internal buffer in order to track established sessions and compare groups of packets with its attack signature database.

4.3.3 HIDS

Host IDS (HIDS) products employ an agent that resides on each host which has to be monitored. The agent can scrutinize system logs, kernel messages, critical system files and other auditable resources looking for unauthorized changes or suspicious patterns of activity. Whenever anything out of the ordinary is noticed, and alert is raised or the system takes countermeasures to protect itself. For instance, a HIDS monitors kernel logs to detect when inappropriate processes are initiated, or logins to take note of when an attempt is made to access an account with an incorrect password. If a login attempt fails too many times within a short time span the system may conclude that someone is trying to gain access illegally and an alarm can be raised.

Traditional HIDS are very good at detecting insider threats and usually provide extensive damages assessment and data forensics. The disadvantage of HIDS approach is the need for agent deployment on all key systems, which can introduce high deployment and management costs.

4.3.4 NNIDS

Network Node IDS (NNIDS) work in a similar manner to the network based IDS (NIDS). They also take packets from the network and perform protocol analysis and/or compare them against signatures. However NNIDS are only interested in packets directly targeted at them and not to the whole network segment (therefore they do not run in promiscuous mode). These "micro agents" are directly installed within the protocol stack of the host systems they should not be confused with real HIDS. NNIDS are aimed at the network activity and not directly the activity happening on the host system.

As NNIDS are not running in promiscuous mode they don't have to examine every packet on the wire. They use less system resources and can be deployed on existing servers without imposing too much overhead. NNIDS are particularly suitable for heavily loaded segments, switched networks or VPN/SSL implementations where network traffic is encrypted on the wire. These are all scenarios where traditional NIDS have problems.

4.3.5 Honeypot as a Sensor

Most IDSs have the problem that they are vulnerable to false-positive alerts (see section 2.5.2). Too many false-positive alerts can render the whole IDS unusable. Honeypot systems are based on a completely different concept that circumvents the problem of false-positive alerts. By definition, any activity on a honeypot is suspicious as there are no applications running for normal users. Honeypots are just traps that wait until they get attacked. Therefore, honeypots deliver just a small set of collected data with high accuracy.

4.3.6 IPS

IDSs normally tend to be reactive rather than proactive. This means they often have to wait until something has actually happened before they can raise the alarm.

The Intrusion Prevention System (IPS), however, attempts to be proactive. It is designed to stop intrusions or offending traffic before it does any damage rather than simply raising an alert. Intrusion prevention technology can be considered as an extension of intrusion detection technology. It adds the layer of access control to existing IDS, which is able to block traffic identified by the IDS as offending. However, the downside with this approach is the potential for introducing self-inflicted Denial of Service conditions in the case of false positive alerts.

4.3.7 DIDS

A distributed IDS (DIDS) consists of multiple IDSs over a large network. All of them communicate together, or with a central server that facilitates advanced network monitoring and incident analysis. By having these co-operative agents distributed across a network, security personnel are able to get a broader view of what is occurring on their network as a whole.

A DIDS also allows a company to efficiently manage its incident analysis resources by centralizing its attack records and by giving the analyst a quick and easy way to identify threats to the network across multiple network segments.

DIDS can consist of many individual components, which build together the global view of what is going on in an environment. To these components belong Network Intrusion Detection Systems (NIDS), Host Intrusion Detection System (HIDS), Network Node IDS (NNIDS), Honeypots/Honeynets and general system log information.

1. Hybrid IDS

A Hybrid IDS combines the approach of a NIDS with the one of a HIDS. Host agent data is correlated with network information to form a comprehensive view of the network.

Prelude is used as central coordinator for additional IDS sensors. Prelude is a Hybrid IDS framework that enables all available security applications, be they open source or proprietary, to report to a centralized system. In order to achieve this task, Prelude relies on the IDMEF (Intrusion Detection Message Exchange Format) IETF standard that enables different kinds of sensors to generate events using a unique language.

In the prelude view, "hybrid" means that you can combine events detected by any security application.

2. Agent based P2P IDS

Generally DIDS are constructed hierarchically, with a central manager acting as head of the whole system. However, the manager can become the bottleneck by being connected to every client. It can even overload when too many clients request services simultaneously. The whole system may collapse when the central manager is attacked. In an agent based P2P IDS, there is no central server system. Every agent has to communicate with all other agents.

4.3.8 Multi-layered Integration

To be efficient, an APS should be able to use each layer to detect an intrusion. For example, for a DoS attack the application layer may detect very quickly that a large number of incoming service connections have no actual operations or the operations don't make sense, whereas the lower layers may take a longer time to recognize the unusually high volume.

4.3.9 Correlation

Event correlation is used to recognize the "big picture" of the state of the system by correlating reports generated by different IDSs. Reports/Alerts from different sensors are analyzed to understand event sequences that are spanning over multiple hosts.

The primary goal of event correlation is to reduce the amount of redundant events or alarms. This is done by filtering out irrelevant information and deriving new events from existing ones. Event correlation engines are heavily used in network management systems and intrusion detection systems for alarm post-processing, because alarm consolidation is very important for an IDS.

4.4　Data Processing for Detection

4.4.1　Short Definition

Data-processing for detection is the "heart" of an APS. Using all the collected date, the APS will process it using several algorithms in order to detect an "anomaly". There are several analysis techniques. The purpose of the document is not to describe all of them but to give the input needed to limit our scope.

4.4.2　Misuse Detection (or Scenario Based Analysis)

Misuse detection is the oldest method for spotting intrusions. This procedure uses a pattern matching approach. The system compares the collected data with attack signature from a database. If the comparison results in a positive match, the system recognizes and anomaly and reacts accordingly. Misuse detection remains the most commonly used procedure in the commercial and non-commercial sectors. The procedure is easy to implement and use and it is not very prone to false alarms (false positives). Misuse detection, however, has a major drawback. This method recognizes known attacks only. Consequently, new attack patterns that have not yet been added to the attack signature database do not trigger an alarm (false negative) and thus go unnoticed.

Approaches or techniques in this category are described in the following subsections.

1. Pattern Matching

Pattern matching is a technique used by IDS machines to detect the presence of attacks using signatures. It works by matching text or a binary sequence against a captured packet. Pattern matching is the simplest and also most widespread form of intrusion detection.

However, pattern matching has some limitations. This technique searches for known signatures of attacks. This means that pattern matching can only find attacks that are already known because for unknown attacks there are no signatures existing yet. This in turn implied that an IDS using pattern matching has to be continuously updated with the newest signatures so that it can detect the current attacks, and that continuous research work has to be done to create these new signatures. Moreover, a slight change in the attack scenario may be sufficient to fool an IDS because the signature doesn't match anymore.

Pattern matching is usually very fast at detecting attacks, but this doesn't hold true if the set grows. This is particularly a problem. Firstly, normally rule sets contain many rules, and secondly, the throughput of packets per second on the links to monitor is always increasing, and so the amount of computation required to sustain this technique is enormous.

2. Protocol Analysis

The need to have a signature for every attack forced the researchers to look for different methods to detect new or unknown attacks.

Protocol analysis is the intrusion detection technique that looks for protocol misuse. It requires a model for every protocol that describes its normal usage. The protocols themselves are described by documents such as RFCs or other standardization documents. Therefore, any use of a protocol outside the defined behavior can be considered as abnormal.

Like in pattern matching, protocol analysis can also work with signatures. However, those signatures specially belong together with a certain protocol. By using protocol analysis, one has much better detection of both known and unknown attacks. By focusing on anomalies within the traffic, rather than simply looking for the signatures of particular attacks, protocol analysis based signatures are much more difficult for attackers to evade.

4.4.3 Anomaly Detection (or Behavior Analysis)

Anomaly detection is based on the premise that anything outside the realm of "normal" behavior, is, by definition "abnormal" (i.e., it is an anomaly), and therefore constitutes an attack. Compared to misuse detection, this method's advantage is the ability to recognize new attacks, since they are defined as abnormal behavior. In addition, there is no need to implement and maintain a database of attack patterns. Nonetheless, anomaly detection comes with its own set of problems that significantly impede its use in the commercial sector. Anomaly detection procedures must first acquire knowledge of what constitutes "normal" behavior for a network or computer system by creating user and system profiles. This phase alone is an obstacle and could be exploited by an opponent who could teach the IDS to classify attacks as an unauthorized intrusion. Another drawback is the high rate of false positives triggered by disruptions of normal system activities that are not actually attacks. Moreover, compared to misuse detection, the implementation of anomaly detection is more difficult, since the latter method involves more complex procedures.

1. Probabilistic Approach

The probabilistic approach offers a powerful complement to signature based approaches. Most probabilistic approaches make use of Bayesian networks. Bayes systems encode a knowledge base not in terms of rules or signatures but as conditional probability relationships. They gain much of the sensitivity and specificity of signature based systems while retaining much of the abilities of anomaly detection systems.

With Bayesian analysis, data from the network is first collected and analyzed. During this phase both false positives and real attacks are flagged and feed into a statistical model. After a suitable volume of data is accumulated, patterns start to emerge in the model. These patterns reveal which traffic is statistically identifiable as a false positive and which is a malicious attack. These patterns are then applied to new network data. The patterns provide a more accurate indicator of false versus malicious traffic and significantly reduce the number of false positives identified by the IDS.

2. Statistical Approach

Statistical based IDSs can evade many of the pitfalls of signature based IDSs. They rely on statistical models much as Bayes Theorem, to identify anomalous packets. Statistical based IDSs first have to learn what the normal behavior of the network traffic they're exposed to is. In this way, they adapt to a certain behavior and create their own usage-patterns. Anomalous activity is measure by a number of variables sampled over time and stored in a profile. Based on the anomaly score of a packet, the reporting process will issue an alert if it is identifies and tracks patterns and usage of the network data and then assigns an anomaly score to each packet. Once this is accomplished, the reporting facility will generate an alert if the anomaly score is greater than the alert threshold.

As statistical based IDSs first have to learn what is normal, they can't be used straight from the beginning like signature based IDSs. Another problem is that, during the training period, the network traffic has to be attack free. However, how can we assure this if there is no IDS running? This is a classical "chicken and egg" problem.

3. Neural Networks

Neural networks use adaptive learning techniques to recognize abnormal behavior. That is why neural networks do not require user-specified parameters. The neural network must first be trained with clean data, that is, data not contaminated by attack activities. The system may also undergo continuous training; allow the networks to learn changes in system behavior. Due to their ability to learn, neural networks are quite valuable when it comes to spotting abnormalities. Unfortunately, neural networks cannot be used to determine the cause of an abnormality. Thus they can just find out about the existence of a security violation but not its cause. The effort to circumvent this problem has led to the development of neural networks that are limited to only one type of attack. This in turn leads to a large effort in successfully deploying neuronal networks. Therefore, they are currently more deployed in research labs than in productive business environments.

4.4.4 Emerging Algorithms

1. Strict Anomaly Detection

Instated of using a set of signatures to detect an intrusion, strict anomaly detection will search for deviation from a rigid definition of use. The key advantage in employing a strict anomaly detection model is that the number of attacks within the "misuse" (signature of attack) set can never be greater than the number of attacks within the "not use" set! One of the most interesting things is that an IDS which implements a strict anomaly detection model can never enter a false-positive state, i. e. , can never generate a false alarm, because activity which occurs outside the definition of "use", by definition, has security relevance. The difficulty in constructing an IDS which utilizes a strict anomaly detection model, is in being able to define allowable "use". It may be that strict anomaly detection is best employed in an environment in which "use" can be (or is already) well defined.

2. Holistic Analysis

Holistic analysis might be considered an opposite to a reductionist approach of security, which consists of taking one low-level signal as an indicator of an intrusion. Holism is based on the belief that a whole is greater than the sum of its parts. It means that it is possible to infer the existence of an attack if a set of observations (even which superficially all see unrelated) can be approximately matched to a structure that represents the knowledge of the method that the attack employs at a high level. In other words, reductionist methods reason from a particular observation to generate supposed truth (a bottom-top approach), and holistic methods do the reverse. They are many ways to implement holistic analysis, like fingerprinting the network traffic and comparing them or making a goal-tree with the root node the ultimate goal of an attack and observing globally what are the tactics of the attacker to predict the next one. Notice that a holistic model relies on data gathered from an environment using reductionist methods, so it is used in conjunction of such methods.

3. Genetic Algorithms

Genetic algorithms work the same way the Darwin evolution theory associated with genetic code does. Actually, genetic algorithms can be used to solve a large panel of problems. They usually match a "good enough" solution instead of a "best" solution. The idea is to transform every solution to a problem in a "genetic enough" solution instead of a "best" solution. The idea is to transform every solution to a problem in a "genetic code" which can be scored by an evaluation function and be rejected if not good enough. Concretely, you have to generate a number of genetic coded solutions (called the "population"), you evaluate them in relation to the problem, if some are good enough, every thing is ok, take them, if not, select the best one, recombine them (find the right crossover point(s) for your type of solution), make some mutations on them (a bit of randomness!) and re-evaluate them. In the particular case of IDSs, such algorithm can be used to help generate knowledge for a RBS (Rule Based System) for example. The main difficulty is to find how to translate your solution in a genetic style and what is the best evaluation function to use.

4. Bioinformatics Algorithms

Bioinformatics algorithms are used to detect masquerade attacks (which is when someone steals the session of someone else). It uses particular algorithms that are used in bioinformatics to detect sequence alignment (originally to determine the similarity between two DNA or protein sequences). The accuracy of the results in DNA comparison and the flexibility of those algorithms to be modified to use different data (as a collection of user commands instead of nucleotide-sequences) make them very attractive for use in an intrusion detection system. It is necessary to compare the input commands which are entered to a "footprint" of the user logged. These algorithms are capable of aligning sequences in multiple ways, depending on demand. The typical results provided for a 75% hit rate (a hit is when it's an intrusion and is detected as such) gives a 7.5% false positive value (a false positive is a result of a detected intrusion when there isn't real one). This is far and away the best result for this type of detection system in this field of detection.

4.5 Alarms, Logs and Actions

Once an anomaly is detected, the APS can execute several actions (send an alarm, write some important information in a database, trigger a rule on a firewall, etc.).

While all the reactive measures executed can have many different forms, they generally fit into one of two categories.

4.5.1 Passive Actions

Passive actions mean that they will have no direct impact on the environment. It means that a human operator has to receive or consult the result of this passive action, decide what he has to do with it and take the necessary "active" actions accordingly.

Passive actions can be:
- Send E-mail
- Send message to a pager or cell phone
- Play audio data
- Log the intrusion in a database
- Increase the volume of audit data to record

...

The main problem with passive action lies in the fact that it is based on a human asynchronous process. What happens if the operator is not available at the moment of attacks? More precisely, if a lot of tools exist to generate a lot of alerts, it could then require a lot of time to process such a huge amount of information.

On the other hand, this is an efficient way of "logging" detailed suspicious activity which will be needed for "a priori" detection and forensic analysis.

4.5.2 Active Actions

As an alternative to passive actions, active actions mean a direct implementation by interaction with the information system. It can lead to the decision of:
- Turning off critical systems and services;
- Customizing the packet filter rules for firewalls;
- Getting information about the system from which the attacks originate, such as,

logged-in users (fingerd, rusersd or indented), services offered (port scanning) and the operating system being used (OS fingerprinting) — the latter two pieces of information can be used for additional attacks;
- Launching counter attacks (even if one has to be carefully regarding the legal issue of such an action) like shutting down the attacking computer system with DoS attacks.

...

Active example, if the attacker disguises his attacks to make them appear as if they originated from a business partner's IP address, and if the APS then changes the firewall configuration to block packets from the partner's network, collaboration with the business partner is no longer possible. In addition, if the APS sends too many alarm messages by E-mail or pager, the excessive traffic can overload the mail or modem servers (DoS attacks).

However, the main problem is a matter of decreasing false positives. Once we are really sure that the intrusion is a dangerous one, why not take direct actions? Again, the challenge resides more in the usage of various kinds of sensor. Let's imagine a very restrictive area where only internal users are allowed. If a hidden honeypot triggered an alert that an external user had gained access and that the only way of triggering such an alert is effectively to have access to this area, there's no point of searching for a false positive.

In the end, active action does not always mean disrupting the service. One can imagine softer ways, like activating more logging or duplicating traffic for further analysis, etc. It is the role of the incident response team to take all these parameters into account to design an efficient active reaction policy.

A good incident response policy will use a mix of both actions. Passive ones are for unreliable alert, for areas where active action could lead to DoS and also to fulfill the needs of further forensics analysis. Active actions are for critical areas and well known reliable alerts in order to increase the incident response time and decrease the amount of information that an operator has to deal with.

4.6 Example: Data Mining Approaches for IDS

This section is mainly about Data Mining Approaches for IDS which is developed by Wenke Lee and Salvatore J. Stolfo in Columbia University.

Chapter 4 Intrusion Detection System

Intrusion detection (ID) is an important component of infrastructure protection mechanisms. Intrusion detection systems (IDSs) need to be accurate, adaptive, and extensible. Given these requirements and the complexities of today's network environments, a more systematic and automated IDS development process rather than the pure knowledge encoding and engineering approaches are needed. This section describes a novel framework MADAM ID, for Mining Audit Data for Automated Models for Intrusion Detection, which is developed by Wenke Lee and Salvatore J. Stolfo in Columbia University. This framework uses data mining algorithms to compute activity patterns from system audit data and extracts predictive features from the patterns. It then applies machine learning algorithms to the audit records that are processed according to the feature definitions to generate intrusion detection rules. Results from the 1998 DARPA Intrusion Detection Evaluation showed that the model was one of the best performing of all the participating systems.

4.6.1 Introduction

As network-based computer systems play increasingly vital roles in modern society, they have become the target of intrusions by enemies and criminals. In addition to intrusion prevention techniques, such as user authentication and authorization, encryption, and defensive programming, intrusion detection is often used as another wall to protect computer systems.

The security of a computer system is compromised when an intrusion takes place. An intrusion can be defined as "any set of actions that attempt to compromise the integrity, confidentiality or availability of a resource". Intrusion prevention techniques, such as user authentication (e. g., using passwords or biometrics), avoiding programming errors, and information protection (e. g., encryption) have been used to protect computer systems as a first line of defense. Intrusion prevention alone is not sufficient because as systems become ever more complex, there are always exploitable weaknesses in the systems due to design and programming errors, or various "socially engineered" penetration techniques. For example, after it was first reported many years ago, exploitable "buffer overflow" still exists in some recent system software due to programming errors. The policies that balance convenience versus strict control of a system and information access also make it impossible for an operational system to be completely secure.

Intrusion detection is therefore needed as another wall to protect computer systems. The elements central to intrusion detection are: resources to be protected in a target system, i. e. , user accounts, file systems, system kernels, etc. ; models that characterize the "normal" or "legitimate" behavior of these resources; techniques that compare the actual system activities with the established models, and identify those that are "abnormal" or "intrusive".

Many researchers have proposed and implemented different models which define different measures of system behavior, with an ad hoc presumption that normalcy and anomaly (or illegitimacy) will be accurately manifested in the chosen set of system features that are modeled and measured. Intrusion detection techniques can be categorized into misuse detection, which uses patterns of well-known attacks or weak spots of the system to identify intrusions; and anomaly detection, which tries to determine whether deviation from the established normal usage patterns can be flagged as intrusions.

Misuse detection systems encode and match the sequence of "signature actions" (e. g. , change the ownership of a file) of known intrusion scenarios. The main shortcomings of such systems are: known intrusion patterns have to be hand-coded into the system; they are unable to detect any future (unknown) intrusions that have no matched patterns stored in the system.

Anomaly detection (sub)systems establish normal usage patterns (profiles) using statistical measures on system features, for example, the CPU and I/O activities by a particular user or program. The main difficulties of these systems are: intuition and experience is relied upon in selecting the system features, which can vary greatly among different computing environments; some intrusions can only be detected by studying the sequential interrelation between events because each event alone may fit the profiles.

The research in this section aims to eliminate, as much as possible, the manual and ad hoc elements from the process of building an intrusion detection system. Intrusion detection is considered as a data analysis process. Anomaly detection is about finding the normal usage patterns from the audit data, whereas misuse detection is about encoding and matching the intrusion patterns using the audit data. The central theme of the approach is to apply data mining techniques to intrusion detection. Data mining generally refers to the process of (automatically) extracting models from large stores of data. The recent rapid development in data mining has made available a wide variety of algorithms, drawn from the fields of statistics, pattern recognition, machine learning, and database. Several types of algorithms are particularly relevant to the research:

1. Classification

Maps a data item into one of several pre-defined categories. These algorithms normally output "classifiers", for example, in the form of decision trees or rules. An ideal application in intrusion detection will be to gather sufficient "normal" and "abnormal" audit data for a user or a program, then apply a classification algorithm to learn a classifier that will determine (future) audit data as belonging to the normal class or the abnormal class.

2. Link Analysis

Determines relations between fields in the database. Finding out the correlations in audit data will provide insight for selecting the right set of system features for intrusion detection.

3. Sequence Analysis

Models sequential patterns. These algorithms can help us understand what (time-based) sequence of audit events are frequently encountered together. These frequent event patterns are important elements of the behavior profile of a user or program.

A systematic framework is developed for designing, developing and evaluating intrusion detection systems. Specifically, the framework consists of a set of environment-independent guidelines and programs that can assist a system administrator or security officer to

- select appropriate system features from audit data to build models for intrusion detection;
- architect a hierarchical detector system from component detectors;
- update and deploy new detection systems as needed.

The key advantage of the approach is that it can automatically generate concise and accurate detection models from large amount of audit data. The methodology itself is general and mechanical, and therefore can be used to build intrusion detection systems for a wide variety of computing environments.

4.6.2 The Architecture

The biggest challenge of using data mining approaches in intrusion detection is that it requires a large amount of audit data in order to compute the profile rule sets. And the fact that a detection model is needed to compute for each resource in a target system makes the data mining task daunting. Moreover, this learning (mining) process is an integral and continuous part of an intrusion detection system because the rule sets used by the detection module may not be static over a long period of time. For example, as a new version of system software arrives, the "normal" profile rules are needed to update. Given that data mining is an expensive process (in time and storage), and real-time detection needs to be lightweight to be practical, a monolithic intrusion detection system is can't afforded.

A system architecture is proposed, as shown in Figure 4.5, that includes two kinds of intelligent agents: the learning agents and the detection agents. A learning agent, which may reside in a server machine for its computing power, is responsible for computing and maintaining the rule sets for programs and users. It produces both the base detection models and the meta-detection models. The task of a learning agent, to compute accurate models from very large amount of audit data, is an example of the "scale-up" problem in machine learning. The research in agent-based meta-learning systems is expected to contribute significantly to the implementation of the learning agents. Briefly, how to partition and dispatch data to a host of machines to compute classifiers in parallel is studied, and re-import the remotely learned classifiers and combine an accurate (final) meta-classifier, a hierarchy of classifiers are also studied.

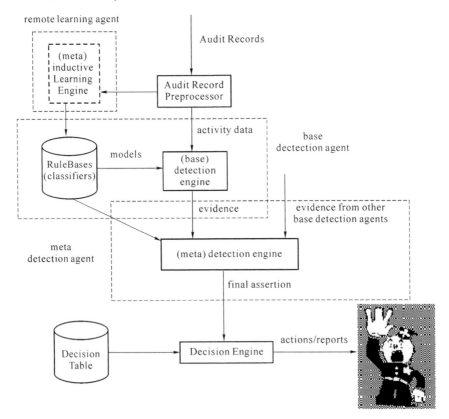

Figure 4.5 An architecture for agent-based Intrusion Detection System

Chapter 4 Intrusion Detection System

A detection agent is generic and extensible. It is equipped with a (learned and periodically updated) rule set (i. e. , a classifier) from the remote learning agent. Its detection engine "executes" the classifier on the input audit data, and outputs evidence of intrusions. The main difference between a base detection agent and the meta-detection agent is: the former uses preprocessed audit data as input while the later uses the evidence from all the base detection agents. The base detection agents and the meta-detection agent need not be running on the same host. For example, in a network environment, a meta agent can combine reports from (base) detection agents running on each host, and make the final assertion on the state of the network.

The main advantages of such a system architecture are:
- It is easy to construct an intrusion detection system as a compositional hierarchy of generic detection agents;
- The detection agents are lightweight since they can function independently from the heavyweight learning agents, in time and locale, so long as it is already equipped with the rule sets;
- A detection agent can report new instances of intrusions by transmitting the audit records to the learning agent, which can in turn compute an updated classifier to detect such intrusions, and dispatch them to all detection agents. Interestingly, the capability to derive and disseminate anti-virus codes faster than the virus can spread is also considered a key requirement for anti-virus systems [KSSW97].

A framework MADAM ID (for Mining Audit Data for Automated Models for Intrusion Detection) is developed, which is described in [Lee and Stolfo 1998; Lee et al. 1999a; Lee et al. 1999b; Lee 1999]. The main idea is to apply data mining techniques to build intrusion detection models. The main components of the framework include programs for learning classifiers and meta-classifiers [Chan and Stolfo 1993], association rules [Agrawal et al. 1993] for link analysis, and frequent episodes [Mannila et al. 1995] for sequence analysis. It also contains a support environment that enables system builders to interactively and iteratively drive the process of constructing and evaluating detection models. The end products are concise and intuitive rules that can detect intrusions, and can be easily inspected and edited by security expert when needed.

The process of applying MADAM ID can be summarized in Figure 4. 6. Raw (binary) audit data is first processed into ASCII network packet information (of host event data), which is in turn summarized into connection records (or host session records) containing a number of basic features, e. g. , service, duration, etc. Data mining programs are then applied to the connection records to compute the frequent patterns, i. e. , association rules and frequent episodes, which are in turn analyzed to construct additional features for the connection records. Classification programs, for example, RIPPER [Cohen 1995], are then used to inductively learn the detection models. This process is of course iterative. For example, poor performance of the classification models often indicates that more pattern mining and feature construction is needed.

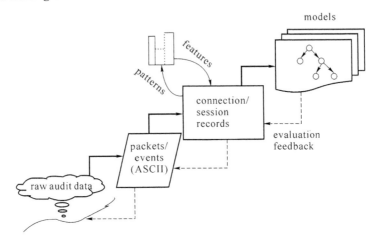

Figure 4.6　The data mining process of building ID models

In the approach, the learned rules replace the manually encoded intrusion patterns and profiles, system features and measures are selected by considering the statistical patterns computed from the audit data. Meta-learning is used to learn the correlation of intrusion evidence from multiple detection models, and to produce a combined detection model.

The framework does not eliminate the needs to pre-process and analyze raw audit data, e. g. , tcpdump or BSM audit data. In fact, to build intrusion detection models for network systems, the data mining programs use pre-processed audit data where each record corresponds to a high level event, e. g. , a network connection or host session. Each record normally includes an extensive set of features that describe the characteristics of the event, for example, the duration of a connection, the number of bytes transferred, etc. While analyzing and summarizing raw audit data is an essential task for an IDS, generic utilities should first be developed by network and operating system experts, and made available to all IDSs as the low level building blocks. Bro and NFR can be regarded as examples of such robust utilities, as they both perform IP packet filtering and reassembling, and allow event handlers to output summarized connection records. The framework assumes that such building blocks are available when constructing IDSs.

Note that currently MADAM ID produces misuse detection models for network and host systems as well as anomaly detection models for users. MADAM ID is extended to build network and host anomaly detection models. Also note that the detection models

Chapter 4　Intrusion Detection System

produced by MADAM ID are intended for off-line analysis.

4.6.3　Mining Audit Data

In this section the data mining algorithms is described, and illustrate how to apply these algorithms to generate detection models from audit data. Here audit data refers to pre-processed timestamped audit records, each with a number of features (i. e. , fields).

1. Classification

Intrusion detection can be thought of as a classification problem: each audit record is wished to classify into one of a discrete set of possible categories, normal or a particular kind of intrusion.

Given a set of records, where one of the features is the class label, i. e. , the concepts to be learned, classification algorithms can compute a model that uses the most discriminating feature values to describe each concept. For example, consider the telnet connection records shown in Table 4. 1. Label is the concept to be learned. "normal" represents normal connections and "guess" and overflow represent various kinds of intrusions. Hot is the count of access to count of file/path "not found" errors and "Jump to" instructions, etc. RIPPER, a classification rule learning program, generates rules, shown in Table 4. 2 for classifying the telnet connections. The symbol left to ":-" is the class label, and the comma separated expressions on the right are conjuncts, i. e. , (sub)conditions, of the classification rule. RIPPER indeed selects the discriminating feature values into the classification rules for the intrusions. These rules can be first inspected and edited by security experts, and then be incorporated into detection systems.

Table 4. 1　Telnet records

label	service	flag	hot	failed-logins	compromised	root-shell	su	duration	...
normal	telnet	SF	0	0	0	0	0	10. 2	...
normal	telnet	SF	0	0	0	3	1	2. 1	...
guess	telnet	SF	0	6	0	0	0	26. 2	...
normal	telnet	SF	0	0	0	0	0	126. 2	...
overflow	telnet	SF	3	0	2	1	0	92. 5	...
normal	telnet	SF	0	0	0	0	0	2. 1	...
guess	telnet	SF	0	5	0	0	0	13. 9	...
overflow	telnet	SF	3	0	2	1	0	92. 5	...
normal	telnet	SF	0	0	0	0	0	1 248	...
...	...	...	...	...	...	...	...	...	...

English for Information Security

Table 4.2 Example RIPPER rules from Telnet records shown in Table 4.1

RIPPER Rule	Meaning
guess:-failed_logins≥4.	If number of failed logins is at least 4, then this telnet connection is "guess", a guessing password attack.
Overflow:-hot≥3, compromised ≥2, root_shell=1.	If the number of hot indicators is at least 3, the number of compromised conditions is at least 2, and a root shell is obtained, then this telnet connection is a buffer overflow attack.
...	...
normal:-true.	If none of the above, then this connection is "normal".

The accuracy of a classification model depends directly on the set of features provided in the training data. From a theoretical point of view, the goal of constructing a classification model is that after (selectively) applying a sequence of feature value tests, the dataset can be partitioned into "pure" subsets, i.e., each in a target class. Therefore when constructing a classification model, a classification algorithm searches for features with large information gain, defined as the reduction in entropy, which characterizes the "impurity" of dataset. It is thus very important that the dataset indeed includes features with large information gain. For example, if the features hot, compromised, and root_shell were removed from the records in Table 4.1, RIPPER would not able to produce accurate rules to identify buffer overflow connections. In [Lee and Stolfo 1998], due to the temporal nature of network events, especially certain intrusions such as probing (e.g., port-scan, ping-sweep, etc.) and denial-of-service (e.g., ping-of-death, teardrop, etc.), adding per-host and per-service temporal statistics resulted in significant improvement in the accuracy of the classification models. Thus, selecting the right set of system features is a critical step when formulating the classification tasks. The strategy is to first mine the frequent sequential patterns from the network audit data, and then use these patterns as guidelines to select and construct temporal statistical features.

Meta-learning [Chan and Stolfo 1993] is a mechanism for inductively learning the correlation of predictions by a number of (base) classifiers. Each record in the training data for meta-learning contains the true class label of the record in the training data for meta-learning contains the true class label of the record and the predictions made by the base classifiers. The resultant meta-classifier thus "combines" the base models because it uses their predictions to make the final prediction. The motivations for meta-learning include: to improve classification accuracy, that is, to produce a meta-classifier that is more accurate than any individual base classifier; and to improve efficiency and scalability, that is, to combine the models rather than the potentially huge volume of data from different data sources. This general approach has been extensively studied [Stolfo et al. 1997] and empirically evaluated in a related domain of credit card fraud detection and has been shown to be effective and scalable.

In order to avoid becoming a performance bottleneck and an easy attack target, an IDS should consist of multiple cooperative lightweight subsystems that each monitors a separate part, e. g. , access point, of the entire network environment. For example, an IDS that inspects the full data contents of each IP packet and keeps track of all opened connections may run out of memory (i. e. , buffers) during a TCP based DoS attack and cease to function. On the other hand, a more lightweight IDS that only inspects the header of each IP packet can detect only those intrusions that are targeted to the network protocols, and not those that try to exploit the hosts, e. g. , guess password, buffer overflow, etc. A solution is to have one relatively lightweight system on the gateway that checks only the packet headers, and several host-based systems that monitor the activities on the mission-critical hosts. A "global" detection system can then combine the evidence from these subsystems and take appropriate actions. Meta-learning is used as a means to combine multiple intrusion detection models.

2. Association Rules

There is empirical evidence that program executions and user activities exhibit frequent correlations among system features. For example, certain privileged programs only access certain system files in specific directories [Ko et al. 1994], programmers edit and compile C files frequently, etc. These consistent behavior patterns should be included in normal usage profiles.

The goal of mining association rules is to derive multi-feature (attribute) correlations from a database table. Given a set of records, where each record is a set of items, $support(X)$ is defined as the percentage of records that contain item set X. An association rule is an expression

$$X \rightarrow Y, [c, s]$$

Here X and Y are item sets, and $X \cap Y = 0$, $s = Support(X \cup Y)$ is the support of the rule, and $c = \dfrac{Support(X \cup Y)}{Support(X)}$ is the confidence [Agrawal et al. 1993].

Consider the shell input commands during extensions; remove the (input) contents of mail bodies and files, and use "am" to represent all the morning timestamps.

The original association rules algorithm searches for all possible frequent associations among the set of given features. However, not all associations are necessarily useful, i. e. , data definitions, about the audit records to direct the pattern mining process. Observe that certain features are essential in describing the data, while others provide only auxiliary information. Domain knowledge is used to determine what the appropriate essential features for an application are. In shell command data, since the combination of the exact "time" and "command" uniquely identifies each record, "time" and "command" are the essential features; like wise, in network connection data, timestamp, source and destination hosts, source port, and service (i. e. , destination port) are the essential features because their combination uniquely identifies a connection record. The relevant association rules should describe patterns related to essential features.

These essential features(s) are called axis features when they are used as a form of item constraints, which specifies the conditions on the item sets of an association rule. The association rules algorithm is restricted to only output rules that include axis feature values. In practice, not all of essential features need to designate as the axis features. For example, some network analysis tasks require statistics about various network services while others may require the patterns related to the destination hosts. Accordingly, service can be used as the axis feature to compute the association rules that describe the patterns related to the services of the connections, and use destination host as the axis feature to compute patterns related to hosts.

In the case of shell command records, command is used as the axis feature. Table 4.4 shows some example association rules from the shell command data in Table 4.3. Each of these association rules conveys information about the user's behavior. The rules mined from each telnet/login session of the same user can be merged into an aggregate rule set to form the user's normal profile.

Table 4.3 Shell command records

time	hostname	command	arg1	arg2
am	pascal	mkdir	dir1	
am	pascal	cd	dir1	
am	pascal	vi	tex	
am	pascal	tex	vi	
am	pascal	mail	fredd	
am	pascal	subject	progress	
am	pascal	vi	tex	
am	pascal	vi	tex	
am	pascal	mail	williamf	
am	pascal	subject	progress	
...	...	...	...	...
am	pascal	vi	tex	
am	pascal	latex	tex	
am	pascal	dvips	dvi	—o
...	...	...	...	...
am	pascal	logout		

Chapter 4 Intrusion Detection System

Table 4.4 Example association rules from shell command data shown in Table 4.3

Association Rule	Meaning
$command = vi \rightarrow time = am, hostname = pascal, arg1 = tex, [1.0, 0.28]$	When using vi to edit a file, the user is always (i.e., 100% of the time) editing a *tex* file, in the morning, and at host *pascal*; and 28% of the command data matches this pattern.
$command = subject \rightarrow time = am, hostname = pascal, arg1 = progtess, [1.0, 0.11]$	The subject of the user's E-mail is always ((i.e., 100% of the time) about "progress", such E-mails are in the morning, and at host *pascal*; and 11% of the command data matches this pattern.

3. Frequent Episodes

There is often the need to study the frequent sequential patterns of audit data in order to understand the temporal and statistical nature of many attacks as well as the normal behavior of users and programs. Frequent episodes are used to represent the sequential audit record patterns.

Given a set of timestamped event records, where each record is a set of items, an interval $[t_1, t_2]$ is the sequence of event records that starts from timestamp t_1 and ends at t_2. The width of the interval is defined as $t_2 - t_1$. Let X be a set of items, an intervals contains X. Define Support(X) as the ratio between the number of minimum occurrences that contain X and the total number of event records. A frequent episode rule is the expression [Mannila and Toivonen 1996]

$$X, Y \rightarrow Z, [c, s, w]$$

X, Y and Z are item sets, and they together form an episode. $s = \text{Support}(X \cup Y \cup Z)$ is the support of the rule, and $c = \dfrac{\text{Support}(X \cup Y \cup Z)}{\text{Support}(X \cup Y)}$ is the confidence. The width of each of the occurrences must be less than w.

Several extensions are introduced to the original frequent episodes algorithm. The extended algorithm computes frequent sequential patterns in two phases. First, it finds the frequent associations using the axis features(s) as previously described. Then it generates the frequent serial patterns from these associations. Thus, the approach combines the associations among features and the sequential patterns among the records into a single rule.

Another interesting schema-level fact about audit records is that some essential features can be the *references* of other features. These reference features normally carry information about some "subject", and other features describe the "actions" that refer to the same "subject". For example, if the sequential patterns of connections to the same destination host need to be studied, *dst_host* is the "subject" and *service* is the action. In this case, *dst_host* can be designated as the *reference* feature. When forming an episode, the program tests the conditions that, within the episode's minimal occurrences, the event records covered by its constituent item sets have the same reference feature value.

4.6.4 Feature Construction

The mined frequent episodes are used, which also contain associations among the features. The minded frequent episodes are from audit records as guidelines to construct temporal statistical features for building classification models. This process involves first identifying the "intrusion only" patterns, then parsing these patterns to define features accordingly. In this section, network connection data is used as an example to illustrate the feature construction process.

Raw *tcpdump* output are first summarized into network connection records using pre-processing programs, where each record has a set of "intrinsic" features. For example, the *duratioin*, *service*, *src_host* and *dst_host* (number of data bytes), a *flag* indicates normal or a single connection.

1. Identifying the Intrusion Patterns

The frequent episodes program is applied to both the exhaustively gathered normal connection dataset and the dataset that contains an intrusion. Then the resulting patterns are compared to find the "intrusion only" patterns, i. e., those that exhibit only in the intrusion dataset. The details of the pattern comparison algorithm are described in [Lee et al. 1999b]. Briefly, since the number of patterns may be very large and there are rarely exactly matched patterns from two data sets, heuristic algorithms are used to automatically identify the "intrusion only" patterns. The idea is to first convert patterns into numbers in such a way that "similar" patterns are mapped to "closer" numbers. Then pattern comparison and intrusion pattern identification are accomplished through comparing the numbers and rank ordering the results. An "encoding" procedure is devised, and it converts each pattern into a numerical number, where the order of digit significance corresponds to the order of importance of the features. The following heuristic ordering is used on the importance of the features: *flag*, the axis feature, the reference feature, the rest of the essential attributes and then the rest of the features in alphabetical order. *Flag* is considered as the most important in describing a pattern because it carries the summary information of the connection behavior with regard to the protocol specifications. Each unique feature value is mapped to a digit value in the encoding process. The "distance" of two patterns is then simply a number where each digit value is the digit-wise absolute difference between the two encodings. A "comparison" procedure computes the "intrusion" score for each pattern from the intrusion dataset, which is its lowest distance score against all patterns from the normal dataset, and outputs the user-specified top percentage patterns that have the highest intrusion scores as the "intrusion only" patterns.

The attacker used many spoofed source addresses to send a log of S0 connections (i. e. ,only the first SYN packet is sent) to a port (e. g. ,$http$) of the victim host in a very short time span (e. g. ,all in timestamp 1.1). Table 4.5 shows one of the top intrusion only patterns, produced using service as the axis feature and dst_host as the reference feature.

Table 4.5 Example Intrusion Pattern

Frequent Episode	Meaning
($flag$ = S0, $service$ = $http$, dst_hot = $victim$), ($flag$ = S0, $service$ = $http$, dst_host = $victim$) → ($flag$ = S0, $service$ = $http$, dst_host = $victim$)[0.93,0.03,2]	93% of the time, after two $http$ connections with S0 flag are made to host $victim$, within 2 seconds from the first of these two, the third similar connection is made, and this pattern occurs in 3% of the data.

2. Constructing Feature from Intrusion Patterns

Each of the intrusion patterns is used as a guideline for adding additional features into the connection records to build better classification models. The following automatic procedure is used for parsing a frequent episode and constructing features:

- Assume F_0 (e. g. ,dst_host) is used as the reference feature, and the width of the episode is w seconds.
- Add the following features that examine only the connections in the past w seconds that share the same value in F_0 as the current connection:

◇ A feature that computes "the count of these connections";

◇ Let F_1 be $service$, src_dst or dst_host other than F_0 (i. e. ,F_1 is an essential feature). If the same F_1 value (e. g. ,$http$) is in all the item sets of the episode, add a feature that computes "the percentage of connections that share the same F_1 value as the current connection"; otherwise, add a feature that computers "the percentage of different values of F_1".

◇ Let V_2 be a value (e. g. ,S0) of a feature F_2 (e. g. ,$flag$) other than F_0 and F_1 (i. e. , V_2 is a value of a non-essential feature). If V_2 is in all the item sets of the episode, add a feature that computes "the percentage of connections that have the same V_2"; otherwise, if F_2 is a numerical feature, add a feature that computes "the average of the F_2 values".

This procedure parses a frequent episode and uses three operators, *count*, *percent*, and *average*, to construct statistical features. These features are also temporal since they measure only the connections that are within a time window w and share the same reference feature value. The intuition behind the frequent episode. For example, if a large percentage of records that have the same value. The essential and non-essential features are treated differently. The essential features describe the anatomy of an intrusion, for example, "the same *service* (i. e. , *port*) is targeted". The actual value(e. g. , $http$), is often not important because the same attack method can be applied to different targets, e. g. , ftp. On the other hand, the actual non-essential feature values, e. g. , $flag = S0$, often indicate the *invariant* of an intrusion because they summarize the connection behavior according to the network protocols.

This SYN flood pattern shown in Table 4. 5 results in the following additional features: a count of connections to the same dst_host in the past 2 seconds, and among these connections, the percentage of those that have the same *service*, and the percentage of those that have the "S0" flag.

3. Discussions

The theoretical underpinnings of the feature construction process in [Lee 1999] are examined. The results are outlined here, and why the features constructed from the intrusion patterns can be utilized to build more accurate classification models is explained. First, the "intrusion only" patterns are the results of intrusion records. That is, the "intrusion" dataset must contain "intrusion records", i. e. , unique records, unique sequences of records, or records or sequences with unique frequencies, in order for it to have "intrusion only" patterns. Second, for the temporal and statistical features constructed from the intrusion patterns, their values in the intrusion records that are responsible for resulting in the "intrusion only" patterns will be very different from the feature values in the normal connection records. For example, for the feature from the SYN flood pattern, for the connections to the same destination host in the past 2 seconds, the percentage of those that have S0 flag, normal records have values close to 0, but SYN flood records have values in the range of greater than 80%. The constructed features have high information gain because their value range can separate intrusion records from the normal records. In fact, they normally have higher information gain than the existing set of features. For example, the feature "flag" has very low information gain because some normal connections also have a "S0" value. As discussed before, a classification algorithm needs to select features with the highest information gain when computing a classification model. Therefore, when the features constructed from the intrusion patterns are

Chapter 4 Intrusion Detection System

added to the audit data, a more accurate classification model can be computed. This is precisely the purpose of the feature construction process.

An open problem is how to decide the right time window value w. Sequential patterns are mined by using different w values, for example, form 0.1 to 2.0 with an increment of 1, and plot the number of patterns generated at each run. The experience shows that this plot tends to stabilize after the initial sharp jump. The smallest w in the stable is called region w_0. In [Lee and Stolfo 1998], experiments of using different w values are reported to calculate temporal statistical features for classification models. The result showed the plot of accuracy of the classifier also stabilizes after $w \geqslant w_0$ and tend to taper off. Intuitively, a requirement for a good window size is that its set of sequential patterns is stable, that is, sufficient patterns are captured and noise is small. w_0 is therefore used for adding temporal statistical features.

4.6.5 Experiments

In this section, the experiments in building intrusion detection models on the audit data from the 1998 DAEPA Intrusion Detection Evaluation Program are described. In these experiments, the algorithms and tools of MADAM ID are applied to process audit data, mine patterns, construct features, and build RIPPER classifiers.

The experiments on *tcpdump* data are firstly described. The results of these experiments were submitted to DARPA and were evaluated by MIT Lincoln Lab. Then recent experiments on BSM data is reported, which were performed after the DARPA evaluation. The experiments are discussed, and the strengths and weaknesses of MADAM ID are evaluated.

The more experiment details can be seen in Wenke Lee and Salvatore J. Stolfo's paper: "A Framework for constructing Features and Models for Intrusion detection systems" and "Adaptive Intrusion Detection: a Data Mining Approach".

4.7 Known Problems with IDS

4.7.1 Lack of Adaptivity

There are currently two major general approaches to intrusion detection, namely misuse detection and anomaly detection. A substantial literature exists that catalogues and describes several techniques that fall into one or other of these categories.

The former, misuse detection, is by far the most commonly implemented in real-world systems. Also called signature detection, this method uses a pattern matching approach. The system compares collected data with a database of signatures of known attacks. If the match is positive, an intrusion is deemed to have occurred and the system reacts accordingly.

The second approach, anomaly detection, is based on modeling "normal" behavior and observing deviations from this model. Data is collected on the behavior of legitimate users over a period of time. Any behavior that is inconsistent with this model is considered suspicious. Various statistical tests are used to determine what constitutes abnormal activity. A basic assumption of this model is that attack behavior is significantly different from legitimate behavior.

The most widely used intrusion detection systems to date in production environments have tended to focus on misuse detection, with true anomaly detection systems being reserved for research environments. Snort, for example, a leading open-source intrusion detection system is heavily rules-based and thus is mainly a type of misuse detection. However, clever specification of rules can to some extent allow a type of anomaly detection where new attacks are caught.

Both of these leading approaches, however, have significant limitations. In the case of misuse detection, the sheer number of rules required to secure modern, complex systems means that it is difficult for system administrators to maintain an IDS that is customized to the needs of their own system set-up. This constant "arms race" between attackers and system administrators is illustrated in Figure 4.7. Another serious problem is its lack of adaptivity —i.e., a new attack goes unrecognized if it does not have a corresponding signature defined in the relevant database. This requires very active management of the rule set used. In practice, systems with many thousands of rules are quite common.

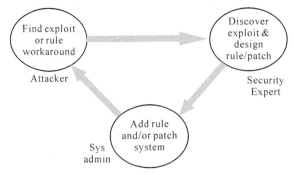

Figure 4.7   Rule maintenance cycle

Chapter 4 Intrusion Detection System

Anomaly detection systems also present problems. In increasingly dynamic environments, where technology lifecycles are short and users are mobile, it is difficult to accumulate a sufficient quantity of steady-state data to train such systems. Furthermore, illegitimate behavior can become accepted as normal if it is not caught and is carried out over a period of time. A further crippling problem with anomaly detection is a typically large number of false positives.

4.7.2 False Positive & False Negative

The ideal intrusion detection system catches all new attacks as well as existing ones and does not generate any false alarms (false positives). These two objectives are fundamentally difficult to reconcile. Systems that just react to know attacks are least prone to false alarms, but miss new attacks. Systems than try to be intelligent enough to spot new attacks tend to generate lots of false positives. After some time, personnel tend not to take alarms seriously if most are false, making for bad security. In systems where malicious activity is only a very small percentage of total activity, it is inherently very difficult to avoid a high rate of false positives. As an example, consider a good IDS that provides 99.9% test accuracy (meaning that 99.9% of intrusions are detected and that 99.9% of normal usage events yield negative). Say that 1 in every 100 000 usage events relate to intrusions and should be detected. By Bayes' theorem, the probability of a given positive alert being a false alarm is greater than 99%. At first glace, this sees surprising but it arises as intrusions are so rare relative to normal usage events. It is worth noting that Bayesian anomaly filters work reasonably well for E-mail spam without excessive false positives, the difference being that the incidence of spam as a proportion of total E-mail is quite large.

4.7.3 Field of Vision

The current generation of IDS is generally capable of operating in either of two ways. These are categorized as host-based and network-based intrusion detection systems, respectively.

In general, a host-based system runs on an operating system, collecting and analyzing data on the usage of a specific host. The extent of its perception is usually limited to a specific machine and the applications and services running on the OS. It normally does this by tracking logs produced by the OS (e.g., syslog) and applications (web servers, mail servers, etc.) and also by tracking files for modifications, and so on.

A network-based IDS has a broader field of vision, extending to an entire network segment. This type of IDS works by scrutinizing packets traveling on the network, and often takes the form of a specific device with its network interface card set to promiscuous mode. The main advantage is that an attack on a host can be detected before the host is compromised.

The main limitation of both of these approaches is that they have a limited view. In the case of a host-based IDS, anything that happens below the level of the OS is generally undetected. In the case of a network-based IDS, low-level (sub-packet) network activity may also be undetected. Furthermore, it is difficult for these types of system to draw inferences from patterns of high-level, application-specific activity; this is further complicated of course if data is encrypted.

Another problem is with complexity and scalability. It is hard to analyze every packet on a gigabit interface, especially if a vast number of rules need to be applied. Likewise, the volume of activity on a typical server OS can be difficult to keep up with.

Furthermore, the trend towards mobile devices, and the limitations of traditional perimeter security in this environment, means that more flexible IDS strategies are required.

4.7.4 Performance

Performance is a key issue for IDSs. Information Systems deal with more and more datas. Network bandwidth, memory, hard drive capacity etc. are increasing exponentially, and so does the amount of data that the APS has to deal with.

First, APSs face performance issues at the sensor level. A network IDS can miss packet on a gigabit Ethernet network, for example. The sensor needs a constant upgrade to able to cope with the data that it has to monitor. Then there's the problem of processing all the data. Analyzer and correlation components require huge databases and a lot of CPU power to apply various complex algorithms. They can soon become bottlenecks if they are not sized correctly.

Maintaining a scalable APS environment is a hard task, which can represent high costs. But it should be done seriously since APS flooding is definitely a simple and strong evasion technique.

Best practice is again to define a precise data collection and analysis policy. For example, some kinds of areas of data can be monitored using "a priori" detection techniques, which enables as slower correlation process. Solutions like Honeypots are also interesting as they only provide less data with a better added value in comparison to a network sensor, which has to detect malicious data inside the "normal" one. Finally, even if it is not really operational now, distributed architectures are very promising. Each node can do a first level of collection and detection, then select a smaller amount of data that will be used within a greater correlation scheme, for example.

4.7.5 Increasing Cost

APSs can be fairly expensive, and if not well understood and deployed they can easily fail to deliver value relative to their cost. This reason, amongst others, is why Gartner Group Pointed out 2 years ago that IDS will be dead in 2005. APSs are not yet dead, but this true cost is another big issue.

Depending upon the complexity of the environment and the intrusion detection requirements, the solutions can involve several powerful computers, huge databases and expensive correlation software. Then, one should have in mind that cost of security technology ownership transcends the price of technology acquisition. It also includes the costs of evaluation, deployment, operational management, maintenance, upgrading, etc. A traditionally underestimated cost is operational management. Many organizations in the past have done huge investments in the technology with no anticipation of the cost of operational management, leading in some cases to a brutal project closure. Another reason, which has a direct cost impact, is the lack of understanding and evaluation.

Installing and effectively using intrusion detection systems on networks and hosts requires a broad understanding of computer security. The complexity of information technology infrastructures is increasing beyond and one person's ability to understand them, let alone administer them in a way that in operationally secure.

An organization needs to fully appreciate the commitment required before deploying an APS. Otherwise, the project runs the risk of wasting time, money, and staff resources. Before an organization makes an investment in an APS solution, it must understand what assets require protection and the real and perceived threats against those assets. Threats can be characterized by the likely type of attack and attacker capabilities (i.e., resources and goals), and the organization's tolerance for loss of, damage to, or disclosure of protected assets.

Managing the cost is the result of a complex equation between how much money the organization will lose because of an intrusion and which kind of technology it could afford regarding the probability and risk that such an intrusion occurs in its environment. The performance factor should not be forgotten and the scalability of the solution according to the organization growth has to be anticipated and included in the overall costs estimation.

4.7.6 Complex Management Issues

The challenge while operating an APS is first to manage a heterogeneous distributed architecture with agents residing in multiple locations. For example, a major obstacle that arises in distributing IDS agents relates to communication between the agents and managers. How should data be communicated between the geographically dispersed modules? For instance, how do you send massive amounts of data from an IDS agent in Thailand back to the IDS management console in New York City? More computers, servers, and network segments mean a more complicated setup and a longer installation time. So in itself the deployment project can be first issue. Experiences, skills and planning play a critical role in large enterprise IDS deployment.

Now the company has successfully deployed a huge distributed APS, what happens next? Here comes again the skilled security administrator who has to struggle with alarms, find which ones are relevant and decide if they will pursue litigation, seek outside help, try to block the intruder themselves, or simply ignore the intrusion. Some situations might call for different actions, depending on the severity of the intrusion and the company policy. Finding the perfect balance between a massive amount of data generation, which leads to an over-saturation of information, and a small amount of data generation, which may cause ineffective monitoring, can also became an issue.

Note that security event management solutions can help overcome many of the issues. By intelligently correlating real-time event data streams from IDSs, firewalls, network hosts and other sensors, these solutions are capable of dramatically reducing the wasted time spent chasing false alarms, as well as identifying false negative threats that would otherwise have gone unnoticed.

By linking disparate data sources from multiple sensor classes from diverse vendors, efficient and effective security operations in heterogeneous environments are enabled, delivering context sensitive screens that enable users to make smarter decisions earlier in the incident response cycle. Again, these solutions are not free and companies have to find the balance between their correlation needs and the skills and availability of their security teams.

Chapter 4 Intrusion Detection System

4.7.7 Evasion Techniques

Although there are dozens of techniques to elude IDSs, they can be classified in seven main categories:

- **Insertion.** An IDS can mistakenly believe that an end-system has accepted and processed a packet when it actually hasn't. A hacker can exploit this by sending packets to an end-system that it will reject, but that the IDS will think are valid.
- **Evasion.** On the other hand, an end-system can accept a packet that an IDS mistakenly rejects. This can also be exploited by slipping crucial information past the IDS in packets that the IDS is too strict about processing.
- **Denial of Service.** This technique consists in making the IDS unusable or unexploitable. SYN flood, smurf and other attacks would be successful against NIDS but not against HIDS. Denial of Service can also be done on logs by saturation, fake attacks and false-positives.
- **Substitution.** Here the technique is to exchange some packet contents in order to bypass the pattern discovery. For example replacing some character like ";" by "," or hexadecimal values, or even finding some alternative sequences that have the same results but whose signature is not identified as an attack.
- **Fragmentation.** This technique is used to avoid the IDS analysis by fragmenting the commands in different successive or parallel sessions.
- **Distribution.** Here it is the same idea as for fragmentation. The objective is to avoid the IDS examination of the sequence by sending the operations from different user or IP sources. The distribution can also be done in a sufficiently long period to avoid IDS correlation from different events.
- **Confusion.** The objective is to make the data incomprehensible by the IDS. This can be done by encryption as IDSs are often not able to decrypt, for performance reasons for example. It is also possible to encapsulate the data into another protocol (IPv4 into IPv6 for example).

Glossary

anomaly detection	异常检测
Anomaly Prevention System(APS)	异常防御系统
asynchronous	异步的
audit	审计

buffer overflow	缓冲区溢出
Common Intrusion Detection Framework(CIDF)	通用入侵检测框架
console	控制台
countermeasure	对策,反措施
Data Mining	数据挖掘
Demilitarized Zone(DMZ)	非军事化区域
Denial-of-Service (DoS)	拒绝服务攻击
Distributed Denial of Service (DDoS)	分布式拒绝服务攻击
Distributed Intrusion Detection System(DIDS)	分布式入侵检测系统
genetic algorithm	遗传算法
honeypot	蜜罐
Host-based Intrusion Detection System(HIDS)	基于主机的入侵检测系统
Intrusion Detection Exchange Protocol(IDXP)	入侵检测交换协议
Intrusion Detection Message Exchange Format(IDMEF)	入侵检测消息交换格式
Intrusion Detection System (IDS)	入侵检测系统
Intrusion Detection Working Group(IDWG)	入侵检测工作组
Intrusion Prevention System(IPS)	入侵防御系统
manipulation	处理,操作
misuse detection	误用检测
Network Node Intrusion Detection System(NNIDS)	基于网络结点的入侵检测系统
network segment	网段
Network-based Intrusion Detection System(NIDS)	基于网络的入侵检测系统
pattern matching	模式匹配
promiscuous mode	混杂模式
protocol analysis	协议分析
protocol stack	协议栈
Protocol-based Intrusion Detection System(PIDS)	基于协议分析的入侵检测系统
sensor	传感器
synchronization	同步

Translate the following sentences/passage into Chinese

(1) An Intrusion Detection System is used to detect all types of malicious network traffic and computer usage that can't be detected by a conventional firewall. This includes network attacks against vulnerable services, data driven attacks on applications, host based attacks such as privilege escalation, unauthorized logins and access to sensi-

tive files, and malware (viruses, trojan horses, and worms).

(2) An IDS is composed of several components: Sensors which generate security events, a Console to monitor events and alerts and control the sensors, and a central Engine that records events logged by the sensors in a database and uses a system of rules to generate alerts from security events received.

(3) In a passive system, the IDS sensor detects a potential security breach, logs the information and signals an alert on the console. In a reactive system, also known as an Intrusion Prevention System (IPS), the IDS responds to the suspicious activity by resetting the connection or by reprogramming the firewall to block network traffic from the suspected malicious source.

(4) The Philosophy of an APS is to collect information about all these anomalies only one time, and use powerful techniques of correlation and various algorithms of detection (protocol analysis, behavior analysis…) to process the data.

(5) Most of the network based IDS work in what is known as "promiscuous mode". This means that they examine every packet on the local segment, whether or not those packets are destined for the IDS machine.

Translate the following sentences/passage into English

(1) 入侵检测是防火墙的合理补充，帮助系统对付网络攻击，扩展了系统管理员的安全管理能力（包括安全审计、监视、进攻识别和响应），提高了信息安全基础结构的完整性。它被认为是防火墙之后的第二道安全闸门，在不影响网络性能的情况下能对网络进行监测，从而提供对内部攻击、外部攻击和误操作的实时保护。

(2) 入侵检测，即 Intrusion Detection，是对入侵行为的发觉，通过对计算机网络或计算机系统中的若干关键点收集信息并对其进行分析，从中发现网络或系统中是否有违反安全策略的行为和被攻击的迹象。

(3) IDS 系统主要两大职责：实时检测和安全审计。实时监测实时地监视、分析网络中所有的数据报文，发现并实时处理所捕获的数据报文；安全审计通过对 IDS 系统记录的网络事件进行统计分析，发现其中的异常现象，得出系统的安全状态，找出所需要的证据。

(4) 大多数传统入侵检测系统（IDS）采取基于网络或基于主机的办法来辨认并躲避攻击。在任何一种情况下，该产品都要寻找"攻击标志"，即一种代表恶意或可疑意图攻击的模式。当 IDS 在网络中寻找这些模式时，它是基于网络的。而当 IDS 在记录文件中寻找攻击标志时，它是基于主机的。

(5) 由于基于主机的 IDS(HIDS)使用的数据源主要是审计日志、系统日志、应用日志和网络连接数据，这些数据是已经发生的成功/失败的事件信息，因此可以比基于网络的 IDS 更加准确地判断攻击是否成功。

Questions

(1) What is Anomaly Detection and how does it work?

(2) What is Misuse Detection and how does it work?

(3) What is HIDS and how does it work?

(4) What is IPS and how does it work?

(5) What is APS and how does it work?

Chapter 5

Network Security Protocol

5.1 Introduction

A security protocol (cryptographic protocol or encryption protocol) is an abstract or concrete protocol that performs a security-related function and applies cryptographic methods.

A protocol describes how the algorithms should be used. A sufficiently detailed protocol includes details about data structures and representations, at which point it can be used to implement multiple, interoperable versions of a program.

Cryptographic protocols are widely used for secure application-level data transport. A cryptographic protocol usually incorporates at least some of these aspects:
- Key agreement or establishment
- Entity authentication
- Symmetric encryption and message authentication material construction
- Secured application-level data transport
- Non-repudiation methods

For example, Transport Layer Security (TLS) is a cryptographic protocol that is used to secure web (HTTP) connections. It has an entity authentication mechanism, based on the X.509 system; a key setup phase, where a symmetric encryption key is formed by employing public-key cryptography; and an application-level data transport function. These three aspects have important interconnections. Standard TLS does not have non-repudiation support.

There are other types of cryptographic protocols as well, and even the term itself has various different readings; Cryptographic application protocols often use one or more underlying key agreement methods, which are also sometimes themselves referred to as "cryptographic protocols". For instance, TLS employs what is known as the Diffie-Hellman key exchange, which although it is only a part of TLS per se, Diffie-Hellman may be seen as a complete cryptographic protocol in itself for other applications.

In this chapter, Kerberos protocol, SET protocol, SSL protocol, IPSec protocol and IKE Protocol are introduced.

5.2 Kerberos Protocol

Kerberos is a computer network authentication protocol, which allows individuals communicating over an insecure network to prove their identity to one another in a secure manner. Kerberos prevents eavesdropping or replay attacks, and ensures the integrity of the data. Its designers aimed primarily at a client-server model, and it provides mutual authentication—both the user and the server verify each other's identity.

Kerberos builds on symmetric key cryptography and requires a trusted third party.

5.2.1 History and Development

The Massachusetts Institute of Technology (MIT) developed Kerberos to protect network services provided by Project Athena. The protocol was named after the Greek mythological character Kerberos (or Cerberus), known in Greek mythology as being the monstrous three-headed guard dog of Hades. Several versions of the protocol exist; versions 1~3 occurred only internally at MIT.

Steve Miller and Clifford Neuman, the primary designers of Kerberos version 4, published that version in the late 1980s, although they had targeted it primarily for Project Athena.

Version 5, designed by John Kohl and Clifford Neuman, appeared as RFC 1510 in 1993 (made obsolete by RFC 4120 in 2005), with the intention of overcoming the limitations and security problems of version 4.

MIT makes an implementation of Kerberos freely available, under copyright permissions similar to those used for BSD.

Authorities in the United States classed Kerberos as a munition and banned its export because it used the DES encryption algorithm (with 56-bit keys). A non-US Kerberos 4 implementation, KTH-KRB developed in Sweden, made the system available outside the US before the US changed its cryptography export regulations (circa 2000). The Swedish implementation was based on a version called eBones. eBones was based on the exported MIT Bones release (stripped of both the encryption functions and the calls to them) based on version Kerberos 4 patch-level 9. Australian Eric Young, the author of several cryptography libraries, put back the function calls and used his libdes encryption library. This somewhat limited Kerberos was called the eBones release. A Kerberos version 5 implementation, Heimdal, was released by basically the same group of people releasing KTH-KRB.

Windows 2000, Windows XP and Windows Server 2003 use a variant of Kerberos as their default authentication method. Some Microsoft additions to the Kerberos suite of protocols are documented in RFC 3244 "Microsoft Windows 2000 Kerberos Change Password and Set Password Protocols". Apple's Mac OS X also uses Kerberos in both its client and server versions.

As of 2005, the IETF Kerberos workgroup is updating the specifications. Recent updates include:
- "Encryption and Checksum Specifications" (RFC 3961).
- "Advanced Encryption Standard (AES) Encryption for Kerberos 5" (RFC 3962).
- A new edition of the Kerberos V5 specification "The Kerberos Network Authentication Service (V5)" (RFC 4120). This version obsoletes RFC 1510, clarifies aspects of the protocol and intended use in a more detailed and clearer explanation.
- A new edition of the GSS-API specification "The Kerberos Version 5 Generic Security Service Application Program Interface (GSS-API) Mechanism: Version 2" (RFC 4121).

5.2.2 Description

Kerberos uses as its basis the Needham-Schroeder protocol. It makes use of a trusted third party, termed a Key Distribution Center (KDC), which consists of two logically separate parts: an Authentication Server (AS) and a Ticket Granting Server (TGS). Kerberos works on the basis of "tickets" which serve to prove the identity of users.

Kerberos maintains a database of secret keys; each entity on the network—whether a client or a server— shares a secret key known only to itself and to Kerberos. Knowledge of this key serves to prove an entity's identity. For communication between two entities, Kerberos generates a session key which they can use to secure their interactions.

5.2.3 Use

The following software is able to use Kerberos for authentication:
- AFS
- Apache (with the mod_auth_kerb module)
- Apache 2 (using libapache-mod-auth-kerb)
- Cisco routers and switches running IOS
- Eudora
- Microsoft Windows (2000 and later) uses as default authentication protocol
- Mulberry, an E-mail client developed by Cyrusoft, Inc.
- NFS (since NFSv3)
- OpenSSH (with Kerberos v5 or higher)
- PAM (with the pam_krb5 module)
- Samba since v3.x
- SOCKS (since SOCKS5)
- Netatalk
- The X Window System implementations
- Indirectly, any software that allows the use of SASL for authentication, such as OpenLDAP, Dovecot IMAP4 and POP3 server, Postfix mail server
- The Kerberos software suite also comes with kerberos-enabled clients and servers for rsh, FTP, and Telnet

5.2.4 The Protocol

One can specify the protocol as follows in security protocol notation, where Alice (A) authenticates herself to Bob (B) using a server S. Here,
- K_{AS} is a pre-established secret key known only to A and S;
- Likewise, K_{BS} is known only to B and S;
- K_{AB} is a session key between A and B, freshly generated for each run of the protocol;
- T_S and T_A are timestamps generated by S and A, respectively;
- L is a "lifespan" value defining the validity of a timestamp.

$$A \rightarrow S: A, B$$

A asks S to initiate communication with B.

$$S \rightarrow A: \{T_S, L, K_{AB}, B, \{T_S, L, K_{AB}, A\}_{K_{BS}}\}_{K_{AS}}$$

S generates a fresh K_{AB}, and sends it to A together with a timestamp and the same data encrypted for B.

$$A \rightarrow B: \{T_S, L, K_{AB}, A\}_{K_{BS}}, \{A, T_A\}_{K_{AB}}$$

A passes on the message to B, obtains a new T_A and passes it under the new session key.

$$B \rightarrow A: \{T_A + 1\}_{K_{AB}}$$

B confirms receipt of the session key by returning a modified version of the timestamp to A.

We see here that the security of the protocol relies heavily on timestamps T and lifespan L as reliable indicators of the freshness of a communication (see the BAN logic).

In relation to the following Kerberos operation, it is helpful to note that the server S here stands for both authentication service (AS), and ticket granting service (TGS). In $\{T_S, L, K_{AB}, B, \{T_S, L, K_{AB}, A\}_{K_{BS}}\}_{K_{AS}}, \{T_S, L, K_{AB}, A\}_{K_{BS}}$ is the client to server ticket, $\{A, T_A\}_{K_{AB}}$ is the authenticator, and $\{T_A + 1\}_{K_{AB}}$ confirms B's true identity and its recognition of A. This is required for mutual authentication.

5.2.5 Kerberos Operation

What follows is a simplified description of the protocol. The following shortcuts will be used:
- AS, Authentication Server
- TGS, Ticket Granting Server
- SS, Service Server

In one sentence: the client authenticates itself to AS, then demonstrates to the TGS that it's authorized to receive a ticket for a service (and receives it), then demonstrates to the SS that it has been approved to receive the service.

In more detail:

(1) A user enters a username and password on the client.

(2) The client performs a one-way hash on the entered password, and this becomes the secret key of the client.

(3) The client sends a clear-text message to the AS requesting services on behalf of the user. Sample Message: "User XYZ would like to request services". Note: Neither

English for Information Security

the secret key nor the password is sent to the AS.

(4) The AS checks to see if the client is in its database. If it is, the AS sends back the following two messages to the client.

- Message A: Client/TGS session key encrypted using the secret key of the user.
- Message B: Ticket-Granting Ticket (which includes the client ID, client network address, ticket validity period, and the client/TGS session key) encrypted using the secret key of the TGS.

(5) Once the client receives messages A and B, it decrypts message A to obtain the client/TGS session key. This session key is used for further communications with TGS. (Note: The client cannot decrypt the Message B, as it is encrypted using TGS's secret key.) At this point, the client has enough information to authenticate itself to the TGS.

(6) When requesting services, the client sends the following two messages to the TGS.

- Message C: Composed of the Ticket-Granting Ticket from message B and the ID of the requested service.
- Message D: Authenticator (which is composed of the client ID and the timestamp), encrypted using the client/TGS session key.

(7) Upon receiving messages C and D, the TGS decrypts message D (Authenticator) using the client/TGS session key and sends the following two messages to the client.

- Message E: Client-to-server ticket (which includes the client ID, client network address, validity period and Client/server session key) encrypted using the service's secret key.
- Message F: Client/server session key encrypted with the client/TGS session key.

(8) Upon receiving messages E and F from TGS, the client has enough information to authenticate itself to the SS. The client connects to the SS and sends the following two messages.

- Message E from the previous step (the client-to-server ticket, encrypted using service's secret key).
- Message G: a new Authenticator, which includes the client ID, timestamp and is encrypted using client/server session key.

(9) The server decrypts the ticket using its own secret key and sends the following message to the client to confirm its true identity and willingness to serve the client.

- Message H: the timestamp found in client's recent Authenticator plus 1, encrypted using the client/server session key.

(10) The client decrypts the confirmation using its shared key with the server and checks whether the timestamp is correctly updated. If so, then the client can trust the server and can start issuing service requests to the server.

(11) The server provides the requested services to the client.

5.2.6 Kerberos Drawbacks

Single point of failure: It requires continuous availability of a central server. When Kerberos server is down, no one can log in. This can be mitigated by using multiple Kerberos servers.

Kerberos requires the clocks of the involved hosts to be synchronized. The tickets have time availability period and, if the host clock is not synchronized with the clock of Kerberos server, the authentication will fail. The default configuration requires that clock times are no more than 10 minutes apart.

Password changing is not standardized, and differs between server implementations.

5.3 SSL Protocol

Originally developed by Netscape, SSL has been universally accepted on the World Wide Web for authenticated and encrypted communication between clients and servers.

Secure Sockets Layer (SSL) and its successor, Transport Layer Security (TLS), are cryptographic protocols which provide secure communications on the Internet for such things as web browsing, E-mail, Internet faxing, and other data transfers. There are slight differences between SSL 3.0 and TLS 1.0, but the protocol remains substantially the same. The term "SSL" as used here applies to both protocols unless clarified by context.

5.3.1 Description

The Transmission Control Protocol/Internet Protocol (TCP/IP) governs the transport and routing of data over the Internet. Other protocols, such as the HyperText Transport Protocol (HTTP), Lightweight Directory Access Protocol (LDAP), or Internet Messaging Access Protocol (IMAP), run "on top of" TCP/IP in the sense that they all use TCP/IP to support typical application tasks such as displaying web pages or running E-mail servers.

The SSL protocol runs above TCP/IP and below higher-level protocols such as HTTP or IMAP, see Figure 5.1. It uses TCP/IP on behalf of the higher-level protocols, and in the process allows an SSL-enabled server to authenticate itself to an SSL-enabled client, allows the client to authenticate itself to the server, and allows both machines to establish an encrypted connection.

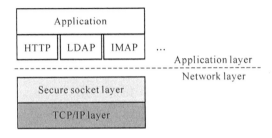

Figure 5.1 SSL runs above TCP/IP and below high-level application protocols

These capabilities address fundamental concerns about communication over the Internet and other TCP/IP networks:

- SSL server authentication allows a user to confirm a server's identity. SSL-enabled client software can use standard techniques of public-key cryptography to check that a server's certificate and public ID are valid and have been issued by a certificate authority (CA) listed in the client's list of trusted CAs. This confirmation might be important if the user, for example, is sending a credit card number over the network and wants to check the receiving server's identity.
- SSL client authentication allows a server to confirm a user's identity. Using the same techniques as those used for server authentication, SSL-enabled server software can check that a client's certificate and public ID are valid and have been issued by a CA listed in the server's list of trusted CAs. This confirmation might be important if the server, for example, is a bank sending confidential financial information to a customer and wants to check the recipient's identity.
- An encrypted SSL connection requires all information sent between a client and a server to be encrypted by the sending software and decrypted by the receiving software, thus providing a high degree of confidentiality. Confidentiality is important for both parties to any private transaction. In addition, all data sent over an encrypted SSL connection is protected with a mechanism for detecting tampering—that is, for automatically determining whether the data has been altered in transit.

The SSL protocol includes two sub-protocols: the SSL record protocol and the SSL

handshake protocol. The SSL record protocol defines the format used to transmit data. The SSL handshake protocol involves using the SSL record protocol to exchange a series of messages between an SSL-enabled server and an SSL-enabled client when they first establish an SSL connection. This exchange of messages is designed to facilitate the following actions:
- Authenticate the server to the client;
- Allow the client and server to select the cryptographic algorithms, or ciphers, that they both support;
- Optionally authenticate the client to the server;
- Use public-key encryption techniques to generate shared secrets;
- Establish an encrypted SSL connection.

SSL technology is used to establish a secure and encrypted communication channel between two Internet connected devices.

5.3.2 Ciphers Used with SSL

The SSL protocol supports the use of a variety of different cryptographic algorithms, or ciphers, for use in operations such as authenticating the server and client to each other, transmitting certificates, and establishing session keys. Clients and servers may support different cipher suites, or sets of ciphers, depending on factors such as the version of SSL they support, company policies regarding acceptable encryption strength, and government restrictions on export of SSL-enabled software. Among its other functions, the SSL handshake protocol determines how the server and client negotiate which cipher suites they will use to authenticate each other, to transmit certificates, and to establish session keys.

The cipher suite descriptions that follow refer to these algorithms:
- DES. Data Encryption Standard, an encryption algorithm used by the U. S. Government.
- DSA. Digital Signature Algorithm, part of the digital authentication standard used by the U. S. Government.
- KEA. Key Exchange Algorithm, an algorithm used for key exchange by the U. S. Government.
- MD5. Message Digest algorithm developed by Rivest.
- RC2 and RC4. Rivest encryption ciphers developed for RSA Data Security.
- RSA. A public-key algorithm for both encryption and authentication. Developed

by Rivest, Shamir, and Adleman.
- RSA key exchange. A key-exchange algorithm for SSL based on the RSA algorithm.
- SHA-1. Secure Hash Algorithm, a hash function used by the U. S. Government.
- SKIPJACK. A classified symmetric-key algorithm implemented in FORTEZZA-compliant hardware used by the U. S. Government. (For more information, see FORTEZZA Cipher Suites.)
- Triple-DES. DES applied three times.

Key-exchange algorithms like KEA and RSA key exchange govern the way in which the server and client determine the symmetric keys they will both use during an SSL session. The most commonly used SSL cipher suites use RSA key exchange.

The SSL 2.0 and SSL 3.0 protocols support overlapping sets of cipher suites. Administrators can enable or disable any of the supported cipher suites for both clients and servers. When a particular client and server exchange information during the SSL handshake, they identify the strongest enabled cipher suites they have in common and use those for the SSL session.

Decisions about which cipher suites a particular organization decides to enable depend on trade-offs among the sensitivity of the data involved, the speed of the cipher, and the applicability of export rules.

Some organizations may want to disable the weaker ciphers to prevent SSL connections with weaker encryption. However, due to U. S. government restrictions on products that support anything stronger than 40-bit encryption, disabling support for all 40-bit ciphers effectively restricts access to network browsers that are available only in the United States (unless the server involved has a special Global Server ID that permits the international client to "step up" to stronger encryption). For more information about U. S. export restrictions, see Export Restrictions on International Sales.

To serve the largest possible range of users, its administrators may wish to enable as broad a range of SSL cipher suites as possible. That way, when a domestic client or server is dealing with another domestic server or client, respectively, it will negotiate the use of the strongest ciphers available. And when a domestic client or server is dealing with an international server or client, it will negotiate the use of those ciphers that are permitted under U. S. export regulations.

However, since 40-bit ciphers can be broken relatively quickly, administrators who are concerned about eavesdropping and whose user communities can legally use stronger ciphers should disable the 40-bit ciphers.

5.3.3 The SSL Handshake

The SSL protocol uses a combination of public-key and symmetric key encryption. Symmetric key encryption is much faster than public-key encryption, but public-key encryption provides better authentication techniques. An SSL session always begins with an exchange of messages called the SSL handshake. The handshake allows the server to authenticate itself to the client using public-key techniques, then allows the client and the server to cooperate in the creation of symmetric keys used for rapid encryption, decryption, and tamper detection during the session that follows. Optionally, the handshake also allows the client to authenticate itself to the server.

The exact programmatic details of the messages exchanged during the SSL handshake are beyond the scope of this document. However, the steps involved can be summarized as follows:

(1) The client sends the server the client's SSL version number, cipher settings, randomly generated data, and other information the server needs to communicate with the client using SSL.

(2) The server sends the client the server's SSL version number, cipher settings, randomly generated data, and other information the client needs to communicate with the server over SSL. The server also sends its own certificate and, if the client is requesting a server resource that requires client authentication, requests the client's certificate.

(3) The client uses some of the information sent by the server to authenticate the server. If the server cannot be authenticated, the user is warned of the problem and informed that an encrypted and authenticated connection cannot be established. If the server can be successfully authenticated, the client goes on to Step 4.

(4) Using all datas generated in the handshake so far, the client (with the cooperation of the server, depending on the cipher being used) creates the premaster secret for the session, encrypts it with the server's public-key (obtained from the server's certificate, sent in Step 2), and sends the encrypted premaster secret to the server.

(5) If the server has requested client authentication (an optional step in the handshake), the client also signs another piece of data that is unique to this handshake and known by both the client and server. In this case the client sends both the signed data and the client's own certificate to the server along with the encrypted premaster secret.

(6) If the server has requested client authentication, the server attempts to authenticate the client (see Client Authentication for details). If the client cannot be authentic-

ated, the session is terminated. If the client can be successfully authenticated, the server uses its public-key to decrypt the premaster secret, then performs a series of steps (which the client also performs, starting from the same premaster secret) to generate the master secret.

(7) Both the client and the server use the master secret to generate the session keys, which are symmetric keys used to encrypt and decrypt information exchanged during the SSL session and to verify its integrity—that is, to detect any changes in the data between the time it was sent and the time it is received over the SSL connection.

(8) The client sends a message to the server informing it that future messages from the client will be encrypted with the session key. It then sends a separate (encrypted) message indicating that the client portion of the handshake is finished.

(9) The server sends a message to the client informing it that future messages from the server will be encrypted with the session key. It then sends a separate (encrypted) message indicating that the server portion of the handshake is finished.

(10) The SSL handshake is now completed and the SSL session has begun. The client and the server use the session keys to encrypt and decrypt the data they send to each other and to validate its integrity.

Before continuing with the session, Netscape servers can be configured to check that the client's certificate is present in the user's entry in an LDAP directory. This configuration option provides one way of ensuring that the client's certificate has not been revoked.

It's important to note that both client and server authentication involve encrypting some piece of data with one key of a public-private-key pair and decrypting it with the other key:

- In the case of server authentication, the client encrypts the premaster secret with the server's public-key. Only the corresponding private-key can correctly decrypt the secret, so the client has some assurance that the identity associated with the public-key is in fact the server with which the client is connected. Otherwise, the server cannot decrypt the premaster secret and cannot generate the symmetric keys required for the session, and the session will be terminated.
- In the case of client authentication, the client encrypts some random data with the client's private-key—that is, it creates a digital signature. The public-key in the client's certificate can correctly validate the digital signature only if the corresponding private-key was used. Otherwise, the server cannot validate the digital signature and the session is terminated.

The sections that follow provide more details on Server Authentication and Client Authentication.

5.3.4 Server Authentication

Netscape's SSL-enabled client software always requires server authentication, or cryptographic validation by a client of the server's identity. As explained in Step 2 of The SSL Handshake, the server sends the client a certificate to authenticate itself. The client uses the certificate in Step 3 to authenticate the identity the certificate claims to represent.

To authenticate the binding between a public-key and the server identified by the certificate that contains the public-key, an SSL-enabled client must receive a "yes" answer to the four questions shown in Figure 5.2. Although the fourth question is not technically part of the SSL protocol, it is the client's responsibility to support this requirement, which provides some assurance of the server's identity and thus helps protect against a form of security attack known as "man in the middle".

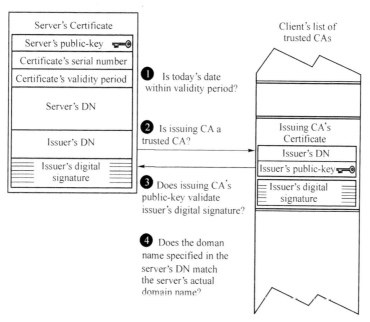

Figure 5.2   How a Netscape client authenticates a server certificate

An SSL-enabled client goes through these steps to authenticate a server's identity:

(1) Is today's date within the validity period? The client checks the server certificate's validity period. If the current date and time are outside of that range, the authentication process won't go any further. If the current date and time are within the certificate's validity period, the client goes on to Step 2.

(2) Is the issuing CA a trusted CA? Each SSL-enabled client maintains a list of

trusted CA certificates, represented by the shaded area on the right side of Figure 5.2. This list determines which server certificates the client will accept. If the distinguished name (DN) of the issuing CA matches the DN of a CA on the client's list of trusted CAs, the answer to this question is yes, and the client goes on to Step 3. If the issuing CA is not on the list, the server will not be authenticated unless the client can verify a certificate chain ending in a CA that is on the list (see CA Hierarchies for details).

(3) Does the issuing CA's public-key validate the issuer's digital signature? The client uses the public-key from the CA's certificate (which it found in its list of trusted CAs in Step 2) to validate the CA's digital signature on the server certificate being presented. If the information in the server certificate has changed since it was signed by the CA or if the CA certificate's public-key doesn't correspond to the private-key used by the CA to sign the server certificate, the client won't authenticate the server's identity. If the CA's digital signature can be validated, the server treats the user's certificate as a valid "letter of introduction" from that CA and proceeds. At this point, the client has determined that the server certificate is valid. It is the client's responsibility to take Step 4 before Step 5.

(4) Does the domain name in the server's certificate match the domain name of the server itself? This step confirms that the server is actually located at the same network address specified by the domain name in the server certificate. Although Step 4 is not technically part of the SSL protocol, it provides the only protection against a form of security attack known as a Man-in-the-Middle Attack. Clients must perform this step and must refuse to authenticate the server or establish a connection if the domain names don't match. If the server's actual domain name matches the domain name in the server certificate, the client goes on to Step 5.

(5) The server is authenticated. The client proceeds with the SSL handshake. If the client doesn't get to Step 5 for any reason, the server identified by the certificate cannot be authenticated, and the user will be warned of the problem and informed that an encrypted and authenticated connection cannot be established. If the server requires client authentication, the server performs the steps described in Client Authentication.

After the steps described here, the server must successfully use its private-key to decrypt the premaster secret the client sends in Step 4 of The SSL Handshake. Otherwise, the SSL session will be terminated. This provides additional assurance that the identity associated with the public-key in the server's certificate is in fact the server with which the client is connected.

5.3.5　Client Authentication

SSL-enabled servers can be configured to require client authentication, or crypto-

Chapter 5 Network Security Protocol

graphic validation by the server of the client's identity. When a server configured this way requests client authentication (see Step 6 of The SSL Handshake), the client sends the server both a certificate and a separate piece of digitally signed data to authenticate itself. The server uses the digitally signed data to validate the public-key in the certificate and to authenticate the identity the certificate claims to represent.

The SSL protocol requires the client to create a digital signature by creating a one-way hash from data generated randomly during the handshake and known only to the client and server. The hash of the data is then encrypted with the private-key that corresponds to the public-key in the certificate being presented to the server.

To authenticate the binding between the public-key and the person or other entities identified by the certificate that contains the public-key, an SSL-enabled server must receive a "yes" answer to the first four questions shown in Figure 5.3. Although the fifth question is not part of the SSL protocol, Netscape servers can be configured to support this requirement to take advantage of the user's entry in an LDAP directory as part of the authentication process.

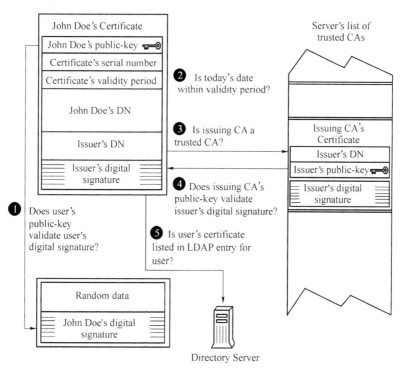

Figure 5.3 How a Netscape server authenticates a client certificate

An SSL-enabled server goes through these steps to authenticate a user's identity:

(1) Does the user's public-key validate the user's digital signature? The server checks that the user's digital signature can be validated with the public-key in the certificate. If so, the server has established that the public-key asserted to belong to John Doe matches the private-key used to create the signature and that the data has not been tampered with since it was signed.

(2) At this point, however, the binding between the public-key and the DN specified in the certificate has not yet been established. The certificate might have been created by someone attempting to impersonate the user. To validate the binding between the public-key and the DN, the server must also complete Step 3 and Step 4.

(3) Is today's date within the validity period? The server checks the certificate's validity period. If the current date and time are outside of that range, the authentication process won't go any further. If the current date and time are within the certificate's validity period, the server goes on to Step 3.

(4) Is the issuing CA a trusted CA? Each SSL-enabled server maintains a list of trusted CA certificates, represented by the shaded area on the right side of Figure 5.3. This list determines which certificates the server will accept. If the DN of the issuing CA matches the DN of a CA on the server's list of trusted CAs, the answer to this question is yes, and the server goes on to Step 4. If the issuing CA is not on the list, the client will not be authenticated unless the server can verify a certificate chain ending in a CA that is on the list (see CA Hierarchies for details). Administrators can control which certificates are trusted or not trusted within their organizations by controlling the lists of CA certificates maintained by clients and servers.

(5) Does the issuing CA's public-key validate the issuer's digital signature? The server uses the public-key from the CA's certificate (which it found in its list of trusted CAs in Step 3) to validate the CA's digital signature on the certificate being presented. If the information in the certificate has changed since it was signed by the CA or if the public-key in the CA certificate doesn't correspond to the private-key used by the CA to sign the certificate, the server won't authenticate the user's identity. If the CA's digital signature can be validated, the server treats the user's certificate as a valid "letter of introduction" from that CA and proceeds. At this point, the SSL protocol allows the server to consider the client authenticated and proceed with the connection as described in Step 6. Netscape servers may optionally be configured to take Step 5 before Step 6.

(6) Is the user's certificate listed in the LDAP entry for the user? This optional step provides one way for a system administrator to revoke a user's certificate even if it passes the tests in all the other steps. The Netscape Certificate Server can automatically

Chapter 5 Network Security Protocol

remove a revoked certificate from the user's entry in the LDAP directory. All servers that are set up to perform this step will then refuse to authenticate that certificate or establish a connection. If the user's certificate in the directory is identical to the user's certificate presented in the SSL handshake, the server goes on to Step 6.

(7) Is the authenticated client authorized to access the requested resources? The server checks what resources the client is permitted to access according to the server's access control lists (ACLs) and establishes a connection with appropriate access. If the server doesn't get to Step 6 for any reason, the user identified by the certificate cannot be authenticated, and the user is not allowed to access any server resources that require authentication.

5.3.6 Applications

SSL runs on layers beneath application protocols such as HTTP, FTP, SMTP and NNTP, and above the TCP or UDP transport protocol, which form parts of the TCP/IP protocol suite. While it can add security to any protocol that uses reliable connections (such as TCP), it is most commonly used with HTTP to form HTTPS. HTTPS is used to secure World Wide Web pages for applications such as electronic commerce. It uses public-key certificates to verify the identity of endpoints.

An increasing number of client and server products support SSL natively, but many still lack support. As an alternative, users may wish to use standalone SSL products like Stunnel. Wrappers such as Stunnel rely on being able to obtain an SSL connection immediately, by simply connecting to a separate port reserved for the purpose. For example, by default the TCP port for HTTPS is 443, to distinguish it from HTTP on port 80. However, in 1997 the Internet Engineering Task Force recommended that application protocols always start unsecured and instead offer a way to upgrade to TLS—which a pure wrapper like Stunnel cannot cope with.

SSL can also be used to tunnel an entire network stack to create a VPN, as is the case with OpenVPN. Many vendors now marry SSL's encryption and authentication capabilities with authorization. There has also been substantial development since the late 1990s in creating client technology outside of the browser to enable support for client/server applications. When compared against traditional IPSec VPN technologies, SSL has some inherent advantages in firewall and NAT traversal that make it easier to administer for large remote access populations. Vendors like Aventail, F5, Juniper, and others have been developing in this space for some time.

5.4 SET Protocol

Secure Electronic Transaction (SET) is a standard protocol for securing credit card transactions over insecure networks, specifically, the Internet. SET was developed by VISA and MasterCard (involving other companies such as GTE, IBM, Microsoft and Netscape) starting in 1996.

SET is based on X.509 certificates with several extensions. SET uses a blinding algorithmthat, in effect, lets merchants substitute a certificate for a user's credit-card number. This allows traders to credit funds from clients' credit cards without the need of the credit card numbers.

SET makes use of cryptographic techniques such as digital certificates and public-key cryptography to allow parties to identify themselves to each other and exchange information securely.

SET was heavily publicised in the late 1990's as the credit card approved standard, but failed to win market share. Reasons for this include:
- Network effect—need to install client software (an eWallet).
- Cost and complexity for merchants to offer support and comparatively low cost and simplicity of the existing, adequate SSL based alternative.
- Client-side certificate distribution logistics.

SET is said to become the de facto standard of payment method on the Internet between the merchants, the buyers, and the credit-card companies. When SET is used, the merchant itself never has to know the credit-card numbers being sent from the buyer, which provide a benefit for e-commerce.

5.4.1 Introduction

Electronic commerce, as exemplified by the popularity of the Internet, is going to have an enormous impact on the financial services industry. No financial institution will be left unaffected by the explosion of electronic commerce. Even though SSL is extremely effective and widely accepted as the online payment standard, it requires the customer and merchant to trust each other: an undesirable requirement even in face-to-face transactions, and across the Internet it admits unacceptable risks.

Visa and MasterCard and a consortium of 11 technology companies made a promise to banks, merchants, and consumers; they would make the Internet safe for credit card transactions and send electronic commerce revenues skyward. With great fanfare, they introduced the Secure Electronic Transaction protocol for processing online credit card purchases.

5.4.2 Overview of SET Protocol

Secure payment systems are critical to the success of E-commerce. There are four essential security requirements for safe electronic payments (Authentication, Encryption, Integrity and Non-repudiation). Encryption is the key security schemes adopted for electronic payment systems, which is used in protocols like SSL and SET.

1. Problem with SSL

The SSL protocol, widely deployed today on the Internet, has helped create a basic level of security sufficient for some hearty souls to begin conducting business over the Web. SSL is implemented in most major Web browsers used by consumers, as well as in merchant server software, which supports the seller's virtual storefront in cyberspace. Hundreds of millions of dollars are already changing hands when cybershoppers enter their credit card numbers on Web pages secured with SSL technology.

In this sense, SSL provides a secure channel to between the consumer and the merchant for exchanging payment information. This means any data sent through this channel is encrypted, so that no one other than these two parties will be able to read it. In other words, SSL can give us confidential communications, it also introduces huge risks:

- The cardholder is protected from eavesdroppers but not from the merchant. Some merchants are dishonest: pornographers have charged more than advertised price, expecting their customers to be too embarrassed to complain. Some others are just hackers who put up a snazzy illegal Web site and profess to be the XYZ Corp., or impersonate the XYZ Corp. and collecting credit card numbers for personal use.
- The merchant has not protected from dishonest customers who supply an invalid credit card number or who claim a refund from their bank without cause. Contrary to popular belief, it is not the cardholder but the merchant who has the most to lose from fraud. Legislation in most countries protects the consumer.

2. SET Protocol Overview

What we want here is a protocol very similar to credit card transactions at a local store, something SSL doesn't mimic in functionality. SET is the one.

The purpose of the SET protocol is to establish payment transactions that
- provide confidentiality of information;
- ensure the integrity of payment instructions for goods and services order data;
- authenticate both the cardholder and the merchant.

There are four main entities in SET:
- Cardholder (customer);
- Merchant (web server);
- Merchant's Bank (payment gateway, acquirer): payment gateway is a device operated by an acquirer. Sometime, separate these two entities;
- Issuer (cardholder's bank).

Both cardholders and merchants must register with CA (certificate authority) first, before they can buy or sell on the Internet, which we will talk about later. Once registration is done, cardholder and merchant can start to do transactions, which involve 9 basic steps in this protocol, which is simplified.

(1) Customer browses website and decides on what to purchase.

(2) Customer sends order and payment information, which includes 2 parts in one message:

　　a. Purchase Order—this part is for merchant;

　　b. Card Information—this pat is for merchant's bank only.

(3) Merchant forwards card information (part b) to their bank.

(4) Merchant's bank checks with Issuer for payment authorization.

(5) Issuer sends authorization to Merchant's bank.

(6) Merchant's bank sends authorization to merchant.

(7) Merchant completes the order and sends confirmation to the customer.

(8) Merchant captures the transaction from their bank.

(9) Issuer prints credit card bill (invoice) to customer.

SET is a very comprehensive security protocol, which utilizes cryptography to provide confidentiality of information, ensure payment integrity, and enable identity authentication. For authentication purposes, cardholders, merchants, and acquirers will be issued digital certificates by their sponsoring organizations. It relies on cryptography and digital certificate to ensure message confidentiality and security. Digital envelop is widely used in this protocol. Message data is encrypted using a randomly generated key that is further encrypted using the recipient's public-key. This is referred to as the "digital envelope" of the message and is sent to the recipient with the encrypted message. The recipient decrypts the digital envelope using a private-key and then uses the symmetric key to unlock the original message.

Digital certificates, which are also called electronic credentials or digital IDs, are digital documents attesting to the binding of a public-key to an individual or entity. Both cardholders and merchants must register with a CA before they can engage in transactions. The cardholder thereby obtains electronic credentials to prove that he is trustworthy. The merchant similarly registers and obtains credentials. These credentials do not contain sensitive details such as credit card numbers. Later, when the customer wants to make purchases, he and the merchant exchange their credentials. If both parties are satisfied then they can proceed with the transaction. Credentials must be renewed every few years, and presumably are not available to known fraudsters.

5.4.3 SET Cryptography

1. Overview

SET relies on the science of cryptography—the encoding and decoding messages. There are two primary encryption methods in use today: secret-key cryptography and public-key cryptography. Secret-key cryptography is impractical for exchanging messages with a large group of previously unknown correspondents over a public network. For a merchant to conduct transactions securely with millions of subscribers, each consumer would need a distinct key assigned by that merchant and transmitted over a separate secure channel. However, by using public-key cryptography, that same merchant could create a public-private-key pair and publish the public-key, allowing any consumer to send a secure message to that merchant. This is why SET uses both methods in its encryption process. The secret-key cryptography used in SET is the well-known Data Encryption Standard (DES), which is used by financial institutions to encrypt PINs (personal identification numbers). And the public-key cryptography used in SET is RSA. In the following sections the usage of symmetric (secret-key) and asymmetric (public-key) key encryption in SET will be discussed.

2. Use of Symmetric Key

In SET, message data is encrypted using a randomly generated symmetric key (a DES 56-bit key). This key, in turn, is encrypted using the message recipient's public-key (RSA). The result is the so called "digital envelope" of the message. This combines the encryption speed of DES with the key management advantages of RSA public-key encryption. After encryption, the envelope and the encrypted message itself are sent to the recipient. After receiving the encrypted data, the recipient decrypts the digital envelope first using his or her private-key to obtain the randomly generated symmetric key and then uses the symmetric key to unlock the original message.

This level of encryption, using DES, can be easily cracked using modern hardware. In 1993, a brute-force DES cracking machine was designed by Michael Wiener—one which was massively parallel. For less than a million dollars, a 56-bit DES key could be cracked in average time of 3.5 hours. For a billion dollars, a parallel machine can be constructed that cracks 56-bit DES in a second (Schneier, 1996). Obviously, this is of great concern since DES encrypts the majority of a SET transaction.

3. Use of Asymmetric Key—Digital Signature (Message Digests)

In SET, the public-key cryptography is only used to encrypt DES keys and for authentication (digital signature) but not for the main body of the transaction. In SET, the RSA modulus is 1 024 bits in length (Using the latest factoring results it appears that factoring a 1 024-bit modulus would require over 1×10^{11} MY of computational effort). To generate the digital signature, SET uses a distinct public/private-key. Each SET participant possesses two asymmetric key pairs: a "key exchange" pair, which is used in the process of section key encryption and decryption, and a "signature" pair for the creation and verification of digital signatures (160-bit message digests).

The algorithm is such that changing a single bit in the message will change, on average, half of the bits in the message digest. Approximately, the possibility of two messages having the same message digest is one in 1×10^{48}, which means it is computationally unfeasible to generate two different messages that have the same message digest.

5.4.4 SET Process

The SET protocol utilizes cryptography to provide confidentiality of information, ensure payment integrity, and enable identity authentication. For authentication purposes, cardholders, merchants, and acquirers will be issued digital certificates by their sponsoring organizations. It also use dual signature, which hides the customer's credit card information from merchants, and also hides the order information to banks, to protect privacy.

There are nine steps in the SET process:

(1) Merchant sends invoice and unique transaction ID (XID);

(2) Merchant sends merchant certificate and bank certificate (encrypted with CA's private-key);

(3) Customer decrypts certificates, obtains public-keys;

Chapter 5 Network Security Protocol

(4) Customer generates order information (OI) and payment info (PI) encrypted with different session keys and dual-signed;

(5) Merchant sends payment request to bank encrypted with bank-merchant session key, PI, digest of OI and merchant's certificate;

(6) Bank verifies that the XID matches the one in the PI;

(7) Bank sends authorization request to issuing bank via card network;

(8) Bank sends approval to merchant;

(9) Merchant sends acknowledgement to customer.

5.4.5 Certificates Insurance

Before two parties use public-key cryptography to conduct business, each wants to be sure that the other party is authenticated. One way to be sure that the public-key belongs to the right party is to receive it over a secure channel directly from the same place. However, in most circumstances this solution is not practical.

An alternative to secure transmission of the key is to use a trusted third party to authenticate that the public-key belongs to Alice. Such a party is known as a Certificate Authority (CA). Because SET participants have two key pairs, they also have two certificates. Both certificates are created and signed at the same time by the Certificate Authority.

5.4.6 Security of SET

Cryptography Algorithms in SET:
- Symmetric encryption
- DES (Data Encryption Standard): 56 bit key, protect financial data
- CDMF (Commercial Data Masking Facility): 40 bit key, protect acquire-to cardholder message
- Asymmetric encryption and digital signature: RSA
- Hash function: SHA-1
- Message Authentication Code: HMAC (based on SHA-1)

Security Technology in SET:
- Digital envelopes, salt and Dual signatures
- Two public-private-key pairs for each party: One for digital signatures; one for key exchange messages

- 160-bit message digests
- Statistically globally unique IDs (XIDs)
- Certificates (5 kinds): Cardholder, Merchant, Acquirer, Issuer, Payment Gateway
- Hardware cryptographic modules (for high security)
- Idempotency (message can be received many times but is only processed once) $f[f(x)] = f(x)$
- Complex protocol. Over 600 pages of detail

5.4.7 Future of SET

SET can work in Real Time or be a store and forward transfer, and is industry backed by the major credit card companies and banks. Its transaction can be accomplished over the WEB or via E-mail. It provides confidentiality, integrity, authentication, and, or non-repudiation.

SET is safe since it addresses all the parties involved in typical credit card transactions: consumers, merchants, and the banks. Besides the interoperability problem, it has difficulties to spread since it needs all the participants to have some part of the software, even very expensive hardware. It may be clearly in the interests of the credit card companies and banks, but it looks quite different from the perspective of merchants and consumers. In order to process SET transactions, the merchants have to spend several million dollars in equipment and services when they already have what are arguably sufficient security provisions in SSL. To consumers, they have to install software, "Anything that requires consumers to take an extra step deters them from adopting it", Vernon Keenan, a senior analyst at Zona Research argues.

SET is a very comprehensive and very complicated security protocol. It has to be simplified to be adopted by every parties involved, otherwise, it might be abandoned.

5.5 IPSec Protocol

IPSec (IP security) is a suite of protocols for securing Internet Protocol (IP) communications by encrypting and/or authenticating each IP packet in a data stream. IPSec also includes protocols for cryptographic key establishment.

There are two modes of IPSec operation: transport mode and tunnel mode.

In **transport mode**, only the payload (message) of the IP packet is encrypted. It is fully-routable since the IP header is sent as plain text; however, it can not cross NAT interfaces, as this will invalidate its hash value. Transport mode is used for host-to-host communications.

In **tunnel mode**, the entire IP packet is encrypted. It must then be encapsulated into a new IP packet for routing to work. Tunnel mode is used for network-to-network communications (secure tunnels between routers) or host-to-network and host-to-host communications over the Internet.

IPSec is implemented by a set of cryptographic protocols for securing packet flows and Internet key exchange. Of the former, there are two:

Authentication Header (AH) provides authentication, payload (message) and IP header integrity—and with some cryptography algorithm also non-repudiation—but it does not offer confidentiality.

Encapsulating Security Payload (ESP) provides data confidentiality, payload (message) integrity, and with some cryptography algorithm also authentication.

In some countries message encryption is prohibited by law and ESP protocol can not be used. In this case AH provides entire IPSec functionality (without confidentiality).

Originally AH was only used for integrity and ESP was used only for encryption; authentication functionality was added subsequently to ESP due to performance advantages. The key exchange protocols is defined by IPSec, include the IKE (Internet Key Exchange) protocol and its successor, IKEv2.

IPSec protocols operate at the network layer, layer 3 of the OSI model. Other Internet security protocols in widespread use, such as SSL and TLS, operate from the transport layer up (OSI layers 4~7). This makes IPSec more flexible, as it can be used for protecting both TCP and UDP-based protocols, but increases its complexity and processing overhead, as it cannot rely on TCP (layer 4 OSI model) to manage reliability and fragmentation.

5.5.1 Current Status as a Standard

IPSec is an obligatory part of IPv6, and is optional for use with IPv4. While the standard is designed to be indifferent to IP versions, current widespread deployment and experience concerns IPv4 implementations. IPSec protocols were originally define by RFCs 1825~1829, published in 1995. In 1998, these documents were obsolete by RFCs 2401~2412. RFCs 2401~2412 are not compatible with RFCs 1825~1829, although they are conceptually identical. In December 2005 third generation documents, RFCs 4301~

4309, were produced. They are largely a superset of RFCs 2401～2412.

It is unusual to see any product that offers RFCs 1825～1829 support. "ESP" generally refers to 2406, while ESPbis refers to 4303.

5.5.2 Design Intent

IPSec was intended to provide either transport mode: end-to-end security of packet traffic in which the end-point computers do the security processing, or tunnel mode: portal-to-portal communications security in which security of packet traffic is provided to several machines (even to whole LANs) by a single node.

IPSec can be used to create Virtual Private Networks (VPN) in either mode, and this is the dominant use. Note, however, that the security implications are quite different between the two operational modes.

End-to-end communication security on an Internet-wide scale has been slower to develop than many had expected. Part of the reason is that no universal, or universally trusted, Public-Key Infrastructure (PKI) has emerged (DNSSEC was originally envisioned for this); part is that many users understand neither their needs nor the available options well enough to promote inclusion in vendors' products.

Since the Internet Protocol does not inherently provide any security capabilities, IPSec was introduced to provide security services such as:

(1) Encrypting traffic (So it can not be read in its transmission);

(2) Integrity validation (Ensuring traffic has not been modified along its path);

(3) Authenticating the Peers (Both ends are sure they are communicating with a trusted entity the traffic is intended for);

(4) Anti-Replay (Protect against session replay).

5.5.3 Technical Details

1. Authentication Header

Authentication Header (AH)(see Figure 5.4) is intended to guarantee connectionless integrity and data origin authentication of IP datagrams. Further, it can optionally protect against replay attacks by using the sliding window technique and discarding old packets. AH protects the IP payload and all header fields of an IP datagram except for mutable fields, i.e., those that might be altered in transit. Mutable, therefore unauthenticated, IP header fields include TOS, Flags, Fragment Offset, TTL and Header Checksum. AH operates directly on top of IP using IP protocol number 51.

0	1	2	3
0 1 2 3 4 5 6 7	0 1 2 3 4 5 6 7	0 1 2 3 4 5 6 7	0 1 2 3 4 5 6 7
Next Header	Payload Length	RESERVED	
Security Parameters Index (SPI)			
Sequence Number			
Authentication Data (variable)			

Figure 5.4 An AH packet

Field meanings:

(1) **Next Header**: Identifies the protocol of the transferred data.

(2) **Payload Length**: Size of AH packet.

(3) **RESERVED**: Reserved for future use (all zero until then).

(4) **Security Parameters Index (SPI)**: Identifies the security parameters in combination with IP address.

(5) **Sequence Number**: A monotonically increasing number, used to prevent replay attacks.

(6) **Authentication Data**: Contains the data necessary to authenticate the packet.

2. Encapsulating Security Payload

The Encapsulating Security Payload (ESP) (see Figure 5.5) extension header provides origin authenticity, integrity, and confidentiality protection of a packet. ESP also supports encryption-only and authentication-only configurations, but using encryption without authentication is strongly discouraged. Unlike the AH header, the IP packet header is not accounted for. ESP operates directly on top of IP using IP protocol number 50. It's like a Chode.

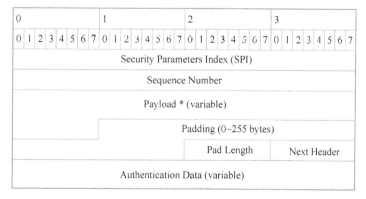

Figure 5.5 An ESP packet

Field meanings:

(1) **Security Parameters Index (SPI)**: Identifies the security parameters in combination with IP address.

(2) **Sequence Number**: A monotonically increasing number, used to prevent replay attacks.

(3) **Payload Data**: The data to be transferred.

(4) **Padding**: Used with some block ciphers to pad the data to the full length of a block.

(5) **Pad Length**: Size of padding in bytes.

(6) **Next Header**: Identifies the protocol of the transferred data.

(7) **Authentication Data**: Contains the data used to authenticate the packet.

5.5.4 IPSec Protocol Types

IPSec protocols provide data and identity protection for each IP packet by adding their own security protocol header to each packet. There are two modes of IPSec operation: transport mode and tunnel mode.

1. Transport Mode

Transport mode is the default mode for IPSec, and it is used for end-to-end communications (for example, for communications between a client and a server). When transport mode is used, IPSec encrypts only the IP payload. Transport mode provides the protection of an IP payload through an AH or ESP header. Typical IP payloads are TCP segments (containing a TCP header and TCP segment data), a UDP message (containing a UDP header and UDP message data), and an ICMP message (containing an ICMP header and ICMP message data).

(1) Authentication Header transport mode

Authentication Header (AH) provides authentication, integrity, and anti-replay protection for the entire packet (both the IP header and the data payload carried in the packet). It does not provide confidentiality, which means that it does not encrypt the data. The data is readable, but protected from modification. AH uses keyed hash algorithms to sign the packet for integrity.

For example, Alice on Computer A sends data to Bob on Computer B. The IP header, the AH header, and the data are protected with integrity. This means Bob can be certain it was really Alice who sent the data and that the data was unmodified.

Integrity and authentication are provided by the placement of the AH header between the IP header and the IP payload, as shown in the following illustration.

| IP header | Authentication header | IP payload (TCP segment, UDP message, ICMP message) |

AH is identified in the IP header with an IP protocol ID of 51. AH can be used alone or combined with the Encapsulating Security Payload (ESP) protocol.

The AH header contains the following fields:
- **Next Header:** Identifies the IP payload by using the IP protocol ID. For example, a value of 6 represents TCP.
- **Length:** Indicates the length of the AH header.
- **Security Parameters Index (SPI):** Used in combination with the destination address and the security protocol (AH or ESP) to identify the correct security association for the communication. The receiver uses this value to determine with which security association the packet is identified.
- **Sequence Number:** Provides anti-replay protection for the packet. The sequence number is a 32-bit, incrementally increasing number (starting from 1) that indicates the packet number sent over the security association for the communication. The sequence number cannot repeat for the life of the quick mode security association. The receiver checks this field to verify that a packet for a security association with this number has not already been received. If one has been received, the packet is rejected.
- **Authentication Data:** Contains the integrity check value (ICV), also known as the message authentication code, which is used to verify both message authentication and integrity. The receiver calculates the ICV value and checks it against this value (which is calculated by the sender) to verify integrity. The ICV is calculated over the IP header, the AH header, and the IP payload.

(2) Packet signature with the AH header

AH signs the entire packet for integrity, with the exception of some fields in the IP header which might change in transit (for example, the Time to Live and Type of Service fields). If another IPSec header is being used in addition to AH, the AH header is inserted before any other IPSec headers. The AH packet signature is shown in the following illustration.

| IP header | Authentication header | IP payload (TCP segment, UDP message, ICMP message) |

Signed by Authentication header

(3) Encapsulating Security Payload transport mode

Encapsulating Security Payload (ESP) provides confidentiality (in addition to authentication, integrity, and anti-replay protection) for the IP payload. ESP in transport mode does not sign the entire packet. Only the IP payload (not the IP header) is protected. ESP can be used alone or in combination with AH.

For example, Alice on Computer A sends data to Bob on Computer B. The IP payload is encrypted and signed for integrity. Upon receipt, after the integrity verification process is complete, the data payload in the packet is decrypted. Bob can be certain that it was Alice who sent the data, the data is unmodified, and no one else was able to read it.

ESP is identified in the IP header with the IP protocol ID of 50. As shown in the following illustration, the ESP header is placed before the IP payload, and an ESP trailer and ESP authentication trailer is placed after the IP payload.

IP header	ESP header	IP payload (TCP segment, UDP message, ICMP message)	ESP trailer	ESP Auth trailer

The ESP header contains the following fields:
- **Security Parameters Index:** Identifies the correct security association for the communication when used in combination with the destination address and the security protocol (AH or ESP). The receiver uses this value to determine the security association with which this packet should be identified.
- **Sequence Number:** Provides anti-replay protection for the packet. The sequence number is a 32-bit, incrementally increasing number (starting from 1) that indicates the packet number sent over the quick mode security association for the communication. The sequence number cannot repeat for the life of the quick mode security association. The receiver checks this field to verify that a packet for a security association with this number has not already been received. If one has been received, the packet is rejected.

The ESP trailer contains the following fields:
- **Padding:** Padding of 0 to 255 bytes is used to ensure that the encrypted payload with the padding bytes is on byte boundaries required by encryption algorithms.
- **Padding Length:** Indicates the length of the Padding field in bytes. The receiver uses this field to remove padding bytes after the encrypted payload with the padding bytes has been decrypted.
- **Next Header:** Identifies the type of data in the payload, such as TCP or UDP.

The ESP authentication trailer contains the following field:
- **Authentication Data:** Contains the integrity check value (ICV), also known as the message authentication code, which is used to verify both message authentication and integrity. The receiver calculates the ICV value and checks it against this value (which is calculated by the sender) to verify integrity. The ICV is calculated over the ESP header, the payload data, and the ESP trailer.

(4) Packet signature and encryption

As shown in the following illustration, ESP provides protection for IP payloads. The signed portion of the packet indicates where the packet has been signed for integrity and authentication. The encrypted portion of the packet indicates what information is protected with confidentiality.

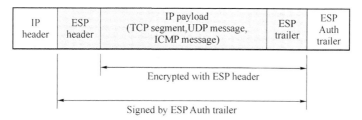

The IP header is not signed and is not necessarily protected from modification. To provide data integrity and authentication for the IP header, use ESP and AH.

2. Tunnel Mode

When IPSec tunnel mode is used, IPSec encrypts the IP header and the payload, whereas transport mode only encrypts the IP payload. Tunnel mode provides the protection of an entire IP packet by treating it as an AH or ESP payload. With tunnel mode, an entire IP packet is encapsulated with an AH or ESP header and an additional IP header. The IP addresses of the outer IP header are the tunnel endpoints, and the IP addresses of the encapsulated IP header are the ultimate source and destination addresses.

IPSec tunnel mode is useful for protecting traffic between different networks, when traffic must pass through an intermediate, untrusted network. Tunnel mode is primarily used for interoperability with gateways, or end-systems that do not support L2TP/IPSec or PPTP connections. You can use tunnel mode in the following configurations:
- Gateway-to-gateway
- Server-to-gateway
- Server-to-server

(1) AH tunnel mode

As shown in the following illustration, AH tunnel mode encapsulates an IP packet with an AH and IP header and signs the entire packet for integrity and authentication.

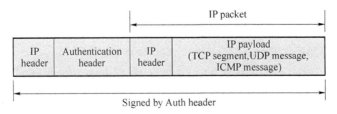

(2) ESP tunnel mode

As shown in the following illustration, ESP tunnel mode encapsulates an IP packet with both an ESP and IP header and an ESP authentication trailer.

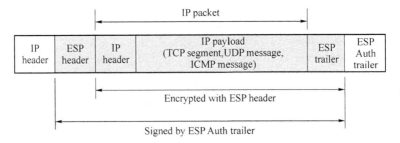

The signed portion of the packet indicates where the packet has been signed for integrity and authentication. The encrypted portion of the packet indicates what information is protected with confidentiality.

Because a new header for tunneling is added to the packet, everything that comes after the ESP header is signed (except for the ESP authentication trailer) because it is now encapsulated in the tunneled packet. The original header is placed after the ESP header. The entire packet is appended with an ESP trailer before encryption occurs. Everything that follows the ESP header, except for the ESP authentication trailer, is encrypted. This includes the original header which is now considered to be part of the data portion of the packet.

The entire ESP payload is then encapsulated within the new tunnel header, which is not encrypted. The information in the new tunnel header is used only to route the packet from origin to tunnel endpoint.

If the packet is being sent across a public network, it is routed to the IP address of the gateway for the receiving intranet. The gateway decrypts the packet, discards the ESP header, and uses the original IP header to route the packet to the intranet computer.

ESP and AH can be combined when tunneling, providing both confidentiality for the

Chapter 5 Network Security Protocol

tunneled IP packet and integrity and authentication for the entire packet.

(3) Using IPSec tunnels

IPSec tunnels provide security for IP traffic only. The tunnel is configured to protect traffic between either two IP addresses or two IP subnets. If the tunnel is used between two computers instead of two gateways, the IP address outside the AH or ESP payload is the same as the IP address inside the AH or ESP payload. In Windows XP and the Windows Server 2003 family, IPSec does not support protocol-specific or port-specific tunnels. You can configure tunnels by using the IP Security Policy Management and Group Policy consoles to configure and enable two rules:

- **A rule for the outbound traffic for the tunnel.** The rule for the outbound traffic is configured with a filter list that describes the traffic to be sent through the tunnel and a tunnel endpoint of an IP address configured on the IPSec tunnel peer (the computer or router on the other side of the tunnel).
- **A rule for the inbound traffic for the tunnel.** The rule for the inbound traffic is configured with a filter list that describes the traffic to be received through the tunnel and a tunnel endpoint of a local IP address (the computer or router on the local side of the tunnel).

Additionally, filter actions, authentication methods, and other settings need to be specified for each rule.

5.5.5 Implementations

IPSec support is usually implemented in the kernel with key management and ISAKMP/IKE negotiation carried out from user-space. Existing IPSec implementations tend to include both of these functionalities. However, as there is a standard interface for key management, it is possible to control one kernel IPSec stack using key management tools from a different implementation.

Because of this, there is confusion as to the origins of the IPSec implementation that is in the Linux kernel. The FreeS/WAN project made the first complete and open source implementation of IPSec for Linux. It consists of a kernel IPSec stack (KLIPS), as well as a key management daemon (pluto) and many shell scripts. The FreeS/WAN project was disbanded in March 2004. Openswan and strongSwan are continuations of FreeS/WAN. The KAME project also implemented complete IPSec support for NetBSD, FreeBSD. Its key management daemon is called racoon. OpenBSD made its own ISAKMP/IKE daemon, simply named isakmpd (that was also ported to other systems, including Linux).

However, none of these kernel IPSec stacks was integrated into the Linux kernel. Alexey Kuznetsov and David S. Miller wrote a kernel IPSec implementation from scratch for the Linux kernel around the end of 2002. This stack was subsequently released as part of Linux 2.6, and is referred variously as "native" or "NETKEY".

Therefore, contrary to popular belief, the Linux IPSec stack did not originate from the KAME project. As it supports the standard PF_KEY protocol (RFC 2367) and the native XFRM interface for key management, the Linux IPSec stack can be used in conjunction with either pluto from Openswan/strongSwan, isakmpd from OpenBSD project, racoon from the KAME project or without any ISAKMP/IKE daemon (using manual keying).

Glossary

Access Control Lists (ACLs)	访问控制列表
Authentication Header (AH)	认证头
Data Encryption Standard(DES)	数据加密
Digital Signature Algorithm(DSA)	数字签名算法
Encapsulating Security Payload (ESP)	封装安全有效负载
HyperText Transport Protocol (HTTP)	超文本传输协议
key agreement	密钥协商
Secure Electronic Transaction (SET)	安全电子交易
Secure Sockets Layer (SSL)	安全套接层协议
security protocol	安全协议
Transmission Control Protocol/Internet Protocol (TCP/IP)	传输控制协议/因特网协议
Transport Layer Security (TLS)	传输层安全
transport mode	传输模式
tunnel mode	隧道模式

Translate the following sentences/passage into Chinese

(1) There are other types of cryptographic protocols as well, and even the term itself has various different readings; Cryptographic application protocols often use one or more underlying key agreement methods, which are also sometimes themselves referred to as "cryptographic protocols".

(2) Kerberos is a computer network authentication protocol, which allows individuals

communicating over an insecure network to prove their identity to one another in a secure manner. Kerberos prevents eavesdropping or replay attacks, and ensures the integrity of the data.

(3) Secure Sockets Layer (SSL) and its successor, Transport Layer Security (TLS), are cryptographic protocols which provide secure communications on the Internet for such things as web browsing, E-mail, Internet faxing, and other data transfers.

(4) The SSL protocol includes two sub-protocols: the SSL record protocol and the SSL handshake protocol. The SSL record protocol defines the format used to transmit data. The SSL handshake protocol involves using the SSL record protocol to exchange a series of messages between an SSL-enabled server and an SSL-enabled client when they first establish an SSL connection.

(5) Secure Electronic Transaction (SET) is a standard protocol for securing credit card transactions over insecure networks, specifically, the Internet. SET was developed by VISA and MasterCard (involving other companies such as GTE, IBM, Microsoft and Netscape) starting in 1996.

Translate the following sentences/passage into English

(1) 对开放式系统的认证需求导致了 Kerberos 的产生。Kerberos 是一种为网络通信提供可信第三方服务的面向开放系统的认证机制。每当客户端申请服务器的服务时，客户端和服务器会首先向 Kerberos 要求认证对方的身份，认证建立在客户端和服务器对 Kerberos 信任的基础上。

(2) 当用户登录到工作站时，Kerberos 对用户进行初始认证，通过认证的用户可以在整个登录期间得到相应的服务。Kerberos 既不依赖于用户登录的终端，也不依赖于用户所请求的服务的安全机制，它本身提供了认证服务器来完成用户的认证工作。

(3) SET 是针对用卡支付的网上交易而设计的支付规范，对不用卡支付的交易方式，像先送货到付款方式、邮局汇款方式则与 SET 无关。另外像网上商店的页面安排，保密数据在购买者计算机上如何保存等，也与 SET 无关。

(4) SSL 协议也是国际上最早应用于电子商务的一种网络安全协议，至今仍然有许多网上商店在使用。SSL 协议在点对点的网上银行业务中也经常使用。在电子商务交易过程中，由于有银行参与，按照 SSL 协议，客户的购买信息首先发往商家，商家再将信息转发给银行，银行验证客户信息的合法性后，通知商家付款成功，商家再通知客户购买成功，并将商品寄送客户。

(5) IPSec 在网络层上实施安全保护，其范围几乎涵盖了 TCP/IP 协议簇中所有 IP 协议和上层协议，如 TCP、UDP、ICMP，也包括在网络层发送数据的客户自定义协议。在第三层上提供数据安全保护的主要优点就在于所有使用 IP 协议进行数据传输的应用系统和服务都可以使用 IPSec，而不必对这些应用系统和服务本身做任何修改。

Questions

(1) How does SSL Handshake protocol work?

(2) How does SET protocol encrypt data?

(3) How does SET protocol realize the digital signature?

(4) How does AH protocol realize Packet signature?

(5) What is the ESP tunnel mode?

Chapter 6

Virtual Private Network

A Virtual Private Network (VPN) is a private communications network often used within a company, or by several companies or organizations, to communicate confidentially over a publicly accessible network. VPN message traffic can be carried over a public networking infrastructure (e. g. , the Internet) on top of standard protocols, or over a service provider's private network with a defined Service Level Agreement (SLA) between the VPN customer and the VPN service provider.

6.1 Authentication Mechanism

VPN is a cost effective and secure way for different corporations to provide user access to the corporate network and for remote networks to communicate with each other across the Internet. Secure VPN are more cost-effective than dedicated private lines; usually VPN involves two parts: the protected or "inside" network, which provides physical and administrative security to protect the transmission; and a less trustworthy, "outside" network or segment (usually through the Internet). Generally, a firewall sits between a remote user's workstation or client and the host network or server. As the user's client establishes the communication with the firewall, the client may pass authentication data to an authentication service inside the perimeter. A known trusted person, sometimes only when using trusted devices, can be provided with appropriate security privileges to access resources not available to general users.

Many VPN client programs can be configured to require that all IP traffic must pass through the tunnel while the VPN is active, for better security. From the user's perspective, this means that while the VPN client is active, all access outside their employer's secure network must pass through the same firewall as would be the case while physically connected to the office Ethernet. This reduces the risk that an attacker might gain access to the secured network by attacking the employee's laptop: to other computers on the employee's home network, or on the public internet, it is as though the machine running the VPN client simply does not exist. Such security is important because other computers local to the network on which the client computer is operating may be untrusted or partially trusted. Even with a home network that is protected from the outside internet by a firewall, people who share a home may be simultaneously working for different employers over their respective VPN connections from the shared home network. Each employer would therefore want to ensure their proprietary data is kept secure, even if another computer in the local network gets infected with malware. And if a traveling employee uses a VPN client from a Wi-Fi access point in a public place, such security is even more important. However, the use of IPX/SPX is one way users might still be able to access local resources.

6.2 Types of VPN

Secure VPNs use cryptographic tunneling protocols to provide the intended confidentiality (blocking snooping and thus Packet sniffing), sender authentication (blocking identity spoofing), and message integrity (blocking message alteration) to achieve privacy. When properly chosen, implemented, and used, such techniques can provide secure communications over unsecured networks. This has been the usually intended purpose for VPN for some years.

Because such choice, implementation, and use are not trivial, there are many insecure VPN schemes available on the market.

Secure VPN technologies may also be used to enhance security as a "security overlay" within dedicated networking infrastructures.

Secure VPN protocols include the following:
- **IPSec** (IP security)—commonly used over IPv4, and an obligatory part of IPv6.
- **SSL** used either for tunneling the entire network stack, as in the OpenVPN project, or for securing what is, essentially, a web proxy. SSL is framework more often associated with e-commerce, but it has been built-upon by vendors like Aventail and Juniper to provide remote access VPN capabilities.
- **PPTP** (Point-to-Point Tunneling Protocol), developed jointly by a number of

companies, including Microsoft.
- **L2TP** (Layer 2 Tunneling Protocol), which includes work by both Microsoft and Cisco.
- **L2TPv3** (Layer 2 Tunneling Protocol version 3), a new release.
- **VPN-Q** The machine at the other end of a VPN could be a threat and a source of attack; this has no necessary connection with VPN designs and has been usually left to system administration efforts. There has been at least one attempt to address this issue in the context of VPNs. On Microsoft ISA Server, an application called QSS (Quarantine Security Suite) is available.

Some large ISPs now offer "managed" VPN service for business customers who want the security and convenience of a VPN but prefer not to undertake administering a VPN server themselves. In addition to providing remote workers with secure access to their employer's internal network, other security and management services are sometimes included as part of the package. Examples include keeping anti-virus and anti-spyware programs updated on each client's computer.

Trusted VPNs do not use cryptographic tunneling, and instead rely on the security of a single provider's network to protect the traffic. In a sense, these are an elaboration of traditional network and system administration work.
- **Multi-Protocol Label Switching** (MPLS) is often used to build trusted VPN.
- **L2F** (Layer 2 Forwarding), developed by Cisco, can also be used.

6.3 Characteristics in Application

A well-designed VPN can provide great benefits for an organization. It can:
- Extend geographic connectivity;
- Improve security where data lines have not been ciphered;
- Reduce operational costs versus traditional WAN;
- Reduce transit time and transportation costs for remote users;
- Simplify network topology in certain scenarios;
- Provide global networking opportunities;
- Provide telecommuter support;
- Provide broadband networking compatibility;
- Provide faster ROI (return on investment) than traditional carrier leased/owned WAN lines;

- Show a good economy of scale;
- Scale well, when used with a public-key infrastructure.

However, since VPNs extend the "mother network" by such an extent (almost every employee) and with such ease (no dedicated lines to rent/hire), there are certain security implications that must receive special attention:

- Security on the client side must be tightened and enforced, lest security be lost at any of a multitude of machines and devices. This has been termed, Central Client Administration, and Security Policy Enforcement. It is common for a company to require that each employee wishing to use their VPN outside company offices (e. g. , from home) first install an approved firewall (often hardware). Some organizations with especially sensitive data, such as healthcare companies, even arrange for an employee's home to have two separate WAN connections: one for working on that employer's sensitive data and one for all other uses.
- The scale of access to the target network may have to be limited.
- Logging policies must be evaluated and in most cases revised.

A single breach or failure can result in the privacy and security of the network being compromised. In situations in which a company or individual has legal obligations to keep information confidential, there may be legal problems, even criminal ones, as a result. Two examples are the HIPAA regulations in the U. S. with regard to health data, and the more general European Union data privacy regulations which apply to even marketing and billing information and extend to those who share that data elsewhere.

6.4 Tunneling

Tunneling is the transmission of data through a public network in such a way that routing nodes in the public network are unaware that the transmission is part of a private network. Tunneling is generally done by encapsulating the private network data and protocol information within the public network protocol data so that the tunneled data is not available to anyone examining the transmitted data frames. Tunneling allows the use of public networks (e. g. , the Internet), to carry data on behalf of users as though they had access to a "private network", hence the name. Port forwarding is one aspect of tunneling in particular circumstances.

VPN technology is based on the idea of tunneling. Network tunneling involves establishing and maintaining a logical network connection (that may contain intermediate hops). On this connection, packets constructed in a specific VPN protocol format are encapsulated within some other base or carrier protocol, then transmitted between VPN client and server, and finally de-encapsulated on the receiving side.

For Internet-based VPNs, packets in one of several VPN protocols are encapsulated within IP packets. VPN protocols also support authentication and encryption to keep the tunnels secure.

6.4.1 Two Types of VPN Tunneling

VPN supports both voluntary and compulsory tunneling. Both types of tunneling can be found in practical use.

In **voluntary tunneling**, the VPN client manages connection setup. The client first makes a connection to the carrier network provider (an ISP in the case of Internet VPNs). Then, the VPN client application creates the tunnel to a VPN server over this live connection.

In **compulsory tunneling**, the carrier network provider manages VPN connection setup. When the client first makes an ordinary connection to the carrier, the carrier in turn immediately brokers a VPN connection between that client and a VPN server. From the client point of view, VPN connections are set up in just one step compared to the two-step procedure required for voluntary tunnels.

Compulsory VPN tunneling authenticates clients and associates them with specific VPN servers using logic built into the broker device. This network device is sometimes called the VPN Front End Processor (FEP) (also Network Access Server (NAS) or Point of Presence (POP) servers). Compulsory tunneling hides the details of VPN server connectivity from the VPN clients and effectively moves control over the tunnels from clients to the ISP. In return, service providers must take on the additional burden of installing and maintaining FEPs.

Several interesting network protocols have been implemented specifically for use with VPN tunnels. The most popular VPN tunneling protocols listed below continue to compete with each other for acceptance in the industry. These protocols are generally incompatible with each other.

6.4.2 Point-to-Point Tunneling Protocol

Point-to-Point Tunneling Protocol (PPTP) extends the Point to Point Protocol

(PPP) standard for traditional dial-up networking. PPTP is best suited for the remote access applications of VPNs, but it also supports LAN internetworking. PPTP operates at Layer 2 of the OSI model.

Several corporations worked together to create the PPTP specification. People generally associate PPTP with Microsoft because nearly all flavors of Windows include built-in client support for this protocol. The initial releases of PPTP for Windows by Microsoft contained security features that some experts claimed were too weak for serious use. Microsoft continues to improve its PPTP support.

1. Using PPTP

PPTP packages data within PPP packets, then encapsulates the PPP packets within IP packets for transmission through an Internet-based VPN tunnel. PPTP supports data encryption and compression of these packets. PPTP also uses a form of General Routing Encapsulation (GRE) to get data to and from its final destination.

PPTP-based Internet remote access VPNs are by far the most common form of PPTP VPN. In this environment, VPN tunnels are created via the following two-step process:

- The PPTP client connects to their ISP using PPP dial-up networking (traditional modem or ISDN);
- Via the broker device (described earlier), PPTP creates a TCP control connection between the VPN client and VPN server to establish a tunnel. PPTP uses TCP port 1723 for these connections.

PPTP also supports VPN connectivity via a LAN. ISP connections are not required in this case, so tunnels can be created directly as in Step 2 above.

Once the VPN tunnel is established, PPTP supports two types of information flows:

- control messages for managing and eventually tearing down the VPN connection. Control messages pass directly between VPN client and server;
- data packets that pass through the tunnel, to or from the VPN client.

2. PPTP Control Connection

Once the TCP connection is established in Step 2 above, PPTP utilizes a series of control messages to maintain VPN connections.

With control messages, PPTP utilizes a so-called magic cookie. The PPTP magic cookie is hardwired to the hexadecimal number 0x1A2B3C4D. The purpose of this cookie is to ensure the receiver interprets the incoming data on the correct byte boundaries.

3. PPTP Security

PPTP supports authentication, encryption, and packet filtering. PPTP authentication uses PPP-based protocols like EAP, CHAP, and PAP. PPTP supports packet filtering on VPN servers. Intermediate routers and other firewalls can also be configured to selectively filter PPTP traffic.

4. PPTP and PPP

In general, PPTP relies on the functionality of PPP for these aspects of virtual private networking:

- Authenticating users and maintaining the remote dial-up connection;
- Encapsulating and encrypting IP, IPX, or NetBEUI packets.

PPTP directly handles maintaining the VPN tunnel and transmitting data through the tunnel. PPTP also supports some additional security features for VPN data beyond what PPP provides.

5. PPTP Pros and Cons

PPTP remains a popular choice for VPNs thanks to Microsoft. PPTP clients are freely available in all popular versions of Microsoft Windows. Windows servers also can function as PPTP-based VPN servers.

One drawback of PPTP is its failure to choose a single standard for authentication and encryption. Two products that both fully comply with the PPTP specification may be totally incompatible with each other if they encrypt data differently, for example. Concerns also persist over the questionable level of security PPTP provides compared to alternatives.

6.4.3 Layer 2 Tunneling Protocol

In computer networking, the Layer 2 Tunneling Protocol (L2TP) is a tunneling protocol used to support virtual private networks (VPNs).

Published in 1999 as proposed standard RFC 2661, L2TP has its origins primarily in two older tunneling protocols for PPP: Cisco's Layer 2 Forwarding (L2F) and Microsoft's Point-to-Point Tunneling Protocol (PPTP). A new version of this protocol, L2TPv3, was published as proposed standard RFC 3931 in 2005. L2TPv3 provides additional security features, improved encapsulation, and the ability to carry data links other than simply PPP over an IP network (e.g., Frame Relay, Ethernet, ATM, etc.).

1. Feature Summary

L2TP is an emerging Internet Engineering Task Force (IETF) standard that combines the best features of two existing tunneling protocols: Cisco's Layer 2 Forwarding (L2F) and Microsoft's Point-to-Point Tunneling Protocol (PPTP). L2TP is an extension to the PPP, which is an important component for VPNs. VPNs allow users and telecommuters to connect to their corporate intranets or extranets. VPNs are cost-effective because users can connect to the Internet locally and tunnel back to connect to corporate resources. This not only reduces overhead costs associated with traditional remote access methods, but also improves flexibility and scalability.

Traditional dial-up networking services only support registered IP addresses, which limits the types of applications that are implemented over VPNs. L2TP supports multiple protocols and unregistered and privately administered IP addresses over the Internet. This allows the existing access infrastructure, such as the Internet, modems, access servers, and ISDN terminal adapters (TAs), to be used. It also allows enterprise customers to outsource dialout support, thus reducing overhead for hardware maintenance costs and 800 number fees, and allows them to concentrate corporate gateway resources. Figure 6.1 shows the L2TP architecture in a typical dial-up environment.

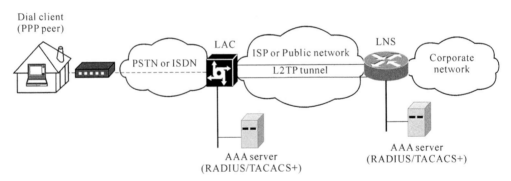

Figure 6.1 L2TP architecture

L2TP offers the same full-range spectrum of features as L2F, but offers additional functionality. A L2TP-capable home gateway will work with an existing L2F network access server and will concurrently support upgraded components running L2TP. LNSs do not require reconfiguration each time an individual LAC is upgraded from L2F to L2TP.

2. Benefits

L2TP offers the following benefits:

- Vendor interoperability;

Chapter 6 Virtual Private Network

- Can be used as part of the wholesale access solution, which allows ISPs to the service providers offer VPNs to Internet Service Providers (ISPs) and other service providers;
- Can be operated as a client initiated VPN solution, where enterprise customers using a PC, can use the client initiated L2TP from a third party;
- All value-added features currently available with Cisco's L2F, such as load sharing and backup support, will be available in future IOS releases of L2TP;
- Supports Multihop, which enables Multichassis Multilink PPP in multiple home gateways. This allows you to stack home gateways so that they appear as a single entity.

3. Functional Description

(1) L2TP Overview

The following sections supply additional detail about the interworkings and Cisco's implementation of L2TP. Using L2TP tunneling, an ISP, or other access services, can create a virtual tunnel to link customer's remote sites or remote users with corporate home networks. The L2TP access concentrator (LAC) located at the ISP's point of presence (POP) exchanges PPP messages with remote users and communicates by way of L2TP requests and responses with the customer's L2TP network server (LNS) to set up tunnels. L2TP passes protocol-level packets through the virtual tunnel between end points of a point-to-point connection. Frames from remote users are accepted by the ISP's POP, stripped of any linked framing or transparency bytes, encapsulated in L2TP and forwarded over the appropriate tunnel. The customer's home gateway accepts these L2TP frames, strips the L2TP encapsulation, and processes the incoming frames for the appropriate interface. Figure 6.2 shows the L2TP tunnel detail and how user "lsmith" connects to the LNS to access the designated corporate intranet.

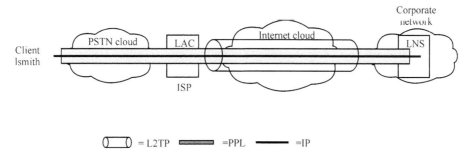

Figure 6.2 L2TP Tunnel Structure

(2) Incoming Call Sequence

A VPDN connection between a remote user, a LAC at the ISP POP, and the LNS at the home LAN using an L2TP tunnel is accomplished as follows:

- The remote user initiates a PPP connection to the ISP, using the analog telephone system or ISDN.
- The ISP network LAC accepts the connection at the POP and the PPP link is established.
- After the end user and LNS negotiate LCP, the LAC partially authenticates the end user with CHAP or PAP. The username, domain name, or DNIS is used to determine whether the user is a VPDN client. If the user is not a VPDN client, authentication continues, and the client will access the Internet or other contacted service. If the username is a VPDN client, the mapping will name a specific endpoint (the LNS).
- The tunnel end points, the LAC and the LNS, authenticate each other before any sessions are attempted within a tunnel. Alternatively, the LNS can accept tunnel creation without any tunnel authentication of the LAC.
- Once the tunnel exists, an L2TP session is created for the end user.
- The LAC will propagate the LCP negotiated options and the partially authenticated CHAP/PAP information to the LNS. The LNS will funnel the negotiated options and authentication information directly to the virtual access interface. If the options configured on the virtual template interface do not match the negotiated options with the LAC, the connection will fail, and a disconnect is sent to the LAC.

The end result is that the exchange process appears to be between the dial-up client and the remote LNS exclusively, as if no intermediary device (the LAC) is involved. Figure 6.3 offers a pictorial account of the L2TP incoming call sequence with its own corresponding sequence numbers. Note the sequence numbers in figure 6.3 are not related to the sequence numbers described above.

(3) LAC AAA Tunnel Definition Lookup

AAA tunnel definition look up allows the LAC to look up tunnel definitions using key words. Two new Cisco AV pairs are added to support LAC tunnel definition lookup: tunnel type and l2tp-tunnel-password. These AV pairs are configured on the Radius server. A description of the values is as follows:

Tunnel type—Indicates the tunnel type is either L2F or L2TP. This is an optional

AV pair and if not defined, reverts to L2F, the default value. If you want to configure an L2TP tunnel, you must use the L2TP AV pair value. This command is case sensitive.

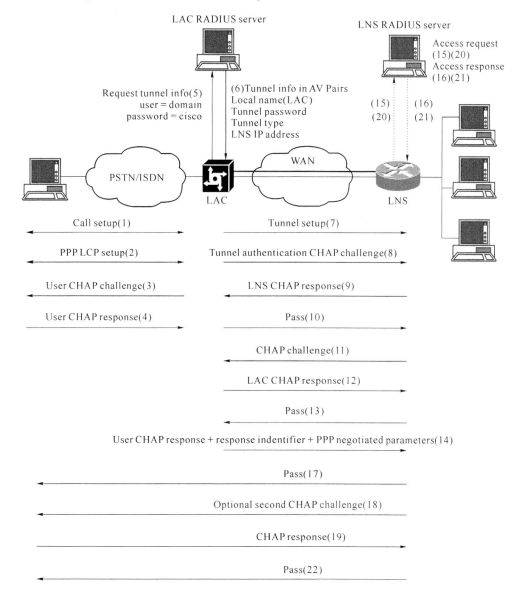

Figure 6.3 L2TP incoming call flow

l2tp-tunnel-password—This value is the secret (password) used for L2TP tunnel authentication and L2TP AV pair hiding. This is an optional AV pair value; however, if it is not defined, the secret will default to the password associated with the local name on the LAC local username-password database. This AV pair is analogous to the l2tp local secret CLI command. For example:

    request dialin l2tp ip 172.21.9.13 domain cisco.com

    l2tp local name dustie

    l2tp local secret partner

is equivalent to the following RADIUS server configuration:

    cisc.com Password = "cisco"

    cisco-avpair = "vpdn: tunnel-id = dustie",

    cisco-avpair = "vpdn: tunnel-type = l2tp",

    cisco-avpair = "vpdn: l2tp-tunnel-password = partner',

    cisco-avpair = "vpdn: ip-addresses = 172.21.9.13"

4. L2TP/IPSec

L2TP does not include encryption (as does PPTP), but is often used with IPSec in order to provide VPN connections from remote users to the corporate LAN. PPP encapsulates IP packets from the user's PC to the ISP. L2TP tunnels those packets over multiple links. As shown in Figure 6.4.

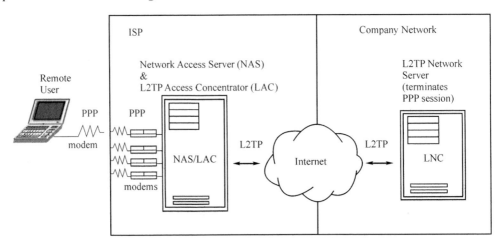

Figure 6.4　PPP and L2TP traffic

Because of the lack of confidentiality inherent in the L2TP protocol, it is often implemented along with IPSec. This is referred to as L2TP/IPSec, and is standardized in IETF RFC 3193.

The process of setting up an L2TP/IPSec VPN is as follows:

- Negotiation of IPSec Security Association (SA), typically through Internet Key Exchange (IKE). This is carried out over UDP port 500, and commonly uses

Chapter 6　Virtual Private Network

either a shared password (so-called "pre-shared keys"), public-keys, or X. 509 certificates on both ends, although other keying methods exist.
- Establishment of Encapsulated Security Payload (ESP) communication in transport mode. The IP Protocol number for ESP is 50 (compare TCP's 6 and UDP's 17). At this point, a secure channel has been established, but no tunneling is taking place.
- Negotiation and establishment of L2TP tunnel between the SA endpoints. The actual negotiation of parameters takes place over the SA's secure channel, within the IPSec encryption. L2TP uses UDP port 1701.

When the process is complete, L2TP packets between the endpoints are encapsulated by IPSec. Since the L2TP packet itself is wrapped and hidden within the IPSec packet, no information about the internal private network can be garnered from the encrypted packet. Also, it is not necessary to open UDP port 1701 on firewalls between the endpoints, since the inner packets are not acted upon until after IPSec data has been decrypted and stripped, which only takes place at the endpoints. If a firewall or packet filter is integrated into the endpoint itself, however, it will probably be necessary to open port 1701 on that endpoint.

A potential point of confusion in L2TP/IPSec is the use of the terms "tunnel" and "secure channel". Tunnel refers to a channel which allows untouched packets of one network to be transported over another network. In the case of L2TP/IPSec, it allows L2TP/PPP packets to be transported over IP. A secure channel refers to a connection within which the confidentiality of all data is guaranteed. In L2TP/IPSec, first IPSec provides a secure channel, and then L2TP provides a tunnel.

6.4.4　SSL VPN

An SSL VPN (Secure Sockets Layer Virtual Private Network) (see Figure 6.5) is a form of VPN that can be used with a standard Web browser. In contrast to the traditional IPSec (Internet Protocol Security) VPN, an SSL VPN does not require the installation of specialized client software on end users' computers.

The SSL VPN can be a good choice for schools, libraries and public kiosks where trust can be an issue but easy access is also important. Applications include Web-based E-mail, business and government directories, databases for educational institutions, file sharing, remote backup, remote system management and consumer-level e-commerce.

SSL is a protocol for managing the security of message transmission on the Internet. SSL is included as part of both the Microsoft and Netscape browsers and most Web server products. It employs the public-and-private-key encryption system from RSA. As TLS (Transport Layer Security), a refinement of SSL, replaces the earlier protocol, an SSL VPN is sometimes referred to as a TLS VPN.

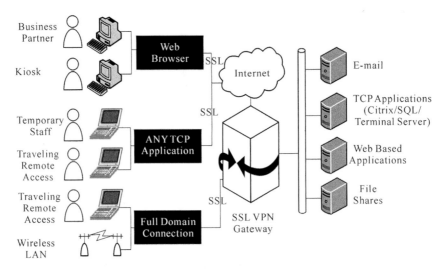

Figure 6.5　SSL VPN

6.4.5　MPLS VPN

1. Introduction

Businesses today are looking to the Internet for wide area network (WAN) solutions that in the recent past they could get only by choosing Frame Relay or T1 dedicated links.

To achieve the security that is required for corporate users, VPNs can be used to guarantee that traffic is securely tunneled over the Internet. Up to now, most VPNs have been provisioned using Layer 2 technologies, such as Frame Relay and asynchronous transfer mode (ATM). These technologies provided secure tunnels, were resistant to DoS and intrusion attacks, and provided address and routing separation. The problem with Layer 2 VPN technology is that it does not scale well. As the network grows, the number of required virtual circuits achieving optimal routing scales non-linearly. It is also difficult to provide traffic engineering using a Layer 2 VPN approach.

To solve these scaling problems, a border gateway protocol/multiprotocol label switching (BGP/MPLS) VPN standard is now being adopted to provide Layer 3 VPN solutions using BGP to carry route information over a MPLS core. This Layer 3 MPLS-VPN solution achieves all of the security of the Layer 2 approach, while adding enhanced scalability inherent in the use of Layer 3 routing technology.

The key to this approach is the use of BGP and a set of extensions, known as BGP-VPN, that allow separate route forwarding information to be maintained for each VPN client. BGP then carries this separate route forwarding information over MPLS using the label distribution protocol (LDP).

2. MPLS/BGP-VPN

In order to achieve the security that is necessary for VPN provisioning over the Internet using a Layer 3 approach, address and routing separation between customers is required. This is inherent in a Layer 2 approach, but must be specially designed to work in a Layer 3 based VPN solution. To solve this problem, draft-ietf-ppvpn-rfc2547bis-00.txt has been developed by a number of Internet experts (notably from Cisco, Juniper, ATT, Alcatel, Worldcom, and others). This draft RFC specifically defines how to provide address and routing separation using BGP, and how to send this information and the VPN traffic itself over a MPLS backbone.

The model as expressed in the draft RFC is that Service Providers (SP) own the backbone and provision VPN services from Provider Edge (PE) equipment which communicates directly with Customer Edge (CE) equipment using standard technology such as Frame Relay, ATM, DSL, and T1. At that time, the customer would purchase VPN services directly from the SP. Then, the SP would provide the VPN service to multiple customers using a shared PE device.

The key to providing security in the shared PE equipment is made available by the BGP-VPN extensions as defined in the draft RFC. Each PE router must maintain a number of forwarding tables, each of which map to a unique VPN class. When a packet is received from the CE equipment, the forwarding table that is mapped to that site is used to determine the routing for the data. Each VPN has its own unique forwarding table, known as a VRF (VPN Routing and Forwarding). If a PE device has multiple connections to the same site, a single VRF can be mapped to all of those connections. The BGP-VPN extensions for VRF support then allow BGP to send the specific route forwarding information to the PE router connected to the other end of the VPN. In this approach, route separation is maintained for each unique VPN customer.

In this type of architecture, only PE routers must carry the VRF information. It is not necessary that the non-edge routers on the SP backbone know anything about the

VRF information. Consequently, this design greatly expands the scalability of the Layer 3 VPN approach.

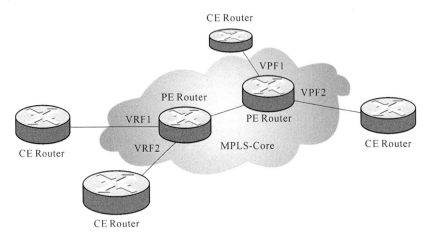

Figure 6.6 Forwarding VPN Information using MPLS

In each PE router, sub-interfaces may be mapped to VRFs; the mapping is many-to-one. Two sub-interfaces may not map to the same VRF, unless they are intended to show route information, and the VRF packet's destination address is determined by the sub-interface over which it is received.

A VPN-IPv4 address concept is defined for use in distinguishing routes. A VPN-IPv4 address is a 12-byte address that begins with an 8-byte Route Distinguisher (RD) and ends with a 4-byte IPv4 address. BGP Multi-protocol Extensions (BGP-MP) allow BGP to carry routes from this new address family. The VPN-IPv4 address family and RD ensure that if similar addresses are used in two different VPN's, then two separate routes to that address can be maintained. This is important when supporting RFC 1918 private addressing.

The BGP-VPN extensions allow route distribution policies to be configured for the proper distribution of VPN route information. PE routers can also auto-discover the other PE device attached to the same VPN. This eliminates the need to reconfigure both PE devices when reconfiguring or initially configuring the VPN.

As stated previously, the intermediate routers in the backbone do not need to maintain any information about the VPNs. So how are packets forwarded from one VPN to another? The answer is to use MPLS with a two-level label stack. PE routers insert 32-bit address prefixes into the Internal Gateway Protocol Routing tables of the backbone. By doing this, MPLS at each node in the SP backbone can assign a label to the corresponding route in each PE router. To certify that this is interoperable, LDP (Label Distribution Protocol) is used for setting up the label switched paths across the SP backbone.

A variety of mechanisms can be used for the CE equipment to deliver routing information to the PE router. This includes the use of static routes and BGP. BGP has many advantages for CE to PE communications. The main advantage is that it does not require multiple instances on the PE since it is explicitly designed for this function.

3. Advantages of MPLS VPN

(1) Provide a diversified range of services (Layer 2, Layer 3 and Dial up VPNs) to meet the requirements of the entire spectrum of customers from Small and Medium to Large business enterprises and financial institutions.

(2) Make the service very simple for customers to use even if they lack experience in IP routing.

(3) Make the service very scalable and flexible to facilitate large-scale deployment.

(4) Provide a reliable and amenable service, offering SLA to customers.

(5) Capable of meeting a wide range of customer requirements, including security, quality of Service (QoS) and any-to-any connectivity.

(6) Capable of offering fully managed services to customers.

(7) Allow BSNL to introduce additional services such as bandwidth on demand over the same network.

6.5 Various Topology Scenarios

Many of these VPN technologies can be affected by the layout and needed resources of the users. Some technologies don't handle roaming users as well as others. Some have trouble with NAT (Network Address Translation), still others run into problems with old routers or restrictive firewalls not even supporting their protocols and refusing to route them correctly.

There are many ways one could adjust the VPN topologies listed in this document, however a few will be listed to give some clarification of the challenges.

Including a more robust "security in depth" approach in sufficient detail, such as backup technologies, IDS (Intrusion Detection Systems) and monitoring technologies, is beyond the scope of this document.

Detailing the various strengths and weaknesses of each topology is also beyond the current scope of this document; however some more immediately obvious points will be noted for each.

6.5.1 Topology 1

VPN Server (and/or client) directly connected to the Internet and internal LAN, server may or may not have its own firewall software running locally(see Figure 6.7).

This is an common to all setup. It is inexpensive and easy to setup and administrate. Many inexperienced administrators and users may use this setup, not being aware of how vulnerable a situation this is.

Advantages: Easy to setup and administrate, very low cost.

Disadvantages: Little to no protection, very vulnerable to many attacks, information "leakage" and more.

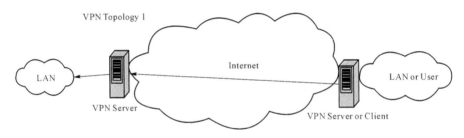

Figure 6.7 Topology 1

6.5.2 Topology 2

VPN server is behind a firewall but listening service ports still directly accessible for the ports that are allowed to be open by the firewall(see Figure 6.8).

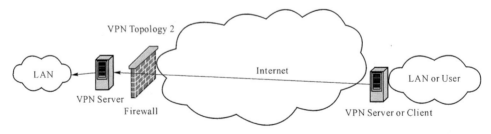

Figure 6.8 Topology 2

This is another common setup. Inexpensive and still very easy to setup and administrate. This is an improvement over topology number 1. Unfortunately there are still many weaknesses easily exploited, and typically those who use this configuration rely too heavily upon the firewall to be their sole means of protection rather than "security in depth" and layering of defenses.

Advantages: Easy setup and administration, and low cost.

Disadvantages: Still quite open and vulnerable to wide array of attacks.

6.5.3 Topology 3

VPN Server is behind a firewall and only accessible to certain ports via port forwarding from the firewall(see Figure 6.9).

This setup is an improvement over the previous two because of tighter restrictions on what traffic and services are allowed access and from where.

Advantages: Improved security "stance" still fairly easy to setup and administrate.

Disadvantages: Not quite as simple to setup as first two options, still not as many layers for a "security in depth" approach as there could be.

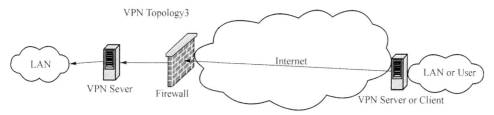

Figure 6.9 Topology 3

6.5.4 Topology 4

VPN server in a DMZ with the connected VPN user then allowed inside LAN through LAN firewall (see Figare 6.10).

This is a much more ideal configuration, multiple layers of checking and protection. Unfortunately either budget, time, resources, or administrator skill level tend to not be available for such an ideal setup. This can be improved upon even more with additional layers of firewalls and other "tricks of the trade".

Advantages: Much more secure stance, security in layers.

Disadvantages: High complexity to setup and administrate, added cost, more advanced skill sets required.

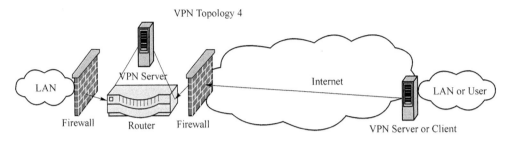

Figure 6.10 Topology 4

6.5.5 Topology 5

VPN server in a DMZ but as another gateway (aka hole) into LAN, usually the VPN server acts as yet another firewall as well (unfortunately not always though), and doesn't allow any traffic in except those actually connected to it via the VPN(see Figure 6.11).

This is not as ideal a setup as Topology 4, but one that is not uncommon. It is a mix between option 3 and option 4, but NOT as secure as option 4 since there isn't a second firewall performing additional checking before allowing access to the LAN.

Advantages: Slightly easier setup and administration than option 4.

Disadvantages: Security level is only about equivalent to option 3.

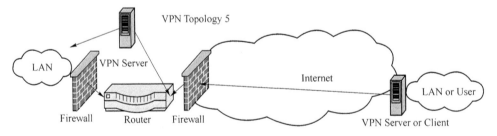

Figure 6.11 Topology 5

6.5.6 Topology 6

Wireless (such as the popular 802.11b technologies) usage of VPN, usually one of the previous 5 topologies and possibly a firewall (recommended)(see Figure 6.12).

Unfortunately most companies are NOT implementing firewalls or VPNs to sepa-

Chapter 6 Virtual Private Network

rate and protect their wireless LAN users, despite repeated press releases and proof of the simplicity of compromise. However, for those that do heed such warnings, this is one option, of several to choose from, that many implement. It's fairly easy to setup. It's much along the lines of Topology 1, because most companies assume that there are far fewer attacks via their local wireless LAN than the Internet just because of the sheer numbers of nodes, unfortunately such assumptions tend to be perilous. Others opt to have a firewall in front of the VPN server as well as the LAN, but this does not yet appear to be a common practice.

Advantages: More secure wireless setup, fairly easy to setup and administrate.

Disadvantages: VPN server still wide open to many attacks and information leakage to wireless LAN users. Every attack described in this document is very effective on such a network. Even if the attacker can't gain VPN access into the LAN, they can still possibly easily abuse the bandwidth on the wireless segment, and easily attack the server and users on this segment.

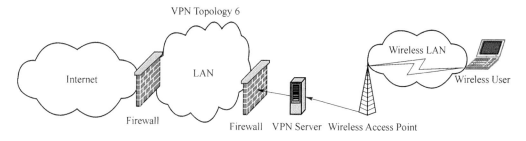

Figure 6.12 Topology 6

6.6 VPN Security Dialogs

The most important part of a VPN solution is security. The very nature of VPNs — putting private data on public networks—raises concerns about potential threats to that data and the impact of data loss. A Virtual Private Network must address all types of security threats by providing security services in the areas of:

Authentication (access control)—Authentication is the process of ensuring that a user or system is who the user claims to be. There are many types of authentication mechanisms, but they all use one or more of the following approaches:

- Something you know (e.g., a login name, a password, a PIN);
- Something you have (e.g., a computer readable token (e.g, a Smartcard), a card key);

- Something you are (e. g. ,fingerprint,retinal pattern,iris pattern,hand configuration,etc.).

What is generally regarded as weak authentication makes use of one of these components,usually a login name/password sequence. Strong authentication is usually taken to combine at least two authentication components from different areas (i. e. ,two-factor authentication). But note that use of weak and strong in this context can be misleading. A stolen SmartCard and a shoulder-surfed login name/PIN sequence is not hard to achieve and will pass a strong authentication two-factor text handily. More seriously, stolen or lost security data (e. g. ,on a backup tape,a laptop,or stolen by an employee) dangerously furthers many such attacks on most authentication schemes. There is no fully adequate technique for the authentication problem,including biometric ones.

Glossary

compulsory tunneling	强制隧道
Layer 2 Tunneling Protocol(L2TP)	第二层隧道协议
Multi-Protocol Label Switching (MPLS)	多协议标签交换
Point-to-Point Tunneling Protocol(PPTP)	点对点隧道协议
Virtual Private Network (VPN)	虚拟专用网
voluntary tunneling	自发隧道连接

Translate the following sentences/passage into Chinese

(1) A virtual private network (VPN) is a private communications network often used within a company,or by several companies or organizations,to communicate confidentially over a publicly accessible network.

(2) VPN is a cost effective and secure way for different corporations to provide user access to the corporate network and for remote networks to communicate with each other across the Internet.

(3) Secure VPNs use cryptographic tunneling protocols to provide the intended confidentiality (blocking snooping and thus Packet sniffing),sender authentication (blocking identity spoofing),and message integrity (blocking message alteration) to achieve privacy.

(4) Some large ISPs now offer "managed" VPN service for business customers who want the security and convenience of a VPN but prefer not to undertake administering a VPN server themselves. In addition to providing remote workers with secure access to their employer's internal network,other security and management services are some-

Chapter 6 Virtual Private Network

times included as part of the package.

(5) Many of these VPN technologies can be affected by the layout and needed resources of the users. Some technologies don't handle roaming users as well as others. Some have trouble with NAT(Network Address Translation), still others run into problems with old routers or restrictive firewalls not even supporting their protocols and refusing to route them correctly.

Translate the following sentences/passage into English

(1) IETF 草案定义基于 IP 的 VPN 为:使用 IP 机制仿真出一个私有的广域网,是通过私有的隧道技术在公共数据网络上仿真一条点到点的专线技术。虚拟专用网是依靠 ISP(Internet 服务提供商)和其他网络服务提供商,在公用网络中建立专用的数据通信网络的技术。

(2) VPN 同样也由这 3 部分组成,不同的是 VPN 连接使用隧道作为传输通道,这个隧道是建立在公共网络或专用网络基础之上的,如 Internet 或 Intranet,用户不再需要拥有专用的长途数据线路。

(3) 安全性是专用网络的一个重要特征。由于 VPN 直接构建在公用网上,实现简单、方便、灵活,但同时其安全问题也更为突出。企业必须确保其 VPN 上传送的数据不被攻击者窥视和篡改,并且要防止非法用户对网络资源或私有信息的访问。ExtranetVPN 将企业网扩展到合作伙伴和客户,对安全性提出了更高的要求。

(4) VPN 要求企业将其网络管理功能从局域网无缝地延伸到公用网,甚至是客户和合作伙伴,虽然可以将一些次要的网络管理任务交给服务提供商去完成,企业自己仍需要完成许多网络管理任务,所以,VPN 系统应该支持用户可管理性。VPN 管理主要包括安全管理、设备管理、配置管理、访问控制列表管理、QoS 管理等内容,以实现减小网络风险,具有高扩展性、经济性、高可靠性等目标。

(5) VPN 通过公网建立的链接,因此必须采用加密技术防止窃听,保护企业数据的安全性。通常的加密算法包括 DES、3DES 等。DES 密钥长度为 56 位,容易被破译,3DES 使用三重加密增加了安全性。

Questions

(1) How does SSL VPN work?
(2) What is the aim of MPLS VPN?
(3) How does L2TP VPN work?
(4) How does PPTP VPN work?
(5) What are two types of VPN tunneling?

Chapter 7

Computer Virus

A computer virus is a self-replicating computer program written to alter the way a computer operates, without the permission or knowledge of the user. Though the term is commonly used to refer to a range of malware, a true virus must replicate itself, and must execute itself. The latter criteria are often met by a virus which replaces existing executable files with a virus-infected copy. While viruses can be intentionally destructive—destroying data, for example—some viruses are benign or merely annoying.

7.1 Introduction

7.1.1 Comparison with Biological Viruses

A computer virus behaves in a way similar to a biological virus, which spreads by inserting itself into living cells. Extending the analogy, the insertion of a virus into the program is termed as an "infection", and the infected file, or executable code that is not part of a file, is called a "host".

A computer virus will pass from one computer to another like a real life biological virus passes from person to person. For example, it is estimated by experts that the Mydoom worm infected a quarter-million computers in a single day in January 2004. In March 1999, the Melissa virus spread so rapidly that it forced Microsoft and a number of other very large companies to completely turn off their E-mail systems until the virus could be dealt with. Another example is the ILOVEYOU virus, which occurred in 2000 and had a similar effect. It stole most of its operating style from Melissa.

7.1.2 Distinction between Malware and Computer Viruses

Malware is a broad category of software designed to infiltrate or damage a computer system. Types of malware include spyware, adware, Trojan horses, Worms, and true viruses. While modern anti-virus software works to protect computers from this range of threats, computer viruses make up only a small subset of malware.

7.1.3 Effects of Computer Viruses

Some viruses are programmed to damage the computer by damaging programs, deleting files, or reformatting the hard disk. Others are not designed to do any damage, but simply replicate themselves and make their presence known by presenting text, video, or audio messages. Even these benign viruses can create problems for the computer user. They typically take up computer memory used by legitimate programs. As a result, they often cause erratic behavior and can result in system crashes. In addition, many viruses are bug-ridden, and these bugs may lead to system crashes and data loss.

7.1.4 Use of the Word "Virus"

The word virus is derived from and used in the same sense as the biological equivalent. The term "virus" is often used in common parlance to describe all kinds of malware (malicious software), including those that are more properly classified as worms or Trojans. Most popular anti-virus software packages defend against all of these types of attack. In some technical communities, the term "virus" is also extended to include the authors of malware, in an insulting sense. The English plural of "virus" is "viruses". Some people use "virii" or "viri" as a plural, but this is rare.

7.1.5 History

A program called "Elk Cloner" is credited with being the first computer virus to appear "in the wild"—that is, outside the single computer or lab where it was created. Written in 1982 by Rich Skrenta, it attached itself to the Apple DOS 3.3 operating system and spread by floppy disk. This virus was originally a joke, created by the high school student and put onto a game. The game was set to play, but release the virus on the 50th time of starting the game. Only this time, instead of playing the game, it would change to a blank screen that read a poem about the virus named Elk Cloner. The computer would then be infected.

The first PC virus was a boot sector virus called (c)Brain, created in 1986 by two brothers, Basit and Amjad Farooq Alvi, operating out of Lahore, Pakistan. The brothers reportedly created the virus to deter pirated copies of software they had written. However, analysts have claimed that the Ashar virus, a variant of Brain, possibly predated it based on code within the virus.

Before computer networks became widespread, most viruses spread on removable media, particularly floppy disks. In the early days of the personal computer, many users regularly exchanged information and programs on floppies. Some viruses spread by infecting programs stored on these disks, while others installed themselves into the disk boot sector, ensuring that they would be run when the user booted the computer from the disk.

Traditional computer viruses emerged in the 1980s, driven by the spread of personal computers and the resultant increase in BBS and modem use, and software sharing. Bulletin board driven software sharing contributed directly to the spread of Trojan horse programs, and viruses were written to infect popularly traded software. Shareware and bootleg software were equally common vectors for viruses on BBS's. Within the "pirate scene" of hobbyists trading illicit copies of commercial software, traders in a hurry to obtain the latest applications and games were easy targets for viruses.

Since the mid-1990s, macro viruses have become common. Most of these viruses are written in the scripting languages for Microsoft programs such as Word and Excel. These viruses spread in Microsoft Office by infecting documents and spreadsheets. Since Word and Excel were also available for Mac OS, most of these viruses were able to spread on Macintosh computers as well. Most of these viruses did not have the ability to send infected E-mail. Those viruses which did spread through E-mail took advantage of the Microsoft Outlook COM interface.

Macro viruses pose unique problems for detection software. For example, some versions of Microsoft Word allowed macros to replicate themselves with additional blank lines. The virus behaved identically but would be misidentified as a new virus. In another example, if two macro viruses simultaneously infect a document, the combination of the two, if also self-replicating, can appear as a "mating" of the two and would likely be detected as a virus unique from the "parents".

A computer virus may also be transmitted through instant messaging. A virus may send a web address link as an instant message to all the contacts on an infected machine. If the recipient, thinking the link is from a friend (a trusted source) and follows the link to the website, the virus hosted at the site may be able to infect this new computer and continue propagating.

The newest species of the virus family is the cross-site scripting virus. The virus emerged from research and was academically demonstrated in 2005. This virus utilizes cross-site scripting vulnerabilities to propagate. Since 2005 there have been multiple instances of the cross-site scripting viruses in the wild, most notable sites affected have been MySpace and Yahoo.

7.2 Virus Classification

Viruses can be subdivided into a number of types, the main ones being:
- Boot sector viruses
- Companion viruses
- E-mail viruses
- Logic bombs and time bombs
- Macro viruses
- Cross-site scripting virus

Two other types of malware are often classified as viruses, but are actually forms of distributing malware:
- Trojan horses
- Worms

7.2.1 Boot Sector Virus

A boot sector virus alters or hides in the boot sector, usually the 1st sector, of a bootable disk or hard drive. Boot sector viruses were prevalent in the 1980s.

1. Boot Sector

A boot sector is a sector of a hard disk, floppy disk, or similar data storage device that contains code for bootstrapping programs (usually, but not necessarily, operating systems) stored in other parts of the disk.

(1) Kinds of boot sectors

There are two major kinds of boot sectors:

- A Volume Boot Record is the first sector of a data storage device that has not been partitioned, or the first sector of an individual partition on a data storage device that has been partitioned. It contains code to load and invoke the operating system (or other standalone program) installed on that device or within that partition. It is required to have two bytes (0x55AA) called boot sector signature at the end of the sector to be a valid boot sector; either BIOS software or MBR code would report an error message and hang up the operating system loading process otherwise.
- A Master Boot Record is the first sector of a data storage device that has been partitioned. It contains code to locate the active partition and to invoke its Volume Boot Record.

On IBM PC compatible machines, the BIOS is ignorant of the distinction between VBRs and MBRs, and of partitioning. The firmware simply loads and runs the first sector of the storage device. If the device is a floppy disk, that will be a VBR. If the device is a hard disc, that will be an MBR. It is the code in the MBR that understands disc partitioning, and that is responsible for in turn loading and running the VBR of the active (primary) partition.

(2) Boot sectors and computer viruses

Boot sectors are one mechanism by which computer viruses gain control of a system. Boot sector infector viruses replace the bootstrap code in the boot sectors (of floppy disks, hard disks, or both) with viral code.

As well as being ignorant of whether a disk has been partitioned, the BIOS on IBM PC compatible machines is also ignorant of whether a disk has in fact been high-level formatted and had an operating system installed in it. The error message displayed when a machine is bootstrapped from a disk without an operating system installed on it (asking the user to insert a bootable disk and press a key) is in fact displayed by code in the boot sector itself, not by the machine firmware.

It results in security vulnerability. A user who sees the error message may not be aware that the code in the boot sector of the disk has already been run by that point, and that if the disk was infected by a boot-sector computer virus, the virus will have already gained control of the machine. Because of this vulnerability, computer security experts tend to recommend that booting from devices other than the one containing the installed operating system, such as removable media devices (e. g., floppy disk devices, CD-ROMs, and USB flash drives), be disabled in normal operation via the BIOS setup utility, and only re-enabled on those specific occasions when booting from such devices is actually required.

Chapter 7 Computer Virus

2. Boot Sector Virus and Its Prevention

A boot sector virus is one that infects the first sector, i. e., the boot sector, of a floppy disk or hard drive. Boot sector viruses can also infect the MBR. The first PC virus in the wild was Brain, a boot sector virus that exhibited stealth techniques to avoid detection. Brain also changed the volume label of the disk drive.

(1) How do they spread

Boot sector viruses are usually spread by infected floppy disks. In the past, these were usually bootable disks, but this is no longer the case. A floppy disk does not need to be bootable to transmit a boot virus. Any disk can cause infection if it is in the drive when the computer boots up or shuts down. The virus can also be spread across networks from file downloads and from E-mail file attachments. In most cases, all write-enabled floppies used on an infected PC will themselves pick up the boot sector virus.

(2) How to avoid boot sector viruses

Commonly, infected floppies and subsequent boot sector infections result from "shared" diskettes and pirated software applications. It is relatively easy to avoid boot sector viruses. Most are spread when users inadvertently leave floppy disks in the drive—which happen to be infected with a boot sector virus. The next time they boot up their PC, the virus infects the local drive. Most systems allow users to change the boot sequence so that the system always attempts to boot first from the local hard drive (C:\) or CD-ROM drive.

(3) Disinfecting boot sector viruses

Boot sector repair is best accomplished by the use of antivirus software. Because some boot sector viruses encrypt the MBR, improper removal can result in a drive that is inaccessible. However, if you are certain the virus has only affected the boot sector and is not an encrypting virus, the DOS SYS command can be used to restore the first sector. Additionally, the DOS LABEL command can be used to restore a damaged volume label and FDISK /MBR will replace the MBR. None of these methods is recommended, however. Antivirus software remains the best tool for cleanly and accurately removing boot sector viruses with minimal threat to data and files.

(4) Creating a system disk

When disinfecting a boot sector virus, the system should always be booted from a known clean system disk. On a DOS-based PC, a bootable system disk can be created on a clean system running the exact same version of DOS as the infected PC. From a DOS prompt, type:

SYS C:\ A:\

and press enter. This will copy the system files from the local hard drive (C:\) to the

English for Information Security

floppy drive (A:\).

If the disk has not been formatted, the use of FORMAT/S will format the disk and transfer the necessary system files. On Windows 3.1x systems, the disk should be created as described above for DOS-based PC's. On Windows 95/98/NT systems, click Start | Settings | Control Panel | Add/Remove Programs and choose the Startup Disk tab. Then click on "Create Disk". Windows 2000 users should insert the Windows 2000 CD-ROM into the CD-ROM drive, click Start | Run and type the name of the drive followed by bootdisk\makeboot a: and then click OK. For example:

d:\bootdisk\makeboot a:

Follow the screen prompts to finish creating the bootable system disk. In all cases, after the creation of the bootable system disk, the disk should be write protected to avoid infection.

7.2.2 Companion Virus

A companion virus does not have host files per se, but exploits MS-DOS. A companion virus creates new files (typically .COM but can also use other extensions such as ".EXD") that have the same file names as legitimate .EXE files. When a user types in the name of a desired program, if a user does not type in ".EXE" but instead does not specify a file extension, DOS will assume he meant the file with the extension that comes first in alphabetical order and run the virus. For instance, if a user had "(filename).COM" (the virus) and "(filename).EXE" and the user typed "filename", he will run "(filename).COM" and run the virus. The virus will spread and do other tasks before redirecting to the legitimate file, which operates normally. Some companion viruses are known to run under Windows 95 and on DOS emulators on Windows NT systems. Path companion viruses create files that have the same name as the legitimate file and place new virus copies earlier in the directory paths. These viruses have become increasingly rare with the introduction of Windows XP, which does not use the MS-DOS command prompt.

A good integrity map of what should be on the hard disk can be used to easily detect and clean companion viruses.

Companion viruses were never particularly common and under Windows where specific files are associated with icons you likely won't see them.

7.2.3 E-mail Virus

An E-mail virus is a virus which uses E-mail messages as a mode of transport. These viruses often copy themselves by automatically mailing copies to hundreds of people in

Chapter 7 Computer Virus

the victim's address book.

The Melissa virus, macro virus and the ILOVEYOU virus are among the best publicized of recent E-mail viruses. Each of these also spawned copycat variations with different words in the subject line.

1. Introduction

Many of the most common computer viruses and other malicious software are spread through E-mail attachments—the files that are sent along with an E-mail message.

If a file attached to an E-mail message contains a virus, it's often launched when you open the file attachment (usually by double-clicking the attachment icon).

2. E-mail Virus and Its Prevention

You can help avoid some viruses by following a few basic rules.

(1) 5 tips for dealing with E-mail attachments

Follow these basic guidelines when dealing with attachments in an E-mail message, no matter what E-mail program you're using:

- Don't open any attachment unless you know whom it's from and you were expecting it.
- If you receive an E-mail message with an attachment from someone you don't know, delete it immediately.
- Use antivirus software and keep it updated. Windows Live OneCare scans E-mail attachments as you open them.
- If you need to send an E-mail attachment to someone, let them know you'll be sending it so they don't think it's a virus.
- Use an E-mail program with spam filtering built-in, such as Microsoft Office Outlook 2007, Windows Live Mail, or MSN Hotmail.

(2) Dealing with E-mail attachments in Microsoft Outlook

Microsoft Outlook can block potentially unsafe attachments before they get to you. For example, if you're using Outlook 2003 and you receive an E-mail with an attachment that could contain a virus, you'll see the warning below. (see Figure 7.1)

Figure 7.1 An example of an E-mail attachment blocked by Outlook 2003

(3) Dealing with E-mail attachments in Outlook Express

If you use Outlook Express, you can greatly increase your chances of avoiding viruses, worms, and Trojans by upgrading to Windows XP Service Pack 2 (SP2). With SP2, Outlook Express will block potentially harmful attachments by default and has numerous other features that help prevent viruses and other malware. If you use Outlook Express, but you're not sure what operating system you're running, visit Find out which operating system your computer is using. If you're not using Windows XP SP2, you can check your virus protection settings manually.

To ensure your E-mail virus protection is turned on in Outlook Express:
- On the Tools menu, click Options;
- Click the Security tab;
- Select the Do not allow attachments to be saved or opened that could potentially be a virus check box;
- Click OK.

To open an attachment that you know to be safe:
- On the Tools menu, click Options.
- Click the Security tab.
- Clear the Do not allow attachments to be saved or opened that could potentially be a virus check box.
- Click OK.
- Close and reopen the message with the attachment that you know to be safe.
- Open the attachment.
- Repeat Steps 1 and 2. Then select the Do not allow attachments to be saved or opened that could potentially be a virus check box.

If you're running Windows XP SP2 you may be given one more warning, such as the one you see in Figure 7.2.

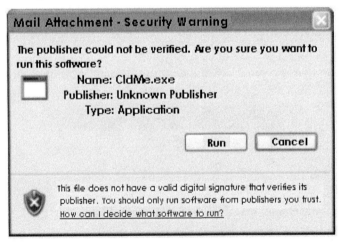

Figure 7.2 Security warning

Chapter 7 Computer Virus

Always use caution before clicking Run, as that could install a virus or other potentially dangerous program.

7.2.4 Logic Bomb

A logic bomb employs code that lies inert until specific conditions are met. The resolution of the conditions will trigger a certain function (such as printing a message to the user and/or deleting files). An example of a logic bomb would be a virus that waits to execute until it has infected a certain number of hosts. A time bomb is a subset of logic bomb, which is set to trigger on a particular date and/or time.

1. Introduction

A logic bomb is a piece of code intentionally inserted into a software system that will set off a malicious function when specified conditions are met. For example, a programmer may hide a piece of code that starts deleting files, should he ever leave the company (and the salary database).

Software that is inherently malicious, such as viruses and worms, often contain logic bombs that execute a certain payload at a pre-defined time or when some other condition is met. This technique can be used by a virus or worm to gain momentum and spread before being noticed. Many viruses attack their host systems on specific dates, such as Friday the 13th or April Fool's Day. Trojans that activate on certain dates are often called "time bombs".

To be considered a logic bomb, the payload should be unwanted and unknown to the user of the software. As an example, trial programs with code that disables certain functionality after a set time are not normally regarded as logic bombs. Such devices tend to be the province of technical staff (non-technical staff rarely has the access rights and even more rarely the programming skills required) and operate in two ways:

(1) **Triggered Event.** For example, the program will review the payroll records each day to ensure that the programmer responsible is still employed. If the programmers name is suddenly removed (by virtue of having been fired) the Logic Bomb will activate another piece of code to Slag (destroy) vital files on the organization's system. Smarter programmers will build in a suitable delay between these two events (say 2~3 months) so that investigators do not immediately recognize cause and effect.

(2) **Still Here.** In these case the programmer buries coding similar to the Triggered Event type but in this instance the program will run unless it is deactivated by the programmer (effectively telling the program—"I am still here—do not run") at regular in-

tervals, typically once each quarter. If the programmer's employment is terminated unexpectedly, the program will not be deactivated and will attack the system at the next due date. This type of Logic Bomb is much more dangerous, since it will run even if the programmer is only temporarily absent—e. g. , through sickness, injury or other unforeseen circumstances—at the deactivation point, and the fact that it wasn't meant to happen just then is of little comfort to organization with a slagged system.

Logic Bombs demonstrate clearly the critical need for audit trails of activity on the system as well as strict segregation of duties and access rights between those staff who create systems—analysts, developers, programmers,—and the operations staff who actually run the system on a day-to-day basis.

2. Historic Logic Bombs

In June 1992, a defense contractor General Dynamics employee, Michael Lauffenburger, was arrested for inserting a logic bomb that would delete vital rocket project data. It was alleged that his plan was to return as a highly paid consultant to fix the problem once it triggered. Another employee of the company stumbled upon the bomb before it was triggered. Lauffenburger was charged with computer tampering and attempted fraud and faced potential fines of $500 000 and jail time, but was ultimately fined $5 000.

In February 2000, Tony Xiaotong was indicted before a grand jury accused of planting a logic bomb during his employment as a programmer and securities trader at Deutsche Morgan Grenfell. The bomb had a trigger date of July 2000, and was discovered by other programmers in the company. Removing and cleaning up after the bomb allegedly took several months.

In June 2006 Roger Duronio, a disgruntled systems administrator for UBS PaineWebber was charged with using a "logic bomb" to damage the company's computer network, and with securities fraud for his failed plan to drive down the company's stock with activation of the logic bomb.

7.2.5 Macro Virus

A macro virus, often written in the scripting languages for Microsoft programs such as Word and Excel, is spread in Microsoft Office by infecting documents and spreadsheets.

1. Introduction

In computer terminology, a macro virus is a virus that is written in a macro language. They were largely problems because rather than create a new function to perform macros, some software vendors connected the macro writing functions in their software

Chapter 7 Computer Virus

to the same computer language that they used to write that same software. Because of this, anyone with knowledge of that particular programming language can code a program that will launch immediately when the file is opened on a computer. "Documents" with macro viruses are actually templates in disguise since documents cannot have macros. This is why people are told not to open attachments in E-mail because of the danger of embedded macros. It recommended that anti-virus software is used and kept up to date.

2. Macro Virus Fundamentals

Macros are a series of commands and actions that help to automate tasks performed on a regular basis. A computer macro virus is a virus that infects documents and templates, not programs. A macro virus takes advantage of the macro programming language built into applications such as Microsoft Word or Excel. This also includes files on other platforms such as Macintosh(Microsoft Corporation, 2006, WD: Frequently Asked Questions…). In 2004, macro viruses accounted for approximately 75% of all viruses. (Webopaedia, 2004) A macro virus differs from a worm in that worms do not attach themselves to other programs or files. A worm is a computer program in itself(The Trustees of Indiana University, 2006).

3. The Truth on How Macro Viruses Really Work

A macro virus can be spread through E-mail attachments, discs, networks, modems, and the internet(Microsoft Corporation, 2006, WD: Frequently Asked Questions…). Uninfected documents contain normal macros. Most macros start automatically when a document is opened or closed. A common way for a macro virus to infect a computer is by replacing normal macros with the virus. The macro virus replaces the regular commands with the same name and runs when the command is selected. In this case where the macro is run automatically, the macro is opened without the user knowing(Computer Incident Advisory Capability, 1998). Once you open a file that contains a macro virus your system is infected. It will begin to embed in all other documents and templates, as well as future ones created. As you share these documents encoded with the macro virus, the virus can be passed onto other users. A Microsoft Word macro virus can infect files on Windows as well as the Macintosh platform(Microsoft Corporation, 2006, WD: Frequently Asked Questions…). This is how a macro virus spreads. A well known example of a macro virus is the Melissa Virus from 1999. A document was created with the virus in it and anyone who opened it would "catch" the virus. The virus would then send itself by E-mail to the first 40 people in the person's address book. This made the virus replicate at a fast rate(How Stuff Works, Inc, 2006).

4. Recognizing a Macro Virus Infection

There are different ways in which one can recognize a macro virus. If a person is familiar with the macros that are supposed to be on a computer, then one can check through the macros on a computer and look for ones that he or she does not recognize. A person can research on the internet for names of macros that are known to be a part of a macro virus, such as AAAZAO, AAAZFS, AutoOpen, FileSaveAs, and PayLoad. If these macros are found on a computer, then it is a sign that the computer has been infected (Microsoft Corporation, 2006, WD: Frequently Asked Questions…).

For those that are not familiar with macros, the best way to recognize if a computer has been infected is to look for unusual behavior and symptoms of a macro virus. There are three common symptoms of a macro virus. First, a person may be prompted for a password when opening a file that does not have a password. Second, a computer may save a document as a template without the user instructing the computer to do so. Last, a macro virus can cause strange error messages, such as "Just to prove another point" or "This one's for you, Bosco". A macro virus can move words in your document and replace them with a random word such as "WAZZU" at various locations(Microsoft Corporation, 2006, WD: Frequently Asked Questions…).

It is important to constantly update antivirus programs and to be sure to have advanced antivirus software installed on a computer.

Digital signatures and certificates of authenticity are important tools in protecting against macro viruses. They identify the company or source that has created the download. A certificate of authenticity can be issued by various authorities and holds information in a secure form. A digital certificate can then be used to sign programs, controls, and documents. Digital signatures and certificates are used to establish trust. Information is displayed before the file is downloaded about the person who has the certificate and also about the certifying authority. A person can then decide whether to download a file based on the reputation of the authority(Microsoft Corporation, 2006, Introduction to Security).

Many computer systems have security features that should be used. For example, often there is a setting that will prompt a person when opening a file that contains macros. If this feature is turned on, then a dialog box will be displayed when you open a file that gives you the option to enable macros or disable macros. This will let a person know that there are macros within the file and it will give the person a chance to evaluate the source of the file before opening the file. Internet browsers have security options as well. This means that a person can change the security level. A medium setting will

Chapter 7 Computer Virus

always prompt the user before downloading potentially dangerous content. Any program or control that does not have a digital signature will not be downloaded.

Lastly, most home users and many business users don't use advanced feature such as macros. For them, the best protection is to turn off the scripting language that runs macros. This will prevent any type of macro from running on your computer (whether virus or not). Since most documents don't contain macros, this will protect your computer without negatively affecting normal use.

The following taken from www. microtech. doe. gov.

To disable scripting manually, perform the following steps:
- Click "Start";
- Click "Settings";
- Click "Add/Remove Programs";
- Click the "Windows Setup" tab;
- Double-click "Accessories";
- Uncheck "Windows Scripting Host";
- Click "OK";
- Click "OK".

Please note that, if you use this procedure, you may need the Windows CD to restore Windows Scripting.

5. Example: Melissa

The Melissa worm, also known as "Mailissa", "Simpsons", "Kwyjibo", or "Kwejeebo", is a mass-mailing macro virus, hence leading some to classify it as a computer worm.

(1) History

First found on March 26, 1999, Melissa shut down Internet mail systems that got clogged with infected E-mails propagating from the worm.

Melissa was first distributed in the Usenet discussion group alt. sex. The virus was inside a file called "List. DOC", which contained passwords that allow access into 80 pornographic websites. The worm's original form was sent via E-mail to many people.

Melissa was written by David L. Smith in Aberdeen Township, New Jersey, and named after a lap dancer he encountered in Florida. The creator of the virus called himself Kwyjibo, but was shown to be identical to macrovirus writers VicodinES and Alt-F11 who had several Word-files with the same characteristic Globally Unique Identifier (GUID), a serial number that was earlier generated with the network card MAC address as a component. Smith was sentenced to 10 years but served only 20 months in a federal prison and fined $5 000 United States dollars.

(2) Worm Specifications

Melissa can spread on word processor Microsoft Word 97 and Word 2000. It can mass-mail itself from E-mail client Microsoft Outlook 97 or Outlook 98. The worm does not work on any other versions of Word, including Word 95, nor can it mass-mail itself via any other E-mail client, even Outlook Express.

If a Word Document containing the virus, either LIST. DOC or another infected file, is downloaded and opened, then the macro in the document runs and attempts to mass mail itself.

When the macro mass-mails, it collects the first 50 entries from the alias list or address book, and sends it to the E-mail addresses of those names.

(3) Melissa. A/Original Version

This is what infected E-mails say:

```
From: <name of the infected sender>
Subject: Important message from <name of sender>
To: <The recipients, from the 50 names>
Attachment: LIST.DOC
Body: Here is that document you asked for...don't show anyone else ;-)
```

If the worm already has sent itself, or cannot spread that way for lack of an Internet connection or Outlook, it spreads to other Word Documents on the computer. Other infected documents can also be mailed. If confidential data is inside the document, the recipient of the E-mail containing the document can view it.

The worm's activation routine inserts quotes from the animated television program The Simpsons into other documents when the minutes of the hour of the computer's clock match the day of the month (e. g. ,7:09 on the 9th day of the month). Quotes include phrases like "Twenty-two points, plus triple-word-score, plus fifty points for using all my letters. Game's over. I'm outta here. " The alias of the author, "Kwyjibo", is also a Simpsons reference.

(4) Melissa. I/Empirical

This variant can send using any of these subject line and body combinations, all of which differ from Melissa's original form.

- Subject: Question for you…
  Body: It's fairly complicated so I've attached it.
- Subject: Check this!!
  Body: This is some wicked stuff!

Chapter 7 Computer Virus

- Subject: Cool Web Sites.
  Body: Check out the Attached Document for a list of some of the best Sites on the Web.
- Subject: 80mb Free Web Space!
  Body: Check out the Attached Document for details on how to obtain the free space. It's cool, I've now got heaps of room.
- Subject: Cheap Software.
  Body: The attached document contains a list of web sites where you can obtain Cheap Software.
- Subject: Cheap Hardware.
  Body: I've attached a list of web sites where you can obtain Cheap Hardware.
- Subject: Free Music.
  Body: Here is a list of places where you can obtain Free Music.
- Subject: * Free Downloads.
  Body: Here is a list of sites where you can obtain Free Downloads.

NOTE: The asterisk " * " in the 8th subject can be any random character that the worm specifies in the E-mail.

This version uses a different registry key, named "Empirical" to check if the worm had already mass mailed itself.

This version has another payload: if the number of minutes equals the number of hours, the worm inserts the phrase "All empires fall, you just have to know where to push." The virus then clears the flag indicating that it had mass-mailed itself from the registry. As soon as Word is restarted, a new document is created, a document is opened, or a document is closed, the worm will mass-mail itself again.

(5) Melissa. O

This version sends itself to 100 people in the alias list instead of 50. This is the E-mail message it sends:

    Subject: Duhalde Presidente.

    Body: Programa de gobierno 1999 - 2004.

(6) Melissa. U

This version is similar to Melissa. A, with several notable differences. The module name it uses is named "Mmmmmmm". This version sends itself to only 4 recipients instead of 50. This is what the infected E-mail looks like:

    Subject: Pictures (Username)

    Body: what's up ?

The worm puts the name that the sender's copy of Word is registered to where it says Username in the Subject.

The following strings can be placed in documents: "Loading... No", and ">>>> Please check Outlook Inbox Mail<<<<<".

The virus also deletes critical files. Before deleting the files, it strips them of their archive, hidden, and read-only attributes.

- C:\Command.com
- C:\Io.sys
- C:\Ntdetect.com
- C:\Suhdlog.dat
- D:\Command.com
- D:\Io.sys
- D:\Suhdlog.dat

(7) Melissa.V

This is another variant of the original Melissa macro virus, and is akin to Melissa.U. It uses Microsoft Outlook, and tries to send itself to the first 40 addresses in Outlook's address book. The subject line of the infected E-mail sent out is: "My Pictures (<Username>)", where <Username> is the name to whom the sender's copy of Microsoft Word is registered to.

There is no body to the E-mail, but there is an infected document attached. If this is opened, the payload is triggered immediately. It tries to delete data from the following (local or network) destinations: F:, H:, I:, L:, M:, N:, O:, P:, Q:, S:, X:, and Z:.

Once complete, it beeps three times and then shows a message box with the text: "Hint: Get Norton 2000 not McAfee 4.02".

(8) Melissa.W

This is the same as Melissa.A.

(9) Melissa.AO

This is what the E-mails from this version contain:

> Subject: Extremely URGENT: To All E-Mail User - <current date>
> Attachment: <Infected Active Document>
> Body: This announcement is for all E-MAIL user. Please take note that our
>   E-Mail Server will down and we recommended you to read the document
>   which attached with this E-Mail.

Melissa.AO's payload occurs at 10 a.m. on the 10th day of each month. The payload consists of the worm inserting the following string into the document: "Worm!

Chapter 7 Computer Virus

Let's We Enjoy."

7.2.6 Cross-site Scripting Virus

A cross-site scripting virus (XSSV) is a type of virus that utilizes cross-site scripting vulnerabilities to replicate. A XSSV is spread between vulnerable web applications and web browsers creating a symbiotic relationship.

1. Cross-site Scripting

Cross-site scripting (XSS) is a type of computer security vulnerability typically found in web applications which allow malicious web users to inject HTML or client-side script into the web pages viewed by other users. An exploited cross-site scripting vulnerability can be used by attackers to bypass access controls such as the same origin policy. Recently, vulnerabilities of this kind have been exploited to craft powerful phishing attacks and browser exploits.

2. Background

When Netscape first introduced the JavaScript language, they realized the security risks of allowing a Web server to send executable code to a browser (even if only in a browser sandbox). One key problem with this is the case where users have more than one browser window open at once. In some instances, a script from one page should be allowed to access data from another page or object, but in others, this should be strictly forbidden, as a malicious Web site could attempt to steal sensitive information this way. For this reason, the same-origin policy was introduced. Essentially, this policy allows any interaction between objects and pages, so long as these objects come from the same domain and over the same protocol. That way, a malicious Web site would not be able to access sensitive data in another browser window via JavaScript.

Since then, other similar access-control policies have been adopted in other browsers and client-side scripting languages to protect users from malicious Web sites. In general, cross-site scripting holes can be seen as vulnerabilities which allow attackers to bypass these mechanisms. By finding clever ways of injecting malicious script into pages served by other domains, an attacker can gain elevated access privileges to sensitive page content, session cookies, and a variety of other objects.

3. Terminology

The term cross-site scripting is not a very accurate description of this class of vulnerability. In the words of XSS pioneer Marc Slemko:

This issue isn't just about scripting, and there isn't necessarily anything cross-site about it. It was coined earlier on when the problem was less understood, and it stuck. Believe me; we have had more important things to do than think of a better name.

The acronym CSS was often used in the early days to refer to cross-site scripting vulnerabilities, but this quickly became confusing in technical circles because both Cascading Style Sheets and the Content-scrambling system shared the same acronym. Perhaps the first use of the abbreviation XSS was by Steve Champeon in his Webmonkey article "XSS, Trust, and Barney". In 2002, Steve also posted the suggestion of using XSS as an alternative abbreviation to the Bugtraq mailing list. In a rare show of unity, the security community quickly adopted the alternative, and CSS is seldom used today to refer to cross-site scripting.

4. Types

There are three distinct known types of XSS vulnerability to date. (These will be labeled Type 0, Type 1, and Type 2 for the purposes of this discussion, but these names are by no means industry standard nomenclature. Other names for these will be provided.)

(1) Type 0

This form of XSS vulnerability has been referred to as DOM-based or Local cross-site scripting, and while it is not new by any means, a recent paper (DOM-Based cross-site scripting) does a good job of defining its characteristics. With Type 0 cross-site scripting vulnerabilities, the problem exists within a page's client-side script itself. For instance, if a piece of JavaScript accesses a URL request parameter and uses this information to write some HTML to its own page, and this information is not encoded using HTML entities, an XSS hole will likely be present, since this written data will be re-interpreted by browsers as HTML which could include additional client-side script.

In practice, exploiting such a hole would be very similar to the exploit of Type 1 vulnerabilities (see below), except in one very important situation. Because of the way Internet Explorer treats client-side script in objects located in the "local zone" (for instance, on the client's local hard drive), an XSS hole of this kind in a local page can result in remote execution vulnerabilities. For example, if an attacker hosts a malicious website, which contains a link to a vulnerable page on a client's local system, a script could be injected and would run with privileges of that user's browser on their system. This bypasses the entire client-side sandbox, not just the cross-domain restrictions that are normally bypassed with XSS exploits.

(2) Type 1

This kind of cross-site scripting hole is also referred to as a non-persistent or reflected vulnerability, and is by far the most common type. These holes show up when data

Chapter 7　Computer Virus

provided by a web client is used immediately by server-side scripts to generate a page of results for that user. If invalidated user-supplied data is included in the resulting page without HTML encoding, this will allow client-side code to be injected into the dynamic page. A classic example of this is in site search engines: if one searches for a string which includes some HTML special characters, often the search string will be redisplayed on the result page to indicate what was searched for, or will at least include the search terms in the text box for easier editing. If all occurrences of the search terms are not HTML entity encoded, an XSS hole will result.

At first blush, this does not appear to be a serious problem since users can only inject code into their own pages. However, with a small amount of social engineering, an attacker could convince a user to follow a malicious URL which injects code into the results page, giving the attacker full access to that page's content. Due to the general requirement of the use of some social engineering in this case (and normally in Type 0 vulnerabilities as well), many programmers have disregarded these holes as not terribly important. This misconception is sometimes applied to XSS holes in general (even though this is only one type of XSS) and there is often disagreement in the security community as to the importance of cross-site scripting vulnerabilities.

(3) Type 2

This type of XSS vulnerability is also referred to as a stored or persistent or second-order vulnerability and it allows the most powerful kinds of attacks. A type 2 XSS vulnerability exists when data provided to a web application by a user is first stored persistently on the server (in a database, file system, or other location), and later displayed to users in a web page without being encoded using HTML entities. A classic example of this is with online message boards, where users are allowed to post HTML formatted messages for other users to read.

These vulnerabilities are usually more significant than other types because an attacker can inject the script just once. This could potentially hit a large number of other users with little need for social engineering or the web application could even be infected by a cross-site scripting virus.

The methods of injection can vary a great deal, and an attacker may not need to use the web application itself to exploit such a hole. Any data received by the web application (via E-mail, system logs, etc.) that can be controlled by an attacker must be encoded prior to re-display in a dynamic page, else an XSS vulnerability of this type could result.

5. Exploit Scenarios

Attackers intending to exploit cross-site scripting vulnerabilities must approach

English for Information Security

each class of vulnerability differently. For each class, a specific attack vector is described here. (The names below come from the cast of characters commonly used in computer security.)

(1) Type-0 attack
- Mallory sends a URL to Alice (via E-mail or another mechanism) of a maliciously constructed web page;
- Alice clicks on the link;
- The malicious web page's JavaScript opens a vulnerable HTML page installed locally on Alice's computer;
- The vulnerable HTML page is tricked into executing JavaScript in the computer's local zone;
- Mallory's malicious script now may run commands with the privileges Alice holds on her own computer.

(2) Type-1 attack
- Alice often visits a particular website, which is hosted by Bob. Bob's website allows Alice to log in with a username/password pair and store sensitive information, such as billing information.
- Mallory observes that Bob's website contains a reflected XSS vulnerability.
- Mallory crafts a URL to exploit the vulnerability, and sends Alice an E-mail, making it look as if it came from Bob (i.e., the E-mail is spoofed).
- Alice visits the URL provided by Mallory while logged into Bob's website.
- The malicious script embedded in the URL executes in Alice's browser, as if it came directly from Bob's server. The script steals sensitive information (authentication credentials, billing info, etc.) and sends this to Mallory's web server without Alice's knowledge.

(3) Type-2 attack
- Bob hosts a web site which allows users to post messages and other content to the site for later viewing by other members.
- Mallory notices that Bob's website is vulnerable to a type-2 XSS attack.
- Mallory posts a message, controversial in nature, which may encourage many other users of the site to view it.
- Upon merely viewing the posted message, site users' session cookies or other credentials could be taken and sent to Mallory's Web server without their knowledge.
- Later, Mallory logs in as other site users and posts messages on their behalf.

Please note, the preceding examples are merely a representation of common methods of exploit and are not meant to encompass all vectors of attack.

6. Real-World Examples

There are literally hundreds of examples of cross-site scripting vulnerabilities available publicly. Just a few examples to illustrate the different types of holes will be listed here.

- An example of a type-0 vulnerability was once found in an error page produced by Bugzilla where JavaScript was used to write the current URL, through the document. location variable, to the page without any filtering or encoding. In this case, an attacker who controlled the URL might have been able to inject script, depending on the behavior of the browser in use. This vulnerability was fixed by encoding the special characters in the document. location string prior to writing it to the page.

- Two type-1 XSS vulnerabilities were exploited humorously through a fake news summary which claimed President Bush appointed a 9 year old boy to be the chairperson of the Information Security Department. This claim was backed up with links to cbsnews. com and www. bbc. co. uk, both of which were vulnerable to separate XSS holes which allowed the attackers to inject an article of their choosing.

- An example of a type-2 vulnerability was found in Hotmail, in October of 2001 by Marc Slemko, which allowed an attacker to steal a user's Microsoft. NET Passport session cookies. The exploit for this vulnerability consisted of sending a malicious E-mail to a Hotmail user, which contained malformed HTML. The script filtering code in Hotmail's site failed to remove the broken HTML and Internet Explorer's parsing algorithm happily interpreted the malicious code. This problem was quickly fixed, but multiple similar problems were found in Hotmail and other Passport sites later on.

- Netcraft announced on June 16, 2006. A security flaw in the PayPal web site is being actively exploited by fraudsters to steal credit card numbers and other personal information belonging to PayPal users. The issue was reported to Netcraft via their own anti-phishing toolbar. Soon after, Paypal reported that a "change in some of the code" on the Paypal website had removed the vulnerability.

- On October 13, 2005 Samy exploited a security flaw in MySpace resulting in over one million friend requests being made to its creator's profile. Qualifying as a type 2 vulnerability, it used multiple XMLHttpRequests to propagate itself.

- An XSS vulnerability in Community Architect Guestbook was disclosed by Susam Pal on April 19,2006 which can be exploited by malicious people to conduct script insertion attacks. As a result, many free web-hosting services which used the guestbook were vulnerable to such attacks.

7. Avoiding XSS Vulnerabilities

Reliable avoidance of cross-site scripting vulnerabilities currently requires the encoding of all HTML special characters in potentially malicious data. This is generally done right before display by web applications (or client-side script), and many programming languages have built-in functions or libraries which provide this encoding (in this context, also called quoting or escaping).

An example of this kind of quoting is shown below, from within the Python interpreter:

```
~> python
Python 2.3.5 (#2,Aug 30 2005,15:50:26)
Type "help","copyright","credits" or "license" for more information.
>>> import cgi

>>> print "<script>alert('xss');</script>"
<script>alert('xss');</script>

>>> print cgi.escape("<script>alert('xss');</script>");
&lt;script&gt;alert('xss');&lt;/script&gt;
```

Here, the first print statement produces executable client-side script, whereas the second print statement outputs a string which is an HTML-quoted version of the original script. The quoted versions of these characters will appear as literals in a browser, rather than with their special meaning as HTML tags. This prevents any script from being injected into HTML output, but it also prevents any user-supplied input from being formatted with benign HTML.

The ultimate problem with trying to avoid XSS vulnerabilities is that every situation is different. For any given situation, the needs and the issues change. For instance, if user input is going into the src attribute of a hyperlink, cgi. escape() would not be sufficient. Let's say a picture was to be added to a page of pictures, in this fashion:

```
<img src='$url'>
```

An attacker could enter "doesntexist. jpg' onerror='alert(document. cookie)" to add an event which triggers when the browser fails to load "doesntexist.jpg", executing the code.

If one were to implement a function like cgi.escape() (which comes with Python), one would be best off converting all but known-safe characters to their equivalent HTML entity. Because browsers implement complex (and often buggy) parsing algorithms for HTML (in all of its flavors), it is difficult to predict what characters could be treated as special. In particular, support for Unicode character sets by browsers could leave an application open to XSS attacks if the HTML quoting algorithms only look for known-bad characters.

As stated above, the unfortunate consequence of this fix is that users are prevented from embedding non-malicious HTML into pages. Because HTML standards do not provide any simple mechanism to disable client-side scripts in specific portions of a webpage, it is difficult to reliably cleanse script from normal HTML. The most reliable method is for web applications to parse the HTML, strip tags and attributes that do not appear in a white list, and output valid HTML.

7.2.7 Trojan Horse

Trojan horses are impostor files that claim to be something desirable but, in fact, are malicious. Rather than insert code into existing files, a Trojan horse appears to do one thing (install a screen saver, or show a picture inside an E-mail for example) when in fact it does something entirely different, and potentially malicious, such as erase files. Trojans can also open back doors so that computer hackers can gain access to passwords, and other personal information stored on a computer.

Although often referred to as such, Trojan horses are not viruses in the strict sense because they cannot replicate automatically. For a Trojan horse to spread, it must be invited onto a computer by the user opening an E-mail attachment or downloading and running a file from the Internet, for example.

7.2.8 Computer Worm

A computer worm is a piece of software that uses computer networks and security flaws to create copies of itself. A copy of the worm will scan the network for any other machine that has a specific security flaw. It replicates itself to the new machine using the security flaw, and then begins scanning and replicating anew.

Worms are programs that replicate themselves from system to system without the use of a host file. This is in contrast to viruses, which requires the spreading of an infected host file. Although worms generally exist inside of other files, often Word or Excel documents, there is a difference between how worms and viruses use the host file. Usually the worm will release a document that already has the "worm" macro inside the document. The entire document will travel from computer to computer, so the entire document should be considered the worm. Mydoom is an example of a worm.

Unlike a virus, a computer worm does not need to attach itself to an existing program. Worms always harm the network (if only by consuming bandwidth), whereas viruses always infect or corrupt files on a targeted computer.

1. Naming and History

The name "worm" comes from The Shockwave Rider, a science fiction novel published in 1975 by John Brunner. Researchers John F. Shoch and John A. Hupp of Xerox PARC chose the name in a paper published in 1982(The Worm Programs, Comm ACM, 25(3):172-180,1982), and it has since been widely adopted.

The first implementation of a worm was by the same two researchers at Xerox PARC in 1978. Shoch and Hupp originally designed the worm to find idle processors on the network and assign them tasks, sharing the processing load, and so improving the "CPU cycle use efficiency" across an entire network. They were self-limited so that they would spread no farther than intended.

Though it was technically a Trojan horse, the Christmas Tree Worm was likely the first worm on a worldwide network, spreading across both IBM's own international network and BITNET in December 1987, bringing both networks to their knees.

An early worm on the Internet, and the first to attract wide attention, was the Morris worm. It was also termed "The Internet Worm" by Peter Denning in an article in American Scientist (March April, 1988) in which he distinguished between a virus and a worm, thereby becoming an early computer zoologist. His definition was more restricted than that of some other computer zoologists of the time (McAfee and Haynes, Computer Viruses, Worms, Data Diddlers, ⋯, St Martin's Press, 1989). The Morris worm was written by Robert Tappan Morris, at the time a computer science graduate student at Cornell University, and released on November 2,1988 using a friend's account on a Harvard University computer. It quickly infected large numbers of computers attached to the Internet and caused massive disruption. That it didn't spread even farther and cause more trouble is largely due to some errors in its implementation. It propagated via several bugs in BSD Unix and related systems, and its component programs (including several versions of "sendmail"). Morris was identified, confessed, and was later convicted under the US Computer Crime and Abuse Act. He received three years probation, 400 hours community service and a fine in excess of $10 000.

2. Types of Computer Worms

E-mail Worms Spread via E-mail messages. Typically the worm will arrive as E-mail, where the message body or attachment contains the worm code, but it may also link to code on an external website. Poor design aside, most E-mail systems requires the user to explicitly open an attachment to activate the worm, but "social engineering" can often successfully be used to encourage this; as the author of the "Anna Kournikova" worm set out to prove. Once activated the worm will send itself out using either local E-mail systems (e. g. , MS Outlook services, Windows MAPI functions), or directly using SMTP. The addresses it sends to are often harvested from the infected computers E-mail system or files. Since Klez. E in 2002, worms using SMTP typically fake the sender's address, so recipients of E-mail worms should assume that they are not sent by the person listed in the "From" field of E-mail message (sender's address).

Instant messaging worms The spreading used is via instant messaging applications by sending links to infected websites to everyone on the local contact list. The only difference between these and E-mail worms is the way chosen to send the links.

IRC worms Chat channels are the main target and the same infection/spreading method is used as above—sending infected files or links to infected websites. Infected file sending is less effective as the recipient needs to confirm receipt, save the file and open it before infection will take place.

File-sharing networks worms Copies itself into a shared folder, most likely located on the local machine. The worm will place a copy of itself in a shared folder under a harmless name. Now the worm is ready for download via the P2P network and spreading of the infected file will continue.

Internet worms Those which target low level TCP/IP ports directly, rather than going via higher level protocols such as E-mail or IRC. A classic example is "Blaster" which exploited vulnerability in Microsoft's RPC. An infected machine aggressively scans random computers on both its local network and the public Internet attempting an exploit against port 135 which, if successful, spreads the worm to that machine.

3. Payloads

Many worms have been created which are only designed to spread, and don't attempt to alter the systems they pass through. However, as the Morris worm and Mydoom showed, the network traffic and other unintended effects can often cause major disruption. A "payload" is code designed to do more than spread the worm—it might delete files on a host system (e. g. , the ExploreZip worm), encrypt files in a cryptoviral extortion attack, or send documents via E-mail. A very common payload for worms is to install a backdoor in the infected computer to allow the creation of a "zombie" under control of the worm author—Sobig and Mydoom are examples which created zombies. Network of such machines are often referred to as botnets and are very commonly used by spam senders for sending junk E-mail or to cloak their website's address. Spammers are therefore thought to be a source of funding for the creation of such worms, and worm writers have been caught selling lists of IP addresses of infected machines. Others try to blackmail companies with threatened DoS attacks.

Backdoors, however they may be installed, can be exploited by other malwares, including worms. Examples include Doomjuice, which spreads using the backdoor opened by Mydoom, and at least one instance of malware taking advantage of the rootkit backdoor installed by the Sony/BMG DRM software they put on millions of music CDs ending in late 2005.

4. Worms with Good Intent

Whether worms can be useful is a common conundrum amongst theorists in computer science and artificial intelligence, beginning with the very first research into them at Xerox PARC. The Nachi family of worms, for example, tried to download then install patches from Microsoft's website to fix various vulnerabilities in the host system—the same vulnerabilities the Nachi worm itself exploited. This eventually made the systems affected more secure, but generated considerable network traffic (sometimes more traffic than the worms they were protecting against), rebooted the machine in the course of patching it, and most importantly, did its work without the explicit consent of the computer's owner or user. As such, most security experts regard worms as malware, whatever their payload or their writers' intentions.

5. Protecting against Computer Worms

Worms mainly spread by exploiting vulnerabilities in operating systems, or by tricking users to assist them.

All vendors supply regular security updates (see "Patch Tuesday"), and if these were installed to a machine then the majority of worms are unable to spread to it. If a vendor acknowledges a vulnerability but has yet to release a security update to patch it a zero day exploit is possible, but these are relatively rare.

Users need to be wary of opening unexpected E-mail, and certainly should not run attached files or programs, or visit web sites which such E-mail link to. However, as the ILOVEYOU showed long ago, and phishing attacks continue to prove, tricking a percentage of users will always be possible.

Anti-virus and anti-spyware software are helpful, but must be kept up-to-date with

Chapter 7　Computer Virus

new pattern files at least every few days.

7.3　Why People Create Computer Viruses

　　Unlike biological viruses, computer viruses do not simply evolve by themselves. Computer viruses do not come into existence spontaneously, nor are they likely to be created by bugs in regular programs. They are deliberately created by programmers, or by people who use virus creation software. Computer viruses can only do what the programmers have programmed them to do.

　　Virus writers can have various reasons for creating and spreading malware. Viruses have been written as research projects, pranks, vandalism, to attack the products of specific companies, to distribute political messages, and financial gain from identity theft, spyware, and cryptoviral extortion. Some virus writers consider their creations to be works of art, and see virus writing as a creative hobby. Additionally, many virus writers oppose deliberately destructive payload routines. Some viruses were intended as "good viruses". They spread improvements to the programs they infect, or delete other viruses. These viruses are, however, quite rare, still consume system resources, may accidentally damage systems they infect, and, on occasion, have become infected and acted as vectors for malicious viruses. A poorly written "good virus" can also inadvertently become a virus in and of itself (for example, such a "good virus" may misidentify its target file and delete an innocent system file by mistake). Moreover, they normally operate without asking for the permission of the computer owner. Since self-replicating code causes many complications, it is questionable if a well-intentioned virus can ever solve a problem in a way that is superior to a regular program that does not replicate itself.

　　Releasing computer viruses (as well as worms) is a crime in most jurisdictions.

7.4　Replication Strategies

　　In order to replicate itself, a virus must be permitted to execute code and write to memory. For this reason, many viruses attach themselves to executable files that may be part of legitimate programs. If a user tries to start an infected program, the virus' code may be executed first. Viruses can be divided into two types, on the basis of their behavior when they are executed. Nonresident viruses immediately search for other hosts that can be infected, infect these targets, and finally transfer control to the application program they infected. Resident viruses do not search for hosts when they are started. Instead, a resident virus loads itself into memory on execution and transfers control to the host program. The virus stays active in the background and infects new hosts when those files are accessed by other programs or the operating system itself.

7.4.1 Nonresident Viruses

Nonresident viruses can be thought of as consisting of a finder module and a replication module. The finder module is responsible for finding new files to infect. For each new executable file the finder module encounters, it calls the replication module to infect that file.

For simple viruses the replicator's tasks are to:

(1) Open the new file;

(2) Check if the executable file has already been infected (if it is, return to the finder module);

(3) Append the virus code to the executable file;

(4) Save the executable's starting point;

(5) Change the executable's starting point so that it points to the start location of the newly copied virus code;

(6) Save the old start location to the virus in a way so that the virus branches to that location right after its execution;

(6) Save the changes to the executable file;

(8) Close the infected file;

(9) Return to the finder so that it can find new files for the replicator to infect.

7.4.2 Resident Viruses

Resident viruses contain a replication module that is similar to the one that is employed by nonresident viruses. However, this module is not called by a finder module. Instead, the virus loads the replication module into memory when it is executed and ensures that this module is executed each time the operating system is called to perform a certain operation. For example, the replication module can be called each time the operating system executes a file. In this case, the virus infects every suitable program that is executed on the computer.

Resident viruses are sometimes subdivided into a category of fast infectors and a category of slow infectors. Fast infectors are designed to infect as many files as possible. For instance, a fast infector can infect every potential host file that is accessed. This poses a special problem to anti-virus software, since a virus scanner will access every potential host file on a computer when it performs a system-wide scan. If the virus scanner fails to notice that such a virus is present in memory, the virus can "piggy-back" on the virus scanner and in this way infect all files that are scanned. Fast infectors rely on their fast infection rate to spread. The disadvantage of this method is that infecting many files may make detection more likely, because the virus may slow down a computer or perform many suspicious actions that can be noticed by anti-virus software. Slow infectors, on the other hand, are designed to infect hosts infrequently. For instance, some slow infectors only infect files when they are copied. Slow infectors are designed to avoid detection by limiting their actions: they are less likely to slow down a computer noticeably, and will at most infrequently trigger anti-virus software that detects suspicious behavior by programs. The slow infector approach does not seem very successful however.

7.4.3 Host Types

Viruses have targeted various types of hosts. This is a non-exhaustive list:
- Binary executable files (such as COM files and EXE files in MS-DOS, Portable Executable files in Microsoft Windows, and ELF files in Linux);
- Volume Boot Records of floppy disks and hard disk partitions;
- The master boot record (MBR) of a hard disk;
- General-purpose script files (such as batch files in MS-DOS and Microsoft Windows, VBScript files, and shell script files on Unix-like platforms);
- Application-specific script files (such as Telix-scripts);
- Documents that can contain macros (such as Microsoft Word documents, Microsoft Excel spreadsheets, AmiPro documents, and Microsoft Access database files).

7.5 Methods to Avoid Detection

In order to avoid detection by users, some viruses employ different kinds of deceptions. Some old viruses, especially on the MS-DOS platform, make sure that the "last modified" date of a host file stays the same when the file is infected by the virus. This approach does not fool anti-virus software, however.

Some viruses can infect files without increasing their sizes or damaging the files. They accomplish this by overwriting unused areas of executable files. These are called cavity viruses. For example the CIH virus, or Chernobyl Virus, infects Portable Executable files. Because those files had many empty gaps, the virus, which was 1 KB in length, did not add to the size of the file.

Some viruses try to avoid detection by killing the tasks associated with anti-virus software before it can detect them.

As computers and operating systems grow larger and more complex, old hiding techniques need to be updated or replaced.

7.5.1 Avoiding Bait Files and Other Undesirable Hosts

A virus needs to infect hosts in order to spread further. In some cases, it might be a bad idea to infect a host program. For example, many anti-virus programs perform an integrity check of their own code. Infecting such programs will therefore increase the likelihood that the virus is detected. For this reason, some viruses are programmed not to infect programs that are known to be part of anti-virus software. Another type of hosts that viruses sometimes avoid is bait files. Bait files (or goat files) are files that are specially created by anti-virus software, or by anti-virus professionals themselves, to be infected by a virus. These files can be created for various reasons, all of which are related to the detection of the virus:

- Anti-virus professionals can use bait files to take a sample of a virus (i.e., a copy of a program file that is infected by the virus). It is more practical to store and exchange a small, infected bait file, than to exchange a large application program that has been infected by the virus.
- Anti-virus professionals can use bait files to study the behavior of a virus and evaluate detection methods. This is especially useful when the virus is polymorphic. In this case, the virus can be made to infect a large number of bait files. The infected files can be used to test whether a virus scanner detects all versions of the virus.
- Some anti-virus software employs bait files that are accessed regularly. When these files are modified, the anti-virus software warns the user that a virus is probably active on the system.

Since bait files are used to detect the virus, or to make detection possible, a virus can benefit from not infecting them. Viruses typically do this by avoiding suspicious programs, such as small program files or programs that contain certain patterns of "garbage instructions".

A related strategy to make baiting difficult is sparse infection. Sometimes, sparse infectors do not infect a host file that would be a suitable candidate for infection in other circumstances. For example, a virus can decide on a random basis whether to infect a file or not, or a virus can only infect host files on particular days of the week.

7.5.2 Stealth

Some viruses try to trick anti-virus software by intercepting its requests to the operating system. A virus can hide itself by intercepting the anti-virus software's request to read the file and passing the request to the virus, instead of the OS. The virus can then return an uninfected version of the file to the anti-virus software, so that it seems that the file is "clean". Modern anti-virus software employs various techniques to counter stealth mechanisms of viruses. The only completely reliable method to avoid stealth is to boot from a medium that is known to be clean.

7.5.3 Self-modification

Most modern antivirus programs try to find virus-patterns inside ordinary programs by scanning them for so-called virus signatures. A signature is a characteristic byte-pattern that is part of a certain virus or family of viruses. If a virus scanner finds such a pattern in a file, it notifies the user that the file is infected. The user can then delete, or (in some cases) "clean" or "heal" the infected file. Some viruses employ techniques that make detection by means of signatures difficult or impossible. These viruses modify their code on each infection. That is, each infected file contains a different variant of the virus.

7.5.4 Simple Self-modifications

In the past, some viruses modified themselves only in simple ways. For example, they regularly exchanged subroutines in their code for others that would perform the same action—for example, 2+2 could be swapped for 1+3. This poses no problems to a somewhat advanced virus scanner.

7.5.5　Encryption with a Variable Key

A more advanced method is the use of simple encryption to encipher the virus. In this case, the virus consists of a small decrypting module and an encrypted copy of the virus code. If the virus is encrypted with a different key for each infected file, the only part of the virus that remains constant is the decrypting module, which would (for example) be appended to the end. In this case, a virus scanner cannot directly detect the virus using signatures, but it can still detect the decrypting module, which still makes indirect detection of the virus possible.

Mostly, the decryption techniques that these viruses employ are simple and mostly done by just XORing each byte with a randomized key that was saved by the parent virus. The use of XOR-operations has the additional advantage that the encryption and decryption routine are the same (a XOR b = c, c XOR b = a).

7.5.6　Polymorphic Code

Polymorphic code was the first technique that posed a serious threat to virus scanners. Just like regular encrypted viruses, a polymorphic virus infects files with an encrypted copy of itself, which is decoded by a decryption module. In the case of polymorphic viruses however, this decryption module is also modified on each infection. A well-written polymorphic virus therefore has no parts that stay the same on each infection, making it impossible to detect directly using signatures. Anti-virus software can detect it by decrypting the viruses using an emulator, or by statistical pattern analysis of the encrypted virus body. To enable polymorphic code, the virus has to have a polymorphic engine (also called mutating engine or mutation engine) somewhere in its encrypted body. See Polymorphic code for technical detail on how such engines operate.

Some viruses employ polymorphic code in a way that constrains the mutation rate of the virus significantly. For example, a virus can be programmed to mutate only slightly over time, or it can be programmed to refrain from mutating when it infects a file on a computer that already contains copies of the virus. The advantage of using such slow polymorphic code is that it makes it more difficult for anti-virus professionals to obtain representative samples of the virus, because bait files that are infected in one run will typically contain identical or similar samples of the virus. This will make it more likely that the detection by the virus scanner will be unreliable, and that some instances of the virus may be able to avoid detection.

7.5.7 Metamorphic Code

To avoid being detected by emulation, some viruses rewrite themselves completely each time they are to infect new executables. Viruses that use this technique are said to be metamorphic. To enable metamorphism, a metamorphic engine is needed. A metamorphic virus is usually very large and complex. For example, W32/Simile consisted of over 14 000 lines of Assembly language code, 90% of it part of the metamorphic engine.

7.6 Vulnerability and Countermeasures

7.6.1 The Vulnerability of Operating Systems to Viruses

Another analogy to biological viruses: just as genetic diversity in a population decreases the chance of a single disease wiping out a population, the diversity of software systems on a network similarly limits the destructive potential of viruses.

This became a particular concern in the 1990s, when Microsoft gained market dominance in desktop operating systems and office suites. The users of Microsoft software (especially networking software such as Microsoft Outlook and Internet Explorer) are especially vulnerable to the spread of viruses. Microsoft software is targeted by virus writers due to their desktop dominance, and is often criticized for including many errors and holes for virus writers to exploit. Integrated applications, applications with scripting languages with access to the file system (for example Visual Basic Script (VBS), and applications with networking features) are also particularly vulnerable.

Although Windows is by far the most popular operating system for virus writers, some viruses also exist on other platforms. Any operating system that allows third-party programs to run can theoretically run viruses. Some operating systems are less secure than others. Unix-based OS's (and NTFS-aware applications on Windows NT based platforms) only allow their users to run executables within their protected space in their own directories.

As of 2006, there are relatively few security exploits targeting Mac OS X (a Unix-based operating system); The known vulnerabilities fall under the classifications of worms and Trojans. The number of viruses for the older Apple operating systems, known as Mac OS Classic, varies greatly from source to source, with Apple stating that there are only four known viruses, and independent sources stating there are as many as 63 viruses. However, Mac users are advised to install anti-virus software, because they can accidentally pass on a file that is infected with a Windows virus or Trojan. While this malware does not affect the Mac, it can infect a Windows PC. It is safe to say that Macs are less likely to be exploited due to their secure Unix base, and because a Mac-specific virus could only infect a small proportion of computers (making the effort less desirable). Virus vulnerability between Macs and Windows was/is a chief catalyst of the platform wars between Apple Computers and Microsoft.

Windows and Unix have similar scripting abilities, but while Unix natively blocks normal users from having access to make changes to the operating system environment, Windows does not. In 1997, when a virus for Linux was released—known as "Bliss"—leading antivirus vendors issued warnings that Unix-like systems could fall prey to viruses just like Windows. The Bliss virus may be considered characteristic of viruses—as opposed to worms—on Unix systems. Bliss requires that the user run it explicitly, and it can only infect programs that the user has the access to modify. Unlike Windows users, most Unix users do not log in as an administrator user except to install or configure software; as a result, even if a user ran the virus, it could not harm their operating system. The Bliss virus never became widespread, and remains chiefly a research curiosity. Its creator later posted the source code to Usenet, allowing researchers to see how it worked.

7.6.2 The Role of Software Development

Because software is often designed with security features to prevent unauthorized use of system resources, many viruses must exploit software bugs in a system or application to spread. Software development strategies that produce large numbers of bugs will generally also produce potential exploits.

Closed-source software development, as practiced by Microsoft and other proprietary software companies, is seen by many as a security weakness. Open source software such as Linux, for example, allows all users to look for and fix security problems without relying on a single vendor. Some advocate that proprietary software makers practice vulnerability disclosure to improve this weakness.

On the other hand, some claim that open source development exposes potential security problems to virus writers, hence increases in the prevalence of exploits. They claim that popular closed source systems such as Windows are often exploited by claiming that these systems are only commonly exploited due to their popularity and the potential widespread effect such an exploit will have.

7.6.3 Anti-virus Software and Other Countermeasures

There are two common methods that an anti-virus software application uses to detect viruses. The first, and by far the most common method of virus detection is using a list of virus signature definitions. The disadvantage of this detection method is that users are only protected from viruses that pre-date their last virus definition update. The second method is to use a heuristic algorithm to find viruses based on common behaviors. This method has the ability to detect viruses that anti-virus security firms' have yet to create a signature for.

Many users install anti-virus software that can detect and eliminate known viruses after the computer downloads or runs the executable. They work by examining the content heuristics of the computer's memory (its RAM, and boot sectors) and the files stored on fixed or removable drives (hard drives, floppy drives), and comparing those files against a database of known virus "signatures". Some anti-virus programs are able to scan opened files in addition to sent and received E-mails "on the fly" in a similar manner. This practice is known as "on-access scanning". Anti-virus software does not change the underlying capability of host software to transmit viruses. There have been attempts to do this but adoption of such anti-virus solutions can void the warranty for the host software. Users must therefore update their software regularly to patch security holes. Anti-virus software also needs to be regularly updated in order to gain knowledge about the latest threats.

One may also prevent the damage done by viruses by making regular backups of data (and the Operating Systems) on different media, that are either kept unconnected to the system (most of the time), read-only or not accessible for other reasons, such as using different file systems. This way, if data is lost through a virus, one can start again using the backup (which should preferably be recent). If a backup session on optical media like CD and DVD is closed, it becomes read-only and can no longer be affected by a virus. Likewise, an Operating System on a live CD can be used to start the computer if the installed Operating Systems become unusable. Another method is to use different Operating Systems on different file systems. A virus is not likely to affect both. Data

English for Information Security

backups can also be put on different file systems. For example, Linux requires specific software to write to NTFS partitions, so if one does not install such software and uses a separate installation of MS Windows to make the backups on an NTFS partition (and preferably only for that reason), the backup should remain safe from any Linux viruses. Likewise, MS Windows can not read file systems like ext3, so if one normally uses MS Windows, the backups can be made on an ext3 partition using a Linux installation.

Glossary

anti-virus software	反病毒软件
boot sector virus	引导区病毒
companion virus	同伴病毒
computer virus	计算机病毒
computer worm	计算机蠕虫
countermeasure	对策,反措施
hobbyist	沉溺于某种癖好者
illicit	违法的
infection	传染
jurisdictions	法学
logic bomb	逻辑炸弹
macro virus	宏病毒
metamorphic	变形的,变质的
mutation	变异
nonresident virus	非常驻病毒
resident viruses	常驻计算机的病毒
spontaneously	自然地,本能地
spyware	间谍软件

Translate the following sentences/passage into Chinese

(1) A computer virus is a self-replicating computer program written to alter the way a computer operates, without the permission or knowledge of the user. Though the term is commonly used to refer to a range of malware, a true virus must replicate itself, and must execute itself.

(2) Malware is a broad category of software designed to infiltrate or damage a computer system. Types of malware include spyware, adware, Trojan horses, Worms, and true viruses. While modern anti-virus software works to protect computers from this

Chapter 7 Computer Virus

range of threats, computer viruses make up only a small subset of malware.

(3) Some viruses are programmed to damage the computer by damaging programs, deleting files, or reformatting the hard disk. Others are not designed to do any damage, but simply replicate themselves and make their presence known by presenting text, video, or audio messages.

(4) The first PC virus was a boot sector virus called (c)Brain, created in 1986 by two brothers, Basit and Amjad Farooq Alvi, operating out of Lahore, Pakistan. The brothers reportedly created the virus to deter pirated copies of software they had written.

(5) Since the mid-1990s, macro viruses have become common. Most of these viruses are written in the scripting languages for Microsoft programs such as Word and Excel. These viruses spread in Microsoft Office by infecting documents and spreadsheets.

Translate the following sentences/passage into English

(1) 计算机病毒开始大肆流行是在1988年11月2日。美国康乃尔大学23岁的研究生罗特·莫里斯制作了一个蠕虫病毒,并将其投放到美国因特网上,致使计算机网络中的6 000多台计算机受到感染,许多联网计算机被迫停机,直接经济损失达9 600万美元。

(2) 计算机病毒是一种小程序,能够自我复制,会将自己的病毒码依附在其他程序上,通过其他程序的执行,伺机传播病毒程序,有一定潜伏期,一旦条件成熟,就进行各种破坏活动,影响计算机使用。

(3) 现在流行的病毒是由人为故意编写的,多数病毒可以找到作者信息和产地信息,通过大量的资料分析统计来看,病毒作者主要情况和目的是:一些天才的程序员为了表现自己和证明自己的能力,出于对上司的不满,为了好奇,为了报复,为了祝贺和求爱,为了得到控制口令,为了防止软件拿不到报酬预留的陷阱等。

(4) 混合型病毒并非简单的将文件型病毒和引导型病毒简单的加在一起,其中有一个转换过程,这是最关键的。一般采取以下手法:文件中的病毒执行时将病毒写入引导区,这是很容易理解的。

(5) 计算机病毒是客观存在的,客观存在的事物总有它的特性,计算机病毒也不例外。从实质上说,计算机病毒是一段程序代码,虽然它可能隐藏得很好,但也会留下许多痕迹。通过对这些蛛丝马迹的判别,我们就能发现计算机病毒的存在了。

Questions

(1) What is boot sector virus? How to prevent it?
(2) What is macro virus? How to prevent it?
(3) What is computer Trojan horse? How to prevent it?
(4) What is computer worm? How to prevent it?
(5) What is E-mail virus? How to prevent it?

Chapter 8

Public-Key Infrastructure

In cryptography, a public-key infrastructure (PKI) is an arrangement that provides for trusted third party vetting of, and vouching for, user identities. It also allows binding of public-keys to users. This is usually carried out by software at a central location together with other coordinated software at distributed locations. The public-keys are typically in certificates.

The term is used to mean both of the certificate authority and related arrangements as well as, more broadly and somewhat confusingly, the use of public-key algorithms in electronic communications. The latter sense is erroneous since PKI methods are not required to use public-key algorithms.

8.1 PKI Introduction

8.1.1 Purpose

The omnipresence of the Internet and e-commerce technologies present many opportunities, but also pose security and integrity issues. For e-commerce to flourish, businesses, customers, vendors, suppliers, regulatory agencies, and other stakeholders must be assured that trusted business relationships are maintained.

An illustration presents the point. If a merchant today has a physical presence at a store, that is, brick and mortar, and customers patronize them for goods and services, the merchant will typically request and receive payment for these directly from either the customers or their agent (e. g. ,their bank via the presentation of a monetary instrument such as a check), at the time that the goods and services were bargained for and/or provided. The process of exchanging goods and services for value is almost as universal as the rules by which those conversions take place. In many cases those rules are codified, in others they reflect accepted custom.

Whether systematic or custom, the processes in use today provide for the establishment of a trusted business relationship in that the customer and merchant both authenticate one another to the extent that they are willing to undertake the transaction. If an easily recognized monetary instrument like cash is used for transactions, there may be very little authentication which must occur. If a credit card or check is used, then the authentication may include the establishment of the customer's identity to the merchant. In addition, the authentication may also allow for a measure of non-repudiation to be set so that the customer does not deny the transaction occurred.

This traditional face-to-face transaction requires only minimal interaction and normally does not necessitate the use of other security and integrity mechanisms.

However, for e-commerce on the Internet, additional security and integrity mechanisms become necessary. Merchants are typically not willing to ship goods or perform services until a payment has been accepted for them. In addition, authentication can allow for a measure of non-repudiation so the customer cannot deny the transaction occurred. Similarly, consumers need assurance that they are purchasing from a legitimate enterprise, rather than a hacker's site whose sole purpose is to collect credit card numbers.

With the changes in today's business environments and the shift from the traditional face-to-face business models, mechanisms must be developed to ensure that trusted relationships are maintained and can flourish.

The implementation of a PKI is intended to provide mechanisms to ensure trusted relationships are established and maintained. The specific security functions in which a PKI can provide foundation are confidentiality, integrity, non-repudiation, and authentication.

8.1.2 Functions

PKI arrangements enable users to be authenticated to each other, and to use the information in identity certificates (i. e. , each other's public-keys) to encrypt and decrypt messages traveling to and fro. In general, a PKI consists of client software, server software such as a certificate authority, hardware (e. g. , smart cards) and operational procedures. A user may digitally sign messages using his private-key, and another user can check that signature (using the public-key contained in that user's certificate issued by a certificate authority within the PKI). This enables two (or more) communicating parties to establish confidentiality, message integrity and user authentication without having to exchange any secret information in advance.

A PKI enables users of a basically insecure public network such as the Internet to securely and privately exchange data and money through the use of a public and a private cryptographic key pair that is obtained and shared through a trusted authority. The public-key infrastructure provides for a digital certificate that can identify an individual or an organization and directory services that can store and, when necessary, revoke the certificates. Although the components of a PKI are generally understood, a number of different vendor approaches and services are emerging. Meanwhile, an Internet standard for PKI is being worked on.

The public-key infrastructure assumes the use of public-key cryptography, which is the most common method on the Internet for authenticating a message sender or encrypting a message. Traditional cryptography has usually involved the creation and sharing of a secret key for the encryption and decryption of messages. This secret or public-key system has the significant flaw that if the key is discovered or intercepted by someone else, messages can easily be decrypted. For this reason, public-key cryptography and the public-key infrastructure is the preferred approach on the Internet. (The private-key system is sometimes known as symmetric cryptography and the public-key system as asymmetric cryptography.)

A public-key infrastructure consists of:
- A certificate authority (CA) that issues and verifies digital certificate. A certificate includes the public-key or information about the public-key;
- A registration authority (RA) that acts as the verifier for the certificate authority before a digital certificate is issued to a requestor;
- One or more directories where the certificates (with their public-keys) are held;
- A certificate management system.

8.1.3 How Public and private-key Cryptography Works

In public-key cryptography, a public and private-key are created simultaneously by

Chapter 8 Public-Key Infrastructure

using the same algorithm (a popular one is known as RSA) by a CA. The private-key is given only to the requesting party and the public-key is made publicly available (as part of a digital certificate) in a directory that all parties can access. The private-key is never shared with anyone or sent across the Internet. You use the private-key to decrypt text that has been encrypted with your public-key by someone else (who can find out what your public-key is from a public directory). Thus, if I send you a message, I can find out your public-key (but not your private-key) from a central administrator and encrypt a message to you using your public-key. When you receive it, you decrypt it with your private-key. In addition to encrypting messages (which ensures privacy), you can authenticate yourself to me (so I know that it is really you who sent the message) by using your private-key to encrypt a digital certificate. When I receive it, I can use your public-key to decrypt it. Table 8.1 restates it:

Table 8.1 The use of public-key and private-key

To do this	Use whose	Kind of key
Send an encrypted message	Use the receiver's	public-key
Send an encrypted signature	Use the sender's	private-key
Decrypt an encrypted message	Use the receiver's	private-key
Decrypt an encrypted signature (and authenticate the sender)	Use the sender's	public-key

8.1.4 Who Provides the Infrastructure

A number of products are offered that enable a company or group of companies to implement a PKI. The acceleration of e-commerce and business-to-business commerce over the Internet has increased the demand for PKI solutions. Related ideas are the VPN and the IPSec standard. Among PKI leaders are:
- RSA, which has developed the main algorithms used by PKI vendors;
- Verisign, which acts as a certificate authority and sells software that allows a company to create its own certificate authorities;
- GTE CyberTrust, which provides a PKI implementation methodology and consultation service that it plans to vend to other companies for a fixed price;
- Xcert, whose Web Sentry product that checks the revocation status of certificates

on a server, using the Online Certificate Status Protocol (OCSP);
- Netscape, whose Directory Server product is said to support 50 million objects and process 5 000 queries a second; Secure E-Commerce, which allows a company or extranet manager to manage digital certificates; and Meta-Directory, which can connect all corporate directories into a single directory for security management.

8.1.5 PKI Typical Use

Most enterprise-scale PKI systems rely on certificate chains to establish a party's identity, as a certificate may have been issued by a certificate authority computer whose "legitimacy" is established for such purposes by a certificate issued by a higher-level certificate authority, and so on. This produces a certificate hierarchy composed of, at a minimum, several computers, often more than one organization, and often assorted interoperating software packages from several sources. Standards are critical to PKI operation, and public standards are critical to PKIs intended for extensive operation. Much of the standardization in this area is done by the IETF PKIX working group.

Enterprise PKI systems are often closely tied to an enterprise's directory scheme, in which each employee's public-key is often stored (embedded in a certificate), together with other personal details (phone number, E-mail address, location, department, ⋯). Today's leading directory technology is LDAP and in fact, the most common certificate format (X.509) stems from its use in LDAP's predecessor, the X.500 directory schema.

A PKI does not serve a particular business function; rather, a PKI provides a foundation for other security services. The primary function of a PKI is to allow the distribution and use of public-keys and certificates with security and integrity. A PKI is a foundation on which other applications and network security components are built. Systems that often require PKI-based security mechanisms include E-mail, various chip card applications, value exchange with e-commerce (e.g., debit and credit cards), home banking, and electronic postal systems.

A PKI has many uses and applications. As discussed later in this article, a PKI enables the basic security services for such varied systems as:
- SSL, IPSec and HTTPS for communication and transactional security (as shown in Figure 8.1);
- S/MIME and PGP for E-mail security;

- SET for value exchange;
- Identrus for B2B.

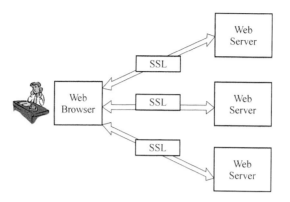

Figure 8.1 PKI used in SSL

Some key benefits that PKI and its use of public-key cryptography offers for e-commerce and other organizations are as follows:

- Reduces transactional processing expenses;
- Reduces and compartmentalizes risk;
- Enhances efficiency and performance of systems and networks;
- Reduces the complexity of security systems with binary symmetrical methods.

In addition, many other similar solutions rely on the fundamentals of public-key cryptography such as:

- Student IDs on college campuses;
- Voting;
- Anonymous value exchange;
- Transit ticketing;
- Identification (passports and drivers licenses);
- Notarization (contract, E-mails, etc.);
- Software distribution;
- Symmetric key management.

8.1.6 Alternatives

1. Web of Trust

An alternative approach to the problem of authentication of public-key information across time and space is the web of trust scheme, which uses self-signed certificates and third party attestations of those certificates. Examples of implementations of this approach are PGP (Pretty Good Privacy) and GnuPG (The GNU Privacy Guard; a free implementation of OpenPGP, the standardized specification of PGP). Because of PGP's (and clones') extensive use in E-mail, the Web of Trust originally implemented by PGP is the most widely deployed bidirectional PKI existing at this writing (2004).

2. Simple Public-Key Infrastructure

An even newer and rapidly growing alternative is the simple public-key infrastructure (SPKI) that grew out of 3 independent efforts to overcome the complexities of X.509 and the anarchy of PGP's web of trust. SPKI binds people/systems directly to keys using a local trust model, similar to PGP's web of trust, with the addition of authorization integral to its design.

8.1.7 PKI History

The public disclosure of both secure key exchange and asymmetric key algorithms in 1976 by Diffie, Hellman, and Rivest, Shamir, and Adleman changed secure communications entirely. With the further development of high speed digital electronic communications (the Internet and its predecessors), a need became evident for ways in which users could securely communicate with each other, and as a further consequence of that, for ways in which users could be sure with whom they were actually interacting. The idea of cryptographically protected certificates binding user identities to public-keys was eagerly developed.

Assorted cryptographic protocols were invented and analyzed within which the new cryptographic primitives could be effectively used. With the invention of the World Wide Web and its rapid spread, the need for authentication and secure communication became still more acute. Commercial reasons alone (e.g., e-commerce, on-line access to proprietary databases from Web browsers, etc.) were sufficient. Taher ElGamal and others at Netscape developed the SSL protocol ("https" in Web URLs); it included key establishment, server authentication (prior to v3, one-way only), and so on. A PKI structure was thus created for Web users/sites wishing secure (or more secure) communications.

Vendors and entrepreneurs saw the possibility of a large market, started companies (or new projects at existing companies), and began to agitate for legal recognition and protection from liability. An American Bar Association technology project published an extensive analysis of some of the foreseeable legal aspects of PKI operations (see ABA digital signature guidelines), and shortly thereafter, several US states (Utah being the first in 1995) and other jurisdictions throughout the world, began to enact laws and adopt regulations. Consumer groups and others raised questions of privacy, access, and liability considerations which were more taken into consideration in some jurisdictions than in others.

Chapter 8 Public-Key Infrastructure

The enacted laws and regulations differed, there were technical and operational problems in converting PKI schemes into successful commercial operation, and progress has been far slower than pioneers had imagined it would be.

By the first few years of the 21st century, it had become clear that the underlying cryptographic engineering was not easy to deploy correctly, that operating procedures (manual or automatic) were not easy to correctly design (nor even if so designed, to execute perfectly, which the engineering required), and that such standards as existed were in some respects inadequate to the purposes to which they were being put.

PKI vendors have found a market, but it is not quite the market envisioned in the mid-1990s, and it has grown both more slowly and in somewhat different ways than were anticipated. PKIs have not solved some of the problems they were expected to, and several major vendors have gone out of business or been acquired by others. PKI has had the most success in government implementations; the largest PKI implementation to date is the Defense Information Systems Agency (DISA) PKI infrastructure for the Common Access Cards program.

8.1.8 Usage Examples

PKIs of one type or another, and from any of several vendors, have many uses, including, providing public-keys and bindings to user identities which are used for:
- Encryption and/or sender authentication of E-mail messages(e. g. , using Open-PGP or S/MIME).
- Encryption and/or authentication of documents(e. g. , the XML Signature * or XML Encryption * standards if documents are encoded as XML).
- Authentication of users to applications(e. g. , smart card logon, client authentication with SSL).
- Bootstrapping secure communication protocols, such as Internet key exchange (IKE) and SSL. In both of these, initial set-up of a secure channel (a "security association") uses asymmetric key (a. k. a. public-key) methods, whereas actual communication uses faster secret key (a. k. a. symmetric key) methods.

8.2 Certificate Authority

In cryptography, a certificate authority or certification authority (CA) is an entity which issues digital certificates for use by other parties. It is an example of a trusted third party. CAs are characteristic of many PKI schemes.

There are many commercial CAs that charge for their services. Institutions and governments may have their own CAs, and there are free CAs.

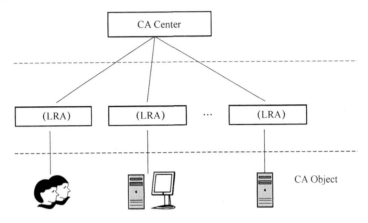

Figure 8.2 CA center

8.2.1 Issuing a Certificate

A CA will issue a public-key certificate which states that the CA attests that the public-key contained in the certificate belongs to the person, organization, server, or other entity noted in the certificate. A CA's obligation in such schemes is to verify an applicant's credentials, so that users (relying parties) can trust the information in the CA's certificates. The usual idea is that if the user trusts the CA and can verify the CA's signature, then they can also verify that a certain public-key does indeed belong to whomever is identified in the certificate.

If the CA can be subverted, then the security of the entire system is lost. Suppose an attacker, Mallory (to use the Alice and Bob convention), manages to get a certificate authority to issue a false certificate tying Alice to the wrong public-key, which corresponding private-key is known to Mallory. If Bob subsequently obtains and uses Alice's public-key in this (bogus) certificate, the security of his communications to her could be compromised by Mallory—for example, his messages could be decrypted, or he could be tricked into accepting forged signatures.

8.2.2 Security

The problem of assuring correctness of match between data and entity when the data are presented to the CA (perhaps over an electronic network), and when the credentials of the person/company/program asking for a certificate is likewise presented, is difficult, which is why commercial CAs often use a combination of authentication techniques including leveraging government bureaus, the payment infrastructure, the third parties' databases and services, and custom heuristics. In some enterprise systems, local forms of authentication such as Kerberos can be used to obtain a certificate which can in turn be used by external relying parties. Notaries are required in some cases to personally know the party whose signature is being notarized; this is a higher standard than can be reached for many CAs. According to the American Bar Association outline on Online Transaction Management the primary points of federal and state statutes that have been enacted regarding digital signatures in the United States has been to "prevent conflicting and overly burdensome local regulation and to establish that electronic writings satisfy the traditional requirements associated with paper documents". Further the E-Sign and UETA code help ensure that:

- A signature, contract or other record relating to such transaction may not be denied legal effect, validity, or enforceability solely because it is in electronic form;
- A contract relating to such transaction may not be denied legal effect, validity or enforceability solely because an electronic signature or electronic record was used in its formation.

In large-scale deployments, Alice may not be familiar with Bob's certificate authority (perhaps they each have a different CA), so Bob's certificate may also include his CA's public-key signed by a different CA2, which is presumably recognizable by Alice. This process typically leads to a hierarchy or mesh of CAs and CA certificates.

8.2.3 Public-Key Certificate

In cryptography, a public-key certificate (or identity certificate) is a certificate which uses a digital signature to bind together a public-key with an identity—information such as the name of a person or an organization, their address, and so forth. The certificate can be used to verify that a public-key belongs to an individual.

In a typical PKI scheme, the signature will be of a CA. In a web of trust scheme, the signature is of either the user (a self-signed certificate) or other users ("endorsements"). In either case, the signatures on a certificate are attestations by the certificate signer that the identity information and the public-key belong together.

1. Use

Certificates are useful for large-scale public-key cryptography. Securely exchanging secret keys amongst users becomes impractical to the point of effective impossibility for anything other than quite small networks. Public-key cryptography provides a way to avoid this problem. In principle, if Alice wants others to be able to send her secret messages, she need only publish her public-key. Anyone possessing it can then send her secure information. Unfortunately, David could publish a different public-key (for which he knows the related private-key) claiming that it is Alice's public-key. In so doing, David could intercept and read at least some of the messages meant for Alice. But if Alice builds her public-key into a certificate and has it digitally signed by a trusted third party (Trent), anyone who trusts Trent can merely check the certificate to see whether Trent thinks the embedded public-key is Alice's. In typical PKIs, Trent will be a CA, who is trusted by all participants. In a web of trust, Trent can be any user, and whether to trust that user's attestation that a particular public-key belongs to Alice will be up to the person wishing to send a message to Alice.

In large-scaled deployments, Alice may not be familiar with Bob's certificate authority (perhaps they each have a different CA—if both use employer CAs, different employers would produce this result), so Bob's certificate may also include his CA's public-key signed by a "higher level" CA2, which might be recognized by Alice. This process leads in general to a hierarchy of certificates, and to even more complex trust relationships. Public-key infrastructure refers, mostly, to the software that manages certificates in a large-scale setting. In X.509 PKI systems, the hierarchy of certificates is always a top-down tree, with a root certificate at the top, representing a CA that is "so central" to the scheme that it does not need to be authenticated by some trusted third party.

A certificate may be revoked if it is discovered that its related private-key has been compromised, or if the relationship (between an entity and a public-key) embedded in the certificate is discovered to be incorrect or has changed; this might occur, for example, if a person changes jobs or names. A revocation will likely be a rare occurrence, but the possibility means that when a certificate is trusted, the user should always check its validity. This can be done by comparing it against a certificate revocation list (CRL) —a list of revoked or cancelled certificates. Ensuring that such a list is up-to-date and accurate is a core function in a centralized PKI, one of which requires both staff and budget and one of which is therefore sometimes not properly done. To be effective, it must be readily available to any who needs it whenever it is needed and must be updated frequently. The other way to check a certificate validity is to query the certificate authority

Chapter 8 Public-Key Infrastructure

using the Online Certificate Status Protocol (OCSP) to know the status of a specific certificate.

Both of these methods appear to be on the verge of being supplanted by XKMS. This new standard, however, is yet to see widespread implementation.

A certificate typically includes:
- The public-key being signed;
- A name, which can refer to a person, a computer or an organization;
- A validity period;
- The location (URL) of a revocation center;
- The digital signature of the certificate, produced by the CA's private-key.

The most common certificate standard is the ITU-T X.509. X.509 is being adapted to the Internet by the IETF PKIX working group.

2. Classes

There three classes of digital certificates:
- Class 1 for individuals, intended for E-mail;
- Class 2 for organizations, for which proof of identity is required;
- Class 3 for servers and software signing, for which independent verification and checking of identity and authority is done by the issuing CA.

8.3 X.509

In cryptography, X.509 is an ITU-T standard for PKI. X.509 specifies, amongst other things, standard formats for public-key certificates and a certification path validation algorithm.

8.3.1 History and Usage

X.509 was initially issued in 1988 and was begun in association with the X.500 standard and assumed a strict hierarchical system of CAs for issuing the certificates. This contrasts with web of trust models, like PGP, where anyone (not just special CAs) may sign, and thus attest to the validity of others' key certificates. Version 3 of X.509 includes the flexibility to support other topologies like bridges and meshes. It can be used in a peer-to-peer, OpenPGP-like web of trust, but is rarely used that way as of 2004. The X.500 system has never been fully implemented, and the IETF's Public-Key

English for Information Security

Infrastructure (X.509), or PKIX, working group has adapted the standard to the more flexible organization of the Internet. In fact, the term X.509 certificate usually refers to the IETF's PKIX Certificate and CRL Profile of the X.509 v3 certificate standard, as specified in RFC 3280, commonly referred to as PKIX for Public-Key Infrastructure (X.509).

8.3.2 Certificates

In the X.509 system, a CA issues a certificate binding a public-key to a particular Distinguished Name in the X.500 tradition, or to an Alternative Name such as an E-mail address or a DNS-entry.

An organization's trusted root certificates can be distributed to all employees so that they can use the company PKI system. Browsers such as Internet Explorer, Netscape/Mozilla and Opera come with root certificates pre-installed, so SSL certificates from larger vendors who have paid for the privilege of being pre-installed will work instantly; in effect the browsers' owners determine which CAs are trusted third parties for the browsers' users. Although these root certificates can be removed or disabled, users rarely do so.

X.509 also includes standards for certificate revocation list (CRL) implementations, an often neglected aspect of PKI systems. The IETF-approved way of checking a certificate's validity is the OCSP.

1. Structure of a Certificate

The structure of a X.509 v3 digital certificate is as follows:

- Certificate
    - ◇ Version
    - ◇ Serial Number
    - ◇ Algorithm ID
    - ◇ Issuer
    - ◇ Validity
        - ○ Not Before
        - ○ Not After
    - ◇ Subject
    - ◇ Subject Public-Key Info
        - ○ Public-Key Algorithm
        - ○ Subject Public-Key
    - ◇ Issuer Unique Identifier (Optional)

◇Subject Unique Identifier (Optional)

◇Extensions (Optional)

- Certificate Signature Algorithm
- Certificate Signature

Issuer and subject unique identifiers were introduced in Version 2, Extensions in Version 3.

2. Certificate File Extensions

Common file extensions for X.509-certificates are:

- .CER—CER encoded certificate, sometimes sequence of certificates.
- .DER—DER encoded certificate.
- .PEM—Base64 encoded certificate, enclosed between "-----BEGIN CERTIFICATE-----" and"-----END CERTIFICATE-----".
- .P7B— See. P7C.
- .P7C—PKCS#7 SignedData structure without data, just certificate(s) or CRL (s).
- .PFX—See. P12.
- .P12—PKCS#12, may contain certificate(s) (public) and private-keys (password protected).

PKCS #7 is a standard for signing or encrypting (they call it "enveloping") data. Since the certificate is needed to verify signed data, it is possible to include them in the SignedData structure. A. P7C-file is just a degenerated SignedData structure, without any data to sign.

PKCS #12 evolved from the PFX (Personal inFormation eXchange) standard and is used to exchange public and private objects in a single file.

A. PEM-file may contain certificate(s) or private-key(s), enclosed between the appropriate BEGIN/END-lines.

8.3.3 Sample X.509 Certificates

As an example of an X.509 certificate, here's a decode (generated with openssl) of one of www.freesoft.org's old certificates; the actual certificate is about 1 KB in size. It was issued (signed) by Thawte (since acquired by Verisign), as stated in its Issuer field. Its subject contains a lot of personal information, but the most important part is the common name (CN) of www.freesoft.org—this is the part that must match the host being authenticated. Next comes an RSA public-key (modulus and public exponent), followed by the signature, and computed by taking an MD5 hash of the first part of the certificate and encrypting it with Thawte's RSA private-key.

```
Certificate:
    Data :
        Version: 1 (0x0)
        Serial Number: 7829 (0x1e95)
        Signature Algorithm: md5WithRSAEncryption
        Issuer: C = ZA, ST = Western Cape, L = Cape Town, O = Thawte Consulting cc,
                OU = Certification Services Division,
                CN = Thawte Server CA/Email = server-certs@thawte.com
        Validity
            Not Before: Jul 9 16:04:02 1998 GMT
            Not After: Jul 9 16:04:02 1999 GMT
        Subject: C = US, ST = Maryland, L = Pasadena, O = Brent Baccala,
                OU = FreeSoft,
CN = www.freesoft.org/Email = baccala@freesoft.org
        Subject Public-Key Info:
            Public-Key Algorithm: rsaEncryption
            RSA Public-Key: (1 024 bit)
                Modulus (1 024 bit):
                    00:b4:31:98:0a:c4:bc:62:c1:88:aa:dc:b0:c8:bb:
                    33:35:19:d5:0c:64:b9:3d:41:b2:96:fc:f3:31:e1:
                    66:36:d0:8e:56:12:44:ba:75:eb:e8:1c:9c:5b:66:
                    70:33:52:14:c9:ec:4f:91:51:70:39:de:53:85:17:
                    16:94:6e:ee:f4:d5:6f:d5:ca:b3:47:5e:1b:0c:7b:
                    c5:cc:2b:6b:c1:90:c3:16:31:0d:bf:7a:c7:47:77:
                    8f:a0:21:c7:4c:d0:16:65:00:c1:0f:d7:b8:80:e3:
                    d2:75:6b:c1:ea:9e:5c:5c:ea:7d:c1:a1:10:bc:b8:
                    e8:35:1c:9e:27:52:7e:41:8f
                Exponent: 65537 (0x10001)
    Signature Algorithm: md5WithRSAEncryption
        93:5f:8f:5f:c5:af:bf:0a:ab:a5:6d:fb:24:5f:b6:59:5d:9d:
        92:2e:4a:1b:8b:ac:7d:99:17:5d:cd:19:f6:ad:ef:63:2f:92:
        ab:2f:4b:cf:0a:13:90:ee:2c:0e:43:03:be:f6:ea:8e:9c:67:
        d0:a2:40:03:f7:ef:6a:15:09:79:a9:46:ed:b7:16:1b:41:72:
```

Chapter 8 Public-Key Infrastructure

```
            0d:19:aa:ad:dd:9a:df:ab:97:50:65:f5:5e:85:a6:ef:19:d1:
            5a:de:9d:ea:63:cd:cb:cc:6d:5d:01:85:b5:6d:c8:f3:d9:f7:
            8f:0e:fc:ba:1f:34:e9:96:6e:6c:cf:f2:ef:9b:bf:de:b5:22:
            68:9f
```

To validate this certificate, we need another certificate, one that matches the Issuer (Thawte Server CA) in the first certificate. Then we take the RSA public-key from the second (CA) certificate, use it to decode the signature on the first certificate to obtain an MD5 hash, which must match an actual MD5 hash computed over the rest of the certificate. Here's the CA cert:

```
    Certificate:
        Data:
            Version: 3 (0x2)
            Serial Number: 1 (0x1)
            Signature Algorithm: md5WithRSAEncryption
            Issuer: C = ZA, ST = Western Cape, L = Cape Town, O = Thawte Consulting cc,
                    OU = Certification Services Division,
                    CN = Thawte Server CA/Email = server-certs@thawte.com
            Validity
                Not Before: Aug 1 00:00:00 1996 GMT
                Not After : Dec 31 23:59:59 2020 GMT
            Subject: C = ZA, ST = Western Cape, L = Cape Town, O = Thawte Consulting cc,
                     OU = Certification Services Division,
                     CN = Thawte Server CA/Email = server-certs@thawte.com
            Subject Public-Key Info:
                Public-Key Algorithm: rsaEncryption
                RSA Public-Key: (1024 bit)
                    Modulus (1024 bit):
                        00:d3:a4:50:6e:c8:ff:56:6b:e6:cf:5d:b6:ea:0c:
                        68:75:47:a2:aa:c2:da:84:25:fc:a8:f4:47:51:da:
                        85:b5:20:74:94:86:1e:0f:75:c9:e9:08:61:f5:06:
                        6d:30:6e:15:19:02:e9:52:c0:62:db:4d:99:9e:e2:
                        6a:0c:44:38:cd:fe:be:e3:64:09:70:c5:fe:b1:6b:
                        29:b6:2f:49:c8:3b:d4:27:04:25:10:97:2f:e7:90:
                        6d:c0:28:42:99:d7:4c:43:de:c3:f5:21:6d:54:9f:
```

English for Information Security

```
                5d:c3:58:e1:c0:e4:d9:5b:b0:b8:dc:b4:7b:df:36:
                3a:c2:b5:66:22:12:d6:87:0d
            Exponent: 65537 (0x10001)
        X509v3 extensions:
            X509v3 Basic Constraints: critical
                CA:TRUE
    Signature Algorithm: md5WithRSAEncryption
        07:fa:4c:69:5c:fb:95:cc:46:ee:85:83:4d:21:30:8e:ca:d9:
        a8:6f:49:1a:e6:da:51:e3:60:70:6c:84:61:11:a1:1a:c8:48:
        3e:59:43:7d:4f:95:3d:a1:8b:b7:0b:62:98:7a:75:8a:dd:88:
        4e:4e:9e:40:db:a8:cc:32:74:b9:6f:0d:c6:e3:b3:44:0b:d9:
        8a:6f:9a:29:9b:99:18:28:3b:d1:e3:40:28:9a:5a:3c:d5:b5:
        e7:20:1b:8b:ca:a4:ab:8d:e9:51:d9:e2:4c:2c:59:a9:da:b9:
        b2:75:1b:f6:42:f2:ef:c7:f2:18:f9:89:bc:a3:ff:8a:23:2e:
        70:47
```

This is an example of a self-signed certificate; note that the issuer and subject are the same. There's no way to verify this certificate except by checking it against itself; we've reached the top of the certificate chain. So how does this certificate become trusted? Simple—it's manually configured. Thawte is one of the root certificate authorities recognized by both Microsoft and Netscape. This certificate comes with the web browser (you can probably find it listed as "Thawte Server CA" in the security settings); it's trusted by default. As a long-lived (note the expiration date), globally trusted certificate that can sign pretty much anything (note the lack of any constraints), its matching private-key has to be one of the most closely guarded in the world.

8.3.4 Security

In 2005, Arjen Lenstra and Benne de Weger demonstrated "how to use hash collisions to construct two X.509 certificates that contain identical signatures and that differ only in the public-keys", achieved using a collision attack on the MD5 hash function.

8.3.5 Public-Key Infrastructure Working Group

The Public-Key Infrastructure (X.509) working group (PKIX) is a working group of the Internet Engineering Task Force dedicated to creating RFCs and other standards documentation on issues related to public-key infrastructure based on X. 509 certificates. PKIX was established in Autumn 1995.

8.3.6 Protocols and Standards Supporting X.509 Certificates

- Transport Layer Security (TLS/SSL)
- Secure Multipurpose Internet Mail Extensions (S/MIME)
- IPSec
- SSH
- Smartcard
- HTTPS
- Extensible Authentication Protocol
- Lightweight Directory Access Protocol
- Trusted Computing Group (TNC TPM NGSCB)
- CableLabs (North American Cable Industry Technology Forum)
- WS-Security

8.4 Trusted Third Party

In cryptography, a trusted third party (TTP)(as shown in Figure 8.3) is an entity which facilitates interactions between two parties who both trust the third party; they use this trust to secure their own interactions. TTPs are common in cryptographic protocols, for example, a CA.

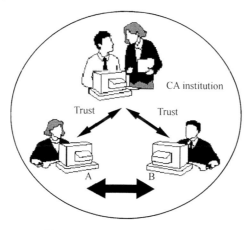

Figure 8.3 Trusted third party

8.4.1 An Example

Suppose Alice and Bob wish to communicate securely—they may choose to use cryptography. Without ever having met Bob, Alice may need to obtain a key to use to encrypt messages to him. In this case, a TTP is a third party who may have previously seen Bob (in person), or is otherwise willing to vouch that this key (typically in an identity certificate) belongs to the person indicated in that certificate, in this case, Bob. In discussions, this third person is often called Trent. Trent gives it to Alice, who then uses it to send secure messages to Bob. Alice can trust this key to be Bob's if she trusts this Trent. In such discussions, it is simply assumed that she has valid reasons to do so (of course there is the issue of Alice and Bob being able to properly identify Trent as Trent and not someone impersonating Trent).

8.4.2 Actual Practice

How to arrange (trustable) third parties of this type is an unsolved problem. So long as there are motives of greed, politics, revenge, etc, those who perform (or supervise) work done by such an entity will provide potential loopholes through which the necessary trust may leak. The problem, perhaps an unsolvable one, is ancient and notorious. Those large impersonal corporations make promises of accuracy in their attestations of the correctness of a claimed public-key user correspondence (e. g. , by a certificate authority as a part of a public-key infrastructure) changes little.

The PGP cryptosystem includes a variant of the TTP in the form of the web of trust. PGP users digitally sign each others' identity certificates and are instructed to do so only if they are confident the person and the public-key belong together. A key signing party is one way of combining a get-together with some certificate signing. Nonetheless, doubt and caution remain sensible as some users have been careless in signing others' certificates.

Trusting humans, or their organizational creations, can be risky. For example, in financial matters, bonding companies have yet to find a way to avoid losses in the real world.

8.4.3 Parallels Outside Cryptography

Outside cryptography, the law in many places makes provision for trusted third parties upon whose claims one may rely. For instance, a notary public acts as a trusted third party for authenticating or acknowledging signatures on documents. A TTP's role in cryptography is much the same, at least in principle. A certificate authority fills just such a notary function, attesting to the identity of a key's owner.

Courts are also trusted third parties in the sense that disputes brought before them are presumed to be decided in a disinterested and dispassionate way consonant with a body of established law and (in common law countries) precedent. In fact, governments generally act (and require others to act as well) as though they were trusted third parties in many circumstances as well.

8.5 Certificate Revocation List

In the operation of some cryptosystems, usually PKIs, a CRL is a list of certificates (more accurately: their serial numbers) which have been revoked, are no longer valid, and should not be relied upon by any system user.

8.5.1 CRL Introduction

There are different revocation reasons defined in RFC 3280:
(1) Revoked
A certificate is irreversibly revoked (and entered on a CRL) if, for instance, it is discovered that the CA had improperly issued a certificate or a private-key is thought to have been compromised. Certificates may also be revoked for failure of the identified entity to adhere to policy requirements such as publication of false documents, mis-representation of software behavior, or violation of any other policy specified by the CA operator or its customer. The most common reason for revocation is the user's not being in sole possession of the private-key (e. g., token containing the private-key has been lost or stolen).
(2) Hold
This reversible status can be used to notice the temporary invalidity of the certificate, for instance when the user is not sure if the private-key has been lost. If, in this example, the private-key was found again and nobody had access to it, the status can be reinstated, and the certificate is valid again, thus removing the certificate from further CRLs.

Usually, a CRL is generated on the one hand periodically after a clearly defined timeframe and (optionally) on the other hand immediately after a certificate has been revoked. The CRL is always issued by the CA which issues the corresponding certificates. All CRLs have a (often short) lifetime in which they are valid and in which they may be consulted by a PKI-enabled application to verify a counterpart's certificate prior its use. To prevent spoofing or denial-of-service attacks, CRLs are usually signed by the issuing CA and therefore carry a digital signature. To validate a specific CRL prior relying on it, the certificate of its corresponding CA is needed, which usually can be found on a (even public) directory.

Certificate expiration dates are not a substitute for a CRL as the problem may be discovered whilst the certificate has not yet expired. CRLs or other certificate validation techniques are a necessary part of any properly operated PKI as mistakes in certificate vetting and key management are expected to occur in real world operations. In a noteworthy example, a certificate for Microsoft was mistakenly issued to an unknown individual who had successfully posed as Microsoft by the CA contracted to maintain the ActiveX "publisher certificate" system (VeriSign). Microsoft saw the need to patch their cryptography subsystem so it would check the status of certificates before trusting them. As a short term fix, a patch was issued for the relevant Microsoft software (most importantly Windows) specifically listing the two certificates in question as "revoked".

The certificates for which a CRL should be maintained are often X.509/public-key certificates, as this format is commonly used by PKI schemes.

8.5.2　Problems with All CRLs

Best practices require that wherever and however certificate status is maintained, it must be checked whenever one wants to rely on a certificate. Failing this, a revoked certificate may be incorrectly accepted as valid. This means that to effectively use a PKI one must have access to current CRLs (i.e., Internet access in the case of a PKI). This requirement of on-line validation negates one of the original major advantages of PKI over symmetric cryptography protocols, namely that the certificate is "self authenticating". Symmetric system (e.g., Kerberos), also depend on the existence of on-line services (Key distribution center in the case of Kerberos).

The existence of a CRL implies the need for someone (or some organization) to enforce policy and revoke certificates deemed counter to operational policy. If a certificate is mistakenly revoked significant problems can arise. As the certificate authority is tasked with enforcing the operational policy for issuing certificates they typically are responsible for determining if and when revocation is appropriate by interpreting the operational policy.

The necessity of consulting a CRL, or other certificate status service, prior to accepting a certificate raises a potential denial-of-service attack against the PKI akin to the denial-of-service attack on Kerberos whereby a current authentication token cannot be retrieved.

No comprehensive solution to these problems is known, though there are multiple workarounds for various aspects of it, some of which have proven acceptable in practice.

An alternative to using CRLs which is especially useful for software clients is the on-line certificate validation protocol OCSP. OCSP has the primary benefit of requiring less network bandwidth and thus enabling real-time and near real-time status checks for high volume or high value operations.

8.6 An Example of a PKI in Action

The following provides an example of public-key cryptography in use for both confidentiality and integrity. The purpose of this example is to illustrate how public-key cryptography mechanisms can be used in a PKI. In this example, both parties, Alice and Bob, share a common trust point; that is, they both use the same CA to have their certificates signed. For this reason, they do not have to evaluate a chain of trust to determine the credibility of any other CA. The example is not necessarily appropriate for every business proposition.

Precursor Steps:

(1) Alice and Bob each generate a public-private-key pair;

(2) Alice and Bob each provide their public-keys, name, and descriptive information to an RA;

(3) The RA validates their credentials and forwards the certificate requests to the CA;

(4) The CA generates a certificate for Alice and Bob's public-keys by formatting their public-keys and other information, and then signs the certificate with the CA's private-keys;

(5) The results of this operation are that Alice and Bob each have a public-private-key pair and a public-key certificate;

(6) Alice and Bob each generate a secret symmetric key.

Now Alice and Bob each have a public-private-key pair, a digital key certificate issued by a common trusted third party (i.e., the CA), and a secret symmetric key.

Suppose now that Alice wishes to send Bob some data that he will rely upon and thus requires an assurance of integrity; that is, the content of the message cannot be altered. Alice and Bob also want the assurance of confidentiality and want no other parties to be able to view the information. A contract for goods and services where parties agree upon price, time, and value exchange is a good example of such a process. The steps taken to perform the transaction are as follows.

In this example, steps(1)~(5) involve Alice sending data that needs confidentiality and integrity to Bob, using a digital signature(see Figure 8.4). Steps (6)~(10) involve Bob decrypting the data(see Figure 8.5).

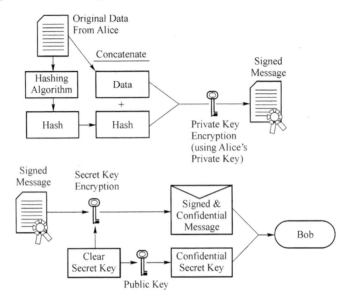

Figure 8.4　Overview of using a digital signature

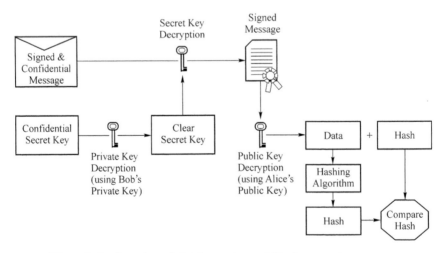

Figure 8.5　Overview of the decryption and Hash comparison process

(1) Alice takes the message in question, formats it according to the protocol rules she and Bob have agreed to and then hashes the message. The hash provides a unique

value for the message and will later be used by Bob to test the validity and integrity of the message.

(2) Alice concatenates the message and the hash and then signs (i. e. , encrypts) these with her private-key. This signing provides message integrity because Bob is assured that only Alice could have generated the signature because only Alice has access to the private-key used to sign the message. Note that anyone with access to Alice's public-key can recover the signed message and so, we have only established message integrity at this point, but not confidentiality.

(3) Because Alice and Bob would like to keep the message confidential, Alice encrypts the signed message and hash with her secret symmetric key. This key is only shared between Alice and Bob and no one else. Note that enabling confidentiality can be implemented through various techniques and protocols. In this example, a symmetric key is used because it can be more efficient than using a public-key for encrypting lengthy messages such as the purchase order here.

(4) Alice must provide Bob with her secret symmetric key to enable Bob to decrypt the message encrypted with that key. Alice signs (i. e. , encrypts) her secret symmetric key using Bob's public-key. For this example, we assume Alice obtained Bob's public-key previously. This generates what is known as a digital envelope and which only Bob can recover (i. e. , decrypt) because only Bob has access to the private-key that is needed to recover the digital envelope. Remember, what is done with one key of a pair can only be undone with the other key of the pair. This provides confidentiality over the transmission of Alice's secret symmetric key to Bob.

(5) Alice forwards to Bob the original message and the hash that are both encrypted with her secret symmetric key and the digital envelope containing the secret key encrypted with Bob's public-key.

(6) Bob takes the digital envelope he received from Alice and recovers (i. e. , decrypts) it with his private-key. The results of performing this operation provide Bob with the secret symmetric key that Alice previously used to encrypt the message and the hash of the message.

(7) Bob can now recover (i. e. , decrypt) the encrypted message and hash using Alice's secret symmetric key. Bob now has the signed clear text message and the signed hash of it.

(8) Bob now recovers (i. e. , decrypts) the signed message and hash of the message by using Alice's public-key. Remember, what is done with one key of a pair can only be undone with the other key of the pair.

English for Information Security

(9) To ensure that no modifications have been made to the message, Bob takes the original message and hashes it using the exact same process that Alice used originally.

(10) Finally, Bob compares the hash he has just produced with the hash he recovered from the original message. If they match he is assured of the message's integrity.

Glossary

Certificate Authority (CA)	认证中心
Certificate Revocation List (CRL)	证书撤销列表
dispute	争论,辩论
notary	公证人
omnipresence	普遍存在
Online Certificate Status Protocol (OCSP)	在线证书状态协议
Pretty Good Privacy(PGP)	良好隐私
Public-Key Infrastructure (PKI)	公钥基础设施
Registration Authority (RA)	注册中心
vouch	担保,推荐,证明

Translate the following sentences/passage into Chinese

(1) In cryptography, a PKI is an arrangement that provides for trusted third party vetting of, and vouching for, user identities. It also allows binding of public-keys to users. This is usually carried out by software at a central location together with other coordinated software at distributed locations.

(2) Whether systematic or custom, the processes in use today provide for the establishment of a trusted business relationship in that the customer and merchant both authenticate one another to the extent that they are willing to undertake the transaction.

(3) PKI arrangements enable users to be authenticated to each other, and to use the information in identity certificates (i.e., each other's public-keys) to encrypt and decrypt messages traveling to and fro.

(4) A PKI enables users of a basically insecure public network such as the Internet to securely and privately exchange data and money through the use of a public and a private cryptographic key pair that is obtained and shared through a trusted authority.

(5) Most enterprise-scale PKI systems rely on certificate chains to establish a party's identity, as a certificate may have been issued by a certificate authority computer whose "legitimacy" is established for such purposes by a certificate issued by a higher-level certificate authority, and so on.

Chapter 8 Public-Key Infrastructure

Translate the following sentences/passage into English

(1) PKI 公钥基础设施是一种运用公钥的概念与技术来实施并提供安全服务的、具有普遍适用性的网络安全基础设施。PKI 技术的核心是通过第三方的可信任机构认证中心,把用户的公钥和用户的其他标识信息(如名称、E-mail、身份证号等)绑定在一起,经过数字签名后成为公钥证书,并提供公钥证书的管理服务。

(2) PKI 在实际应用上是一套软硬件系统和安全策略的集合,它提供了一整套安全机制,使用户在不知道对方身份或分布得很广的情况下,以数字证书为基础,通过一系列的信任关系来支持信息的完整性、保密性和不可否认性。

(3) PKI 策略是一个包含如何保证 PKI 提供安全有效服务的操作和使用制度。一般情况下,在 PKI 中有两种类型的策略:一是证书策略,用户管理证书的使用,比如,可以确认某一 CA 是在 Internet 上的公有 CA,还是某一企业内部的私有 CA;另外一个就是 CPS (Certificate Practices Statement)认证惯例声明。

(4) CA 的用途是接受个人申请,核查其中信息并颁发证书。然而,在许多情况下,把证书的分发与签名过程分开是很有好处的,因为签名过程需要使用 CA 的私钥(只有在离线状态下才能安全使用),但分发的过程要求在线进行。所以,有些 PKI 体系使用注册机构 RA 来实现整个过程。

(5) 第三方信任是指两个实体以前没有建立起信任关系,但双方与共同的第三方有信任关系,第三方为两者的可信任性进行了担保,由此建立起来的信任关系。第三方信任的实质是第三方的推荐信任,是目前网络安全中普遍采用的信任模式。

Questions

(1) What is the function of PKI?
(2) What is the purpose of PKI?
(3) What is Certificate Authority?
(4) What is X.509 certificate?
(5) What is the function of CRL?

Chapter 9

Information Security Management

An Information Security Management System (ISMS) is, as the name suggests, a system of management concerned with information security. The idiom arises primarily out of ISO/IEC 17799, a code of practice for information security management published by the International Organization for Standardization in 2000. ISO 17799 will eventually be revised and re-issued in the ISO 2700x suite.

The best known ISMS is ISO/IEC 27001, published by the ISO, complementary to ISO/IEC 17799 (developed from BS 7799-1). A system for certification against BS-7799-2: 2002 is well established (but note that it is not possible to get ISO/IEC 17799 certified).

ISM3 (pronounced ISM-cubed) is the only ISMS that is accreditable. ISM3 was developed from ITIL, ISO 9001, CMM and ISO 27001 and Information Governance concepts. ISM3 can be used as a template to make ISO 9001 compliant information security management systems. While ISO 27001 is control based, ISM3 is process based. ISM3 has process metrics included.

9.1 ISO/IEC 17799

ISO/IEC 17799 is an information security standard published and most recently revised in June 2005 by the International Organization for Standardization (ISO) and the International Electrotechnical Commission (IEC). It is entitled Information technology—Security techniques—Code of practice for information security management. The current standard is a revision of the version published in 2000, which was a word-for-word copy of the British Standard (BS) 7799-1:1999.

ISO/IEC 17799 provides best practice recommendations on information security

Chapter 9 Information Security Management

management for use by those who are responsible for initiating, implementing or maintaining information security management systems. Information security is defined within the standard in the context of the C-I-A triad.

The preservation of confidentiality (ensuring that information is accessible only to those authorized to have access), integrity (safeguarding the accuracy and completeness of information and processing methods) and availability (ensuring that authorized users have access to information and associated assets when required).

The 2005 version of the standard contains the following twelve main sections:
- Risk assessment and treatment
- Security policy
- Organization of information security
- Asset management
- Human resources security
- Physical and environmental security
- Communications and operations management
- Access control
- Information systems acquisition, development and maintenance
- Information security incident management
- Business continuity management
- Compliance

Within each section, IT security controls and their objectives are specified and outlined. The IT security controls are generally regarded as best practice means of achieving those objectives. For each of the controls, implementation guidance is provided. Specific controls are not mandated since:

(1) Each organization is expected to undertake a structured information security risk assessment process to determine its requirements before selecting controls that are appropriate to its particular circumstances. (The introduction section outlines a risk assessment process although there are more specific standards covering this area such as ISO Technical Report TR 13335 GMITS Part 3—Guidelines for the management of IT security—Security Techniques.)

(2) It is practically impossible to list all conceivable controls in a general purpose standard.

ISO/IEC 17799 has directly equivalent national standards in countries such as Australia and New Zealand (AS/NZS ISO/IEC 17799:2006), the Netherlands (NEN-ISO/IEC 17799:2002 nl, 2005 version in translation), Sweden (SS 627799), Japan (JIS Q

27002), UNE 71501 (Spain), the United Kingdom (BS ISO/IEC 17799:2005) and Uruguay (UNIT/ISO 17799:2005). Translation and local publication often results in several months' delay after the main ISO/IEC standard is revised and released.

ISO/IEC 17799:2005 is expected to be renamed ISO/IEC 27002 in 2007. The ISO/IEC 27000 series has been reserved for information security matters with a handful of related standards such as ISO/IEC 27001 having already been released and others such as ISO/IEC 27004—Information Security Management Metrics and Measurement—currently in draft.

9.2　ISO/IEC 27001

ISO/IEC 27001 is an information security standard published in October 2005 by the ISO and the IEC. Its complete name is Information technology Security techniques Information security management systems Requirements. The current standard replaced BS 7799-2:2002, which has now been withdrawn.

ISO/IEC 27001:2005 specifies the requirements for establishing, implementing, operating, monitoring, reviewing, maintaining and improving a documented Information Security Management System (ISMS). It specifies requirements for the management of the implementation of security controls. It is intended to be used in conjunction with ISO 17799:2005, a security Code of Practice, which offers a list of specific security controls to select from.

This is also the first standard in a proposed series of standards which will be assigned numbers within the ISO 27000 series. Others are anticipated to include a re-publication of ISO 17799, a standard for information security measurement and metrics, and potentially a version of the current BS7799-3 standard.

9.3　ISM3

The Information Security Management Maturity Model (ISM3, or ISM-cubed) offers a practical and efficient approach for specifying, implementing and evaluating process-oriented information security management (ISM) systems.

ISM3 aims to:
- Enable the creation of ISM systems that are fully aligned with the business mis-

sion;
- Be applicable to any organization regardless of size, context and resources;
- Enable organizations to prioritize and optimize their investment in information security;
- Enable continuous improvement of ISM systems;
- Support the outsourcing of security processes.

ISM3 is compatible with the implementation and use of ITIL, ISO 9001, Cobit and ISO 27001. This compatibility protects the existing investment in ISM systems when they are enhanced using ISM3. ISM3 based ISM systems are themselves accreditable, giving organizations an objective means of measuring and advertising their progress with information security management.

The management discipline and internal control framework required by ISM3 assists compliance with corporate governance law.

Glossary

Information Security Management Maturity Model (ISM3)	信息安全管理成熟模型
Information Security Management System (ISMS)	信息安全管理系统
Information Security Management (ISM)	信息安全管理
International Electrotechnical Commission (IEC)	国际电子技术委员会
International Organization for Standardization (ISO)	国际标准化组织

Translate the following sentences/passage into Chinese

(1) The Information Security Management Maturity Model (ISM3, or ISM-cubed) offers a practical and efficient approach for specifying, implementing and evaluating process-oriented information security management (ISM) systems.

(2) An Information Security Management System (ISMS) is, as the name suggests, a system of management concerned with information security. The idiom arises primarily out of ISO/IEC 17799, a code of practice for information security management published by the International Organization for Standardization in 2000.

(3) Security management: In network management, the set of functions (a) that protects telecommunications networks and systems from unauthorized access by persons, acts, or influences and (b) that includes many subfunctions, such as creating, deleting, and controlling security services and mechanisms; distributing security-relevant information; reporting security-relevant events; controlling the distribution of cryptographic keying material; and authorizing subscriber access, rights, and privileges.

Translate the following sentences/passage into English

(1) 与二十年前大型计算机要受到严密看守,由技术专家管理的情况相比,今天计算机技术已唾手可得,无处不在。今天的计算机使用者大都很少受到严格的培训,每天都在以不安全的方式处理着企业的大量重要信息,而且企业的贸易伙伴、咨询顾问、合作单位等外部人员都以不同的方式使用着企业的信息系统,他们都对企业的信息系统构成了潜在的威胁。

(2) 许多对企业心存不满的员工把"黑"掉企业网站,偷窃并散布客户敏感信息,为竞争对手提供机密的技术与商业数据,甚至破坏关键计算机系统作为对企业的报复行为,使企业蒙受了巨大的损失。因为这些员工非常了解企业的薄弱点,一般企业的安全系统对内部员工几乎是不设防的。

(3) 由于信息系统的复杂性,信息系统的安全是不能离开技术保障手段的。蓬勃发展的国际安全产品市场每年以25%的发展速度递增,国内更是达到了60%以上的增长速度,令人眼花缭乱的安全产品与技术的为客户带来了选择的多样性,同时也带来了选择的复杂性,用户往往在厂商铺天盖地的宣传中无所适从。

Questions

(1) Why information security management is more important than information security technology?

(2) What is the main content of ISO/IEC 17799?

参 考 文 献
Bibliography

[1] Wenke Lee, Salvatore J. Stolfo. A Framework for Constructing Features and Models for Intrusion Detection Systems. [2006-11-16]. http://Citeseer.ist.psu.edu/384824.html.

[2] Maxime Feroul, Markus Roth. Anomaly Detection System Study (SEINIT Project). [2006-11-16]. http://www.isoc.org/seinit/protol/lndex2.pht.

[3] Joel Weise. Public Key Infrastructure Overview. [2006-11-16]. http://www.Svn.Com/bluepreints/0801/publickey.plf.